NINTH EDITION

# CASINO CAMPING

## GUIDE TO RV-FRIENDLY CASINOS

**Published by:**

Roundabout Publications
PO Box 569
LaCygne, KS 66040

800-455-2207

www.RoundaboutPublications.com

JANE KENNY

Published by:

Roundabout Publications
PO Box 569
LaCygne KS 66040

Phone: 800-455-2207
Internet: www.RoundaboutPublications.com

Library of Congress Control Number: 2018964480
ISBN-10: 1-885464-70-3
ISBN-13: 978-1-885464-70-5

# Casino Camping

For Jack: my pilot and my best friend

# Contents

# Introduction

Casino Camping is a parking guide for the many Americans who drive the nation's highways and byways in recreational vehicles. It includes listings of casinos in 33 states, from small neighborhood-style casinos to lavish destination resorts that rival Vegas in amenities and entertainment. All casinos listed in this guide are "RV Friendly," meaning they either have a campground or can accommodate large vehicles in their parking areas. Please see Appendix B for important information about RV parking etiquette, safety and security. Casinos that do not have parking accommodations for RVs are not included in these listings.

## How This Guide Is Organized

This book is organized alphabetically by state. A map at the beginning of each state section identifies casino locations by city. Individual listings are cross-referenced to the map by city name. Each casino listing includes the following information where applicable:

- Name, address, phone number and web site
- **DESCRIPTION:** Brief overview of the facility
- **GAMING:** Specific types of gaming and/or racing offered

- **FOOD & ENTERTAINMENT:** Dining options, entertainment types & venues
- **LODGING:** Hotel, motel and features such as golf, retail shops, etc.
- **CAMPING:** RV Park, parking spaces and other overnight options
- **DIRECTIONS:** Driving directions, usually from the nearest interstate exit.

A chart (see sample below) follows each state map and provides information about each casino including:

1) City in which the casino is located
2) Name of casino
3) RV Park (p) or Spaces (s) & number of sites
4) Availability of free RV overnight parking
5) Hotel, motel or lodge at the casino
6) On-site golf course or driving range
7) Distance to casino if within 10 miles of an Interstate exit

We hope you find the 9th edition of this guide helpful and informative as you travel this beautiful land. Wishing you safe and happy travels.

*Jane Kenny*

| ❶ City | ❷ Casino | ❸ 🚐 | ❹ 🅿 | ❺ 🛏 | ❻ 🏌 | ❼ 🛡 |
|---|---|---|---|---|---|---|
| Camp Verde | Cliff Castle Casino Hotel | p150 | x | x | | 1 |
| Mohave Valley | Spirit Mountain Casino | p120 | | | x | 7 |
| San Carlos | Apache Gold Casino Resort | p60 | | x | x | |
| Somerton | Cocopah Casino Resort | s30 | | x | | |

# It's All Just A Game

Do not go to a casino expecting to win big. Do not expect to make a killing at the table or hit the big jackpot on the slots. Sure it happens, but not for the overwhelming majority of casino players. Many "how-to" articles and books have been written about winning at casinos. Advice from professional gamblers may have some merit for other professionals, but the average casino-goer is not a professional gambler.

Most casino-goers are casual, recreational players. So, for us, a trip to the casino is about playing games as a form of entertainment, to have some fun. In this regard we can see a difference between gaming and gambling. As we learned from the time we first played Monopoly -- or any other fun game -- every game has a winner and a loser. While it is true that you need to know the rules, and, yes, a certain amount of skill may be involved. But, in any game, there are always some who win and some who do not. And, those who play only to win – and expect to win every time they play – are unrealistic. They put themselves under a lot of stress and take the fun out of playing games.

Our winning strategy for playing games at the casino is to set limits on money and time and then relax and have fun. The four simple rules outlined below will also help players avoid becoming compulsive about casino games.

1) Set a dollar limit and stick to it. The amount you set – your bankroll – becomes your personal "price of admission" for that session. If you use up the budgeted bankroll before the end of the session (length of session explained below), stop playing! Come back for another session in a few hours, a few days, weeks, or months – whatever is your style. It is a big mistake to pump more money into an already losing session.

2) Set a time limit for the gaming session and stick to it. No matter what game you play, the odds are in the casino's favor. Longer sessions increase the casino's odds even more. By playing shorter sessions you'll probably keep part or all of your original bankroll. If you are winning when your time limit is up, be disciplined enough to end the session as a winner...and you won't need to ante up your personal pre-set price of admission the next time you play.

3) Never ever set your bankroll at more than you can afford to lose! This simple bit of advice will keep you in the arena of recreational gaming. Be sensible. Avoid becoming compulsive.

4) Relax and have fun. Once you've established the mindset of gaming as entertainment, you can have fun at it, knowing you are disciplined enough to spend no more than the specified amount of money, and no longer than the specified time period. Nowadays casinos offer more fun than ever. Slot machines have moved beyond the boring reels of endless cherries and bars to interactive and entertaining electronic slots. Table game fans, too, have more variety. Today there's a wider range of games and, in many places, low minimums for the novice player.

Table players can benefit most from the "specific bankroll and session time" strategy. Disciplined players can relax and enjoy the camaraderie and games at the tables. And, by applying the strategy outlined above, they're more apt to leave a winner.

What does it mean to leave as a winner? A player who leaves with all or part of his bankroll in his pocket is a winner! Players who have the good common sense to leave when they are even, or slightly ahead, are winners. Be a winner!

# For Some, Gambling Is Not An Option

Problem gamblers tell us that winning is easy... leaving is hard. If you can identify with this, read on.

For the large majority of people gambling is fun – it's not a problem. But for some it can become a problem that interferes with their life and literally takes over. If casino gambling is a form of entertainment for you, then you also need to be aware that there is a progressive illness called compulsive gambling.

Gamblers generally fall into three categories:

1. The casual or occasional gambler for whom casino gaming is a form of entertainment.

2. Professional gamblers who have a studied approach to games with an element of skill so that they have an advantage. Their motivation is economic gain. The professional gambler gambles to live; a compulsive gambler lives to gamble.

3. Problem and compulsive gamblers. The problem gambler cannot resist impulses to gamble and is on the way to becoming a compulsive (pathological) gambler. A person is a compulsive gambler if the gambling behavior takes over to the point where it disrupts and damages his or her personal and professional life. That person should seek help.

Gamblers Anonymous is an organization of compulsive gamblers who seek recovery from the illness. GA lists the following 20 questions and notes that if you answer yes to at least seven of them, you may be a problem gambler:

1. Do you lose time from work due to gambling?
2. Does gambling make your home life unhappy?
3. Does gambling affect your reputation?
4. Do you ever feel remorse after gambling?
5. Do you ever gamble to get money to pay debts or otherwise solve financial difficulties?
6. Does gambling cause a decrease in your ambition or efficiency?
7. After losing do you feel you must return as soon as possible to win back your losses?
8. After a win do you have a strong urge to return and win more?
9. Do you often gamble until your last dollar is gone?
10. Do you ever borrow to finance your gambling?
11. Do you ever sell anything to finance your gambling?
12. Are you reluctant to use your gambling money for other expenses?
13. Does gambling make you careless about the welfare of your family?
14. Do you ever gamble longer than you planned?
15. Do you ever gamble to escape worry or trouble?
16. Do you ever commit or consider committing an illegal act to finance your gambling?
17. Does gambling cause you to have difficulty sleeping?
18. Do arguments, disappointments or frustrations create within you an urge to gamble?
19. Do you have an urge to celebrate good fortune by a few hours of gambling?
20. Do you ever consider self-destruction as a result of your gambling?

Compulsive gambling is a diagnosable and treatable illness. It can be as debilitating as drug or alcohol addiction. A 24-hour help line is available at 1-800-522-4700.

# Alabama

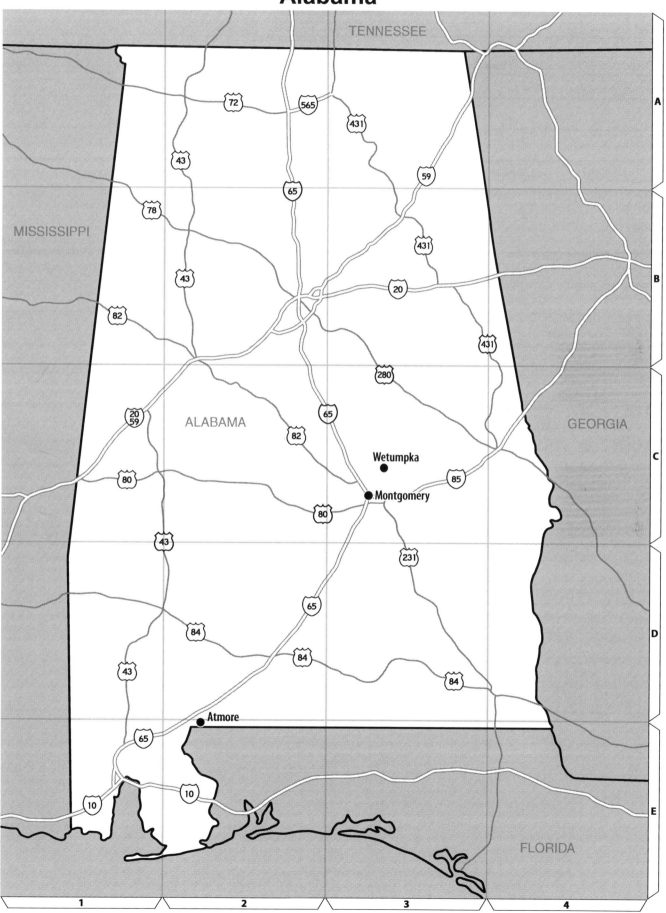

# Alabama

| City | Casino | 📷 | P | 🛏 | 🏌 | 🛡 |
|------|--------|-----|---|-----|---|---|
| Atmore | Wind Creek Casino & Hotel | p28 | x | x | | 1 |
| Montgomery | Wind Creek Casino & Hotel | | x | x | | 9 |
| Wetumpka | Wind Creek Casino & Hotel | | x | x | x | |

Alabama's three Native-American casinos are hosted by Poarch Band of Creek Indians. They have Class II electronic bingo-style gaming machines; no live table games. All are RV-Friendly.

## Atmore

**Wind Creek Casino & Hotel - Atmore**
*303 Poarch Rd*
*Atmore, AL 36502*

www.windcreekatmore.com
251-368-8007

**DESCRIPTION:** Destination resort with RV Park, near the interstate. **GAMING:** gaming machines, all denominations. **FOOD & ENTERTAINMENT:** steakhouse, buffet, cafe, yogurt shop, sports bar entertainment lounge. Ticketed events in amphitheater; movie theater, bowling & arcade. **LODGING:** Luxury hotel. **CAMPING:** RV Park, 28 full-hookup sites, free Wi-Fi. Limited free overnight parking for RVs is also permitted at the back of the west parking lot. **DIRECTIONS:** From I-65 exit 57, the casino complex is one mile east of the interstate.

## Montgomery

**Wind Creek Casino & Hotel - Montgomery**
*1801 Eddie L. Tullis Rd*
*Montgomery, AL 36117*

www.windcreekmontgomery.com
866-946-3360

**DESCRIPTION:** Sprawling casino resort surrounded by a scenic golf course. **GAMING:** slots in all denominations, non-smoking area. **FOOD & ENTERTAINMENT:** Three restaurants, includes BB King's Blues Club. **LODGING:** Luxury hotel, salon, barber shop. **CAMPING:** RVs should park by the golf course, shuttle available. Overnight is OK. **DIRECTIONS:** From I-85 exit 16, follow AL-126 west for 3.3 miles, then north on Wares Ferry Rd for 4.3 miles, then right on Dozier Road for .6 mile and left onto Eddie Tullis Rd for .5 mile.

## Wetumpka

**Wind Creek Casino & Hotel - Wetumpka**
*100 River Oaks Dr*
*Wetumpka, AL 36092*

www.creekcasinowetumpka.com
866-946-3360

**DESCRIPTION:** Largest casino in the state. **GAMING:** slots, video poker, electronic table games. **FOOD & ENTERTAINMENT:** steakhouse, buffet, grill. Ticketed shows in entertainment center. **LODGING:** Luxury hotel. **CAMPING:** Designated area for RV parking in the gravel portion of the lot near the store/smoke shop. Overnight permitted. **DIRECTIONS:** From I-85 exit 6 follow US-231 north for about 13 miles then turn left on River Oaks Blvd.

# Arizona

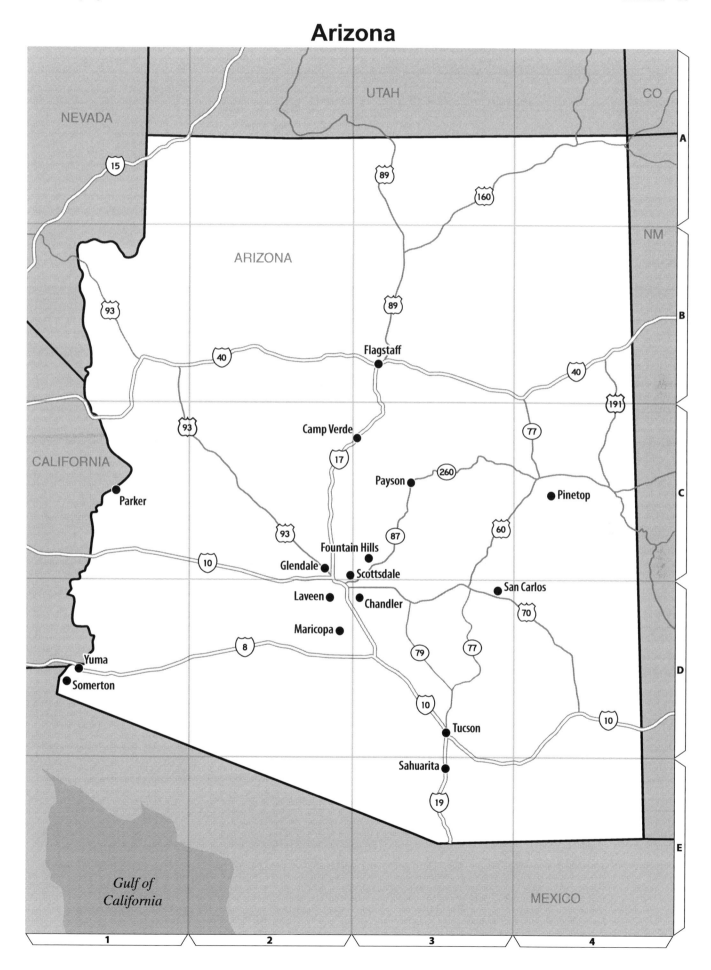

# Arizona

| City | Casino | 🚐 | P | 🛏 | 🏌 | 🛡 |
|------|--------|-----|-----|-----|-----|-----|
| Camp Verde | Cliff Castle Casino Hotel | p150 | x | x | | 1 |
| Chandler | Wild Horse Pass Casinos | | x | x | x | 1 |
| Flagstaff | Twin Arrows Navajo Casino Resort | | x | x | | 2 |
| Fountain Hills | Fort McDowell Casino Resort | p150 | | x | | |
| Glendale | Desert Diamond Casino Resort | | x | x | | 7 |
| Laveen | Vee Quiva Hotel & Casino | | x | x | | 10 |
| Maricopa | Harrah's Ak-Chin | | x | x | | |
| Parker | Blue Water Resort & Casino | p50 | x | x | x | |
| Payson | Mazatzal Hotel & Casino | | x | x | | |
| Pinetop | Hon-Dah Resort Casino | p258 | | x | | |
| Sahuarita | Desert Diamond | | x | | | 1 |
| San Carlos | Apache Gold Casino Resort | p60 | x | x | x | |
| Scottsdale | Talking Stick Resort | | x | x | x | |
| Somerton | Cocopah Casino Resort | s30 | x | x | | |
| Tucson | Casino Del Sol Resort | | x | x | x | 8 |
| Tucson | Casino of the Sun | | x | | | 7 |
| Tucson | Desert Diamond Hotel | | x | x | | 2 |
| Yuma | Paradise Casino | | x | | | 1 |

Native American tribes operate all casinos in the state. Most Arizona casinos now have a full range of gaming as well as other entertainment opportunities.

## Camp Verde

### *Cliff Castle Casino Hotel*
*555 Middle Verde Rd*
*Camp Verde, AZ 86322*

www.cliffcastlecasinohotel.com
928-567-7900

*RV Park: Distant Drums RV Park*
*583 W Middle Verde Rd*
*Camp Verde, AZ 86322*

www.ddrvresort.com
928-554-8000 • 877-577-5507

**DESCRIPTION:** Casino destination resort south of Flagstaff & adjacent to I-17. **GAMING:** open 24/7, slots, video poker, live blackjack, poker room; non-smoking area. **FOOD & ENTERTAINMENT:** steakhouse, casual dining, diner. Shows in outdoor pavilion; live music & dancing in the lounge. **LODGING:** Hotel & lodge. **CAMPING:** RV Park, 158 modern full-hookup sites, west of the interstate, pool/spa, pavilion, country store, shuttle to the casino. Overnight parking in the lower lot near the casino, east of the interstate; obtain parking permit (nominal fee) at the hotel front desk or Castle Club in the casino. **DIRECTIONS:** From I-17 exit 289.

## Chandler

### *Wild Horse Pass Casinos*
*1077 S Kyrene Rd (Lone Butte Casino)*
*5040 Wild Horse Pass Blvd (Wild Horse Pass Casino)*
*Chandler, AZ 85226*

www.wingilariver.com
800-946-4452

**DESCRIPTION:** Two separate casino buildings are both located adjacent to I-10 at exit 162. Wild Horse Pass Casino & Hotel is west of the interstate and Lone Butte, a smaller casino building, is on the east side of the interstate, visible from the highway. Open 24 hours. **GAMING:** Slots, gaming tables, poker room & pai gow poker progressive at both locations; bingo at Lone Butte. **FOOD & ENTERTAINMENT:** Fine dining, casual dining & 24-hour cafes at both locations. Ticketed concerts in Ovations Showroom. Lounge entertainment at both casinos. **LODGING:** Hotel, golf course at Wild Horse Pass. **CAMPING:** Free overnight RV Parking available at Wild Horse complex, north side; first come-first serve, no hookups. Notify Security if you plan to stay overnight; 48-hour stay limit. **DIRECTIONS:** From I-10, exit 162: to Wild Horse go west, follow signs. To Lone Butte: east, then north on 54th St. Free overnight RV parking only in Wild Horse designated lot.

## Flagstaff

### Twin Arrows Navajo Casino Resort
*22181 Resort Blvd*
*Flagstaff, AZ 86004*

www.TwinArrows.com
928-856-7200 • 855-946-8946

**DESCRIPTION:** Native American casino resort off I-40 east of Flagstaff. **GAMING:** open 24/7, slots, live table games, keno, poker room, bingo. **FOOD & ENTERTAINMENT:** steakhouse, buffet, cafe, coffee bar, sports bar. **LODGING:** Hotel, amenities. **CAMPING:** RV parking on south side of the casino; overnight is OK. **DIRECTIONS:** From I-40 exit 219, go north on Twin Arrows Road (becomes Resort Blvd) for 1.2 miles.

## Fountain Hills

### Fort McDowell Casino Resort
*10424 N Fort McDowell Rd*
*Fountain Hills, AZ 85264*

www.fortmcdowellcasino.com
480-789-5300

*RV Park: Eagle View RV Resort*
*9605 N Fort McDowell Rd*

www.eagleviewrvresort.com
480-789-5310

**DESCRIPTION:** Resort features spectacular desert views from RV Park. **GAMING:** 24/7, slots, keno, blackjack & poker, bingo every day. **FOOD & ENTERTAINMENT:** steakhouse, cafe, buffet, three restaurants & deli. golf course. **LODGING:** Luxury hotel. **CAMPING:** Modern RV Resort, 150 full hookup sites, swimming pool/spa, wireless access, clubhouse & fitness center. Free continental breakfast daily. Weekly, monthly rates available. If staying overnight, RVs must check into the RV Park. NO overnight parking at the casino. **DIRECTIONS:** From State Road 87 north (the Beeline), exit at Fort McDowell Road (25 miles northeast of Phoenix.)

## Glendale

### Desert Diamond Casino Resort - West Valley
*9341 W Northern Ave*
*Glendale, AZ 85305*

www.ddcaz.com/westvalley
623-877-7777

**DESCRIPTION:** Casino resort on 135 acres in Glendale. **GAMING:** 24/7, slots, table games, poker room, bingo. **FOOD & ENTERTAINMENT:** restaurant, food court, buffet, coffee shop, lounge, sports bar, event center. **LODGING:** Spa hotel. **CAMPING:** Free RV parking (no hookups). Must check in with Security to obtain a parking permit to be displayed on the vehicle. **DIRECTIONS:** Take exit 8 from the AZ-101 Loop N; go east on W Northern Ave.

## Laveen

### Vee Quiva Hotel & Casino
*15091 S Komatke Ln*
*Laveen, AZ 85339*

www.wingilariver.com/vee-quiva
800-946-4452

**DESCRIPTION:** Modern boutique resort on west side of Phoenix. **GAMING:** 24/7, slots, table games, bingo, poker room. **FOOD & ENTERTAINMENT:** restaurant, food court, coffee shop, entertainment center. Small stage lounge entertainment. **LODGING:** Stylish hotel. **CAMPING:** Free dry camping (no hookups) available on the south side of the lot near the hotel entrance. Check in with Security if you plan to stay overnight. **DIRECTIONS:** From I-10 at exit 139, travel south on 51st Avenue for 10 miles to Komatke Lane.

## Maricopa

### Harrah's Ak-Chin Casino Resort
*15406 N Maricopa Rd*
*Maricopa, AZ 85139*

www.harrahsakchin.com
480-802-5000

**DESCRIPTION:** South of Phoenix, resort hosted by Ak-Chin Indian Community. **GAMING:** 24 hrs, slots & video poker, keno parlor, table games, poker room, bingo hall. **FOOD & ENTERTAINMENT:** steakhouse, buffet, grill, cafe, free lounge entertainment. **LODGING:** Luxury hotel, Native American crafts shop, smoke shop. **CAMPING:** Free RV overnight parking, southeast corner of the lot, no hookups. Please obtain a parking permit from Valet or Security. **DIRECTIONS:** From I-10 exit 164, turn right on to Queen Creek Road for 17 miles to the casino.

## Parker

### Blue Water Resort & Casino
*11300 Resort Dr*
*Parker, AZ 85344*

www.bluewaterfun.com
928-669-7000 • RV Park: 928-669-2433

**DESCRIPTION:** Destination resort on the Colorado River. **GAMING:** open 24 hrs, slots, live gaming tables, keno, bingo. **FOOD & ENTERTAINMENT:** steakhouse, buffet, grill, cantina, cafe, bakery, deli, shows in amphitheater. **LODGING:** Hotel, movie theater, arcade, miniature golf & golf course. **CAMPING:** RV resort, full-hookup sites & cable TV. Boat launches, river fishing. Special events during winter season. Designated free dry camping area is in the upper lot. Overnight RV stays are limited to one night. **DIRECTIONS:** Located

about 160 miles west of Phoenix. From Quartzsite, go north 35 miles on SR-95 into Parker. Turn right at Riverside Drive and go 1.5 miles to the casino.

## Payson

### Mazatzal Hotel & Casino
*Highway 87 - Mile Marker 251*
*Payson, AZ 85541*

www.mazatzal-casino.com
928-474-6044 • 800-777-7529

**DESCRIPTION:** Mountain resort northeast of Phoenix. **GAMING:** slots & card room **FOOD & ENTERTAINMENT:** fine dining, casual grill, coffee bar, lounge. **LODGING:** All-suite hotel. **CAMPING:** For RV parking, inform Security if staying overnight; 3-night stay limit; no hookups. Follow signs to overflow parking & park on the level lots across from the casino, walking distance. **DIRECTIONS:** From Phoenix, go north on SR-87 (the Beeline) to mile marker 251.

## Pinetop

### Hon-Dah Resort Casino
*777 Hwy 260/Jct Hwy 73*
*Pinetop, AZ 85935*

www.hon-dah.com
928-369-0299 • 800-929-8744
RV Park: 928-369-7400

**DESCRIPTION:** Largest casino resort in the White Mountains. **GAMING:** open 24/7, slots, video poker, gaming tables & poker room. **FOOD & ENTERTAINMENT:** restaurant, buffet, snack bar. Free lounge entertainment. Outdoor concerts on festival grounds. **LODGING:** Hotel, cigar bar, gift shop. **CAMPING:** Sunrise RV Park, 258 level wooded sites. RVs required to check into the Park. Summer is busy, reservations suggested. Dry camping permitted only after RV Park is full. **DIRECTIONS:** Located at the junction of Hwy-260 and Hwy-73 (three miles south of Pinetop). From I-40 exit 286, take SR-77 south for 47 miles to Show Low; US-60 west .6 miles; turn left and head southeast 15.8 miles on SR-260.

# Sahuarita

## Desert Diamond
*1100 W Pima Mine Rd*
*Sahuarita, AZ 85629*

www.ddcaz.com
520-294-7777

**DESCRIPTION:** One of three casinos hosted by Tohono O'dham Nation of Southern Arizona. **GAMING:** open 24/7, slots, live blackjack tables, poker and keno. **FOOD & ENTERTAINMENT:** restaurant, buffet, grill, lounge, sports bar, event center. **LODGING:** There is no hotel at this location. **CAMPING:** Free overnight parking for large vehicles at the north end of the lot; shuttle service. RVs must obtain a parking pass if staying overnight. Limit 7 days. **DIRECTIONS:** From I-19 exit 80, the casino is on the north side of Pima Mine Rd.

# San Carlos

## Apache Gold Casino Resort
*5 U.S. Highway 70 (milepost 258)*
*San Carlos, AZ 85550*

www.apache-gold-casino.com
928-475-7800 • 800-272-2438
RV Park: 800-272-2438 Ext. 3515 or 3658

**DESCRIPTION:** Destination resort with casino, RV Park, bass fishing nearby. **GAMING:** open 24/7, slots, video poker, keno, blackjack tables, poker room, bingo. **FOOD & ENTERTAINMENT:** Grill, buffet, lunch and dinner. Live shows in Cabaret. **LODGING:** Best Western hotel **CAMPING:** Mountain View RV Park, 60 extra wide, full-hookup, pull-thru sites, walking distance to the casino, heated pool/spa, laundry, convenience store. Free RV overnight parking is also permitted in the casino lot; upon arrival obtain a parking permit at the convenience store. **DIRECTIONS:** From Globe, go east for six miles on US-70 (a major four-lane road).

# Scottsdale

## Talking Stick Resort
*9800 East Talking Stick Way*
*Scottsdale, AZ 85256*

www.talkingstickresort.com
480-850-7777 • 877-724-4687

**DESCRIPTION:** Lavish, mountain destination resort in Scottsdale. **GAMING:** 24hrs, slots, gaming tables, race book, non-smoking poker room. **FOOD & ENTERTAINMENT:** Six restaurants, fine dining to casual; bars and lounges with live entertainment. Ticketed shows at ballroom, golf course. Salt River Fields, Spring Training home of AZ Diamondbacks. **LODGING:** Luxury hotel, day spa. **CAMPING:** RV camping, no hookups, in the southwest corner of the lot (section "G"). RV parking fee, $25 per day; pay at the gift shop, then get the parking permit from Security. **DIRECTIONS:** Located 15 miles northeast of Phoenix, next to Loop 101. Take exit 44, then east.

# Somerton

## Cocopah Casino Resort
*15318 S Ave B (Rt-95)*
*Somerton, AZ 85350*

www.cocopahresort.com
928-726-8066 • 800-237-5687

**DESCRIPTION:** Resort on a mesa, Sonoran Desert views. **GAMING:** 24-hrs, slots, blackjack tables, bingo every day. **FOOD & ENTERTAINMENT:** restaurant, food court, lounge, sports bar. Entertainment in lounge. Ticketed concerts. **LODGING:** Contemporary hotel. **CAMPING:** 30 spaces designated for RV dry camping at $5 per night. Pay at the cashier's cage. Shuttle service to casino. **DIRECTIONS:** From I-8 near the California border, exit at 16th St. Take 16th Street to Avenue B (US-95). Go seven miles south on Avenue B toward Somerton.

# Tucson

## Casino Del Sol Resort
*5655 W Valencia*
*Tucson, AZ 85757*

www.casinodelsol.com
855-765-7829 • 800-344-9435

**DESCRIPTION:** Destination resort near Tucson. **GAMING:** open 24/7, slots, gaming tables, poker room, bingo daily. **FOOD & ENTERTAINMENT:** steakhouse, buffet, cafe, grille, deli, diner. Shows in amphitheater. Live music in the lounge, golf course. **LODGING:** Luxury hotel, spa. **CAMPING:** Space for RVs near the amphitheater. Free overnight parking for self-contained vehicles (except on concert nights.) The casino requests that RVs not use jacks in the parking lot. **DIRECTIONS:** From I-19 exit 95 (W Valencia Rd exit) go 8 miles west on Valencia.

### Casino of the Sun

*7406 S Camino De Oeste*
*Tucson, AZ 85746*

www.casinosun.com
520-883-1700

**DESCRIPTION:** The smaller 24-hour sister casino to Casino Del Sol. **GAMING:** slots and table games. **FOOD & ENTERTAINMENT:** buffet, full service restaurant. **LODGING:** There is no hotel at this location. Smoke shop and gift shop on site. **CAMPING:** Free RV parking; notify Security if staying overnight. **DIRECTIONS:** From I-19 exit 95 (W Valencia Rd exit), go 7 miles west to Camino De Oeste, turn left.

### Desert Diamond Hotel

*7350 S Nogales Hwy*
*Tucson, AZ 85756*

www.ddcaz.com
520-294-7777 • 866 332-9467

**DESCRIPTION:** Large destination casino resort. **GAMING:** 24-hrs, slots, video poker, gaming tables, bingo, live keno, smoke-free gaming area. **FOOD & ENTERTAINMENT:** steakhouse, buffet, grill, casual dining, sports bar, lounges with live music, special events in the nightclub. **LODGING:** Contemporary hotel. **CAMPING:** Free overnight parking; designated RV area near the hotel, dry camping. Security officer will assist with parking and give you required paperwork to complete for your free stay. **DIRECTIONS:** From I-19 exit 95 take Valencia Rd east to Nogales Hwy, then south on Nogales Hwy, 1 mile.

## Yuma

### Paradise Casino

*450 Quechan Dr*
*Yuma, AZ 85364*

www.paradise-casinos.com
760-572-7777 • 888-777-4946

**DESCRIPTION:** Casino near the California border owned & operated by the Quechan Indian Tribe. **GAMING:** 24-hour slots, bingo every day. **FOOD & ENTERTAINMENT:** restaurant, lounge with live entertainment. Shows in event center. **LODGING:** There is no hotel at this location. **CAMPING:** RVs may park on dirt area designated for large vehicles. Overnight parking is available only for persons in the casino. **DIRECTIONS:** From I-8 exit at 4th Ave and follow casino signs.

**Note**: A casino resort, also operated by the Quechan Tribe, is located in Winterhaven, California, about eight miles west of the Paradise Casino.

# California

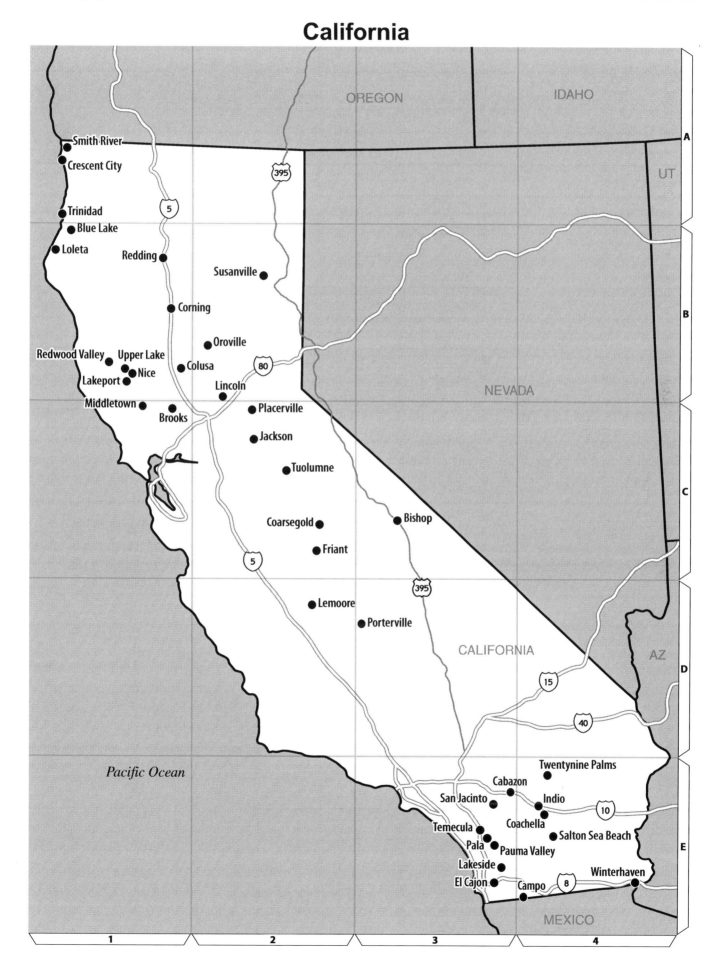

# California

| City | Casino | 🚐 | **P** | 🛏 | 🏌 | 🛡 |
|---|---|---|---|---|---|---|
| Alpine | Viejas Casino | | x | x | | 2 |
| Bishop | Paiute Palace Casino | | | | | |
| Blue Lake | Blue Lake Casino Hotel | | x | x | | |
| Brooks | Cache Creek Casino Resort | | x | x | x | |
| Cabazon | Morongo Casino Resort & Spa | | x | x | | 1 |
| Campo | Golden Acorn Casino | | x | | | 1 |
| Coachella | Augustine Casino | | x | | | 5 |
| Coachella | Spotlight 29 Casino | | x | | | 1 |
| Coarsegold | Chukchansi Gold Resort & Casino | | x | x | | |
| Colusa | Colusa Casino Resort | | x | x | | |
| Corning | Rolling Hills Casino | p72 | x | x | x | 1 |
| Crescent City | Elk Valley Casino | | x | | | |
| El Cajon | Sycuan Casino | | x | x | x | 7 |
| Friant | Table Mountain Casino | | x | | | |
| Indio | Fantasy Springs Resort Casino | | x | x | x | 1 |
| Jackson | Jackson Rancheria Casino Resort | p100 | | x | | |
| Lakeport | Konocti Vista Casino | p74 | x | x | | |
| Lakeside | Barona Resort & Casino | | x | x | x | 10 |
| Lemoore | Tachi Palace Hotel & Casino | | x | x | | |
| Lincoln | Thunder Valley Casino Resort | | x | x | | 7 |
| Loleta | Bear River Casino Hotel | | x | x | | |
| Middletown | Twin Pine Casino & Hotel | | x | x | | |
| Nice | Robinson Rancheria Resort & Casino | | x | x | | |
| Oroville | Feather Falls Casino & Lodge | p43 | | x | | |
| Oroville | Gold Country Casino & Hotel | p77 | x | x | | |
| Pala | Pala Casino Spa Resort | p100 | | x | | 5 |
| Pauma Valley | Casino Pauma | | x | | | |
| Placerville | Red Hawk Casino | | x | | | |
| Porterville | Eagle Mountain Casino | | x | | | |
| Redding | Win-River Casino | p13 | | x | | 8 |
| Redwood Valley | Coyote Valley Casino | | x | | | |
| Salton Sea Beach | Red Earth Casino | | x | | | |
| San Jacinto | Soboba Casino | | x | | x | |
| Smith River | Lucky 7 Casino | | x | x | | |

| City | Casino | 🚐 | 🅿 | 🛏 | 🏌 | 🛡 |
|------|--------|-----|-----|-----|-----|-----|
| Susanville | Diamond Mountain Casino & Hotel | | x | x | | |
| Temecula | Pechanga Resort Casino | p168 | x | x | x | 3 |
| Trinidad | Cher-Ae Heights Casino | | | | | |
| Tuolumne | Black Oak Casino | p85 | x | x | | |
| Twentynine Palms | Tortoise Rock Casino | | x | | | |
| Upper Lake | Running Creek Casino | | x | | | |
| Winterhaven | Quechan Casino Resort | | x | x | | 1 |

Gaming came to the state in 2000, when voters approved legislation to permit casinos on California's Indian lands. Currently, 62 California Tribes host casino gambling, ranging from small country casinos to large, lavish resorts. Some casinos are in remote locations, others near the freeways. Casinos that do not permit RV parking on their property or do not have 24-hour security are not included in this book.

# Alpine

### Viejas Casino
5000 Willows Rd
Alpine, CA 91901

www.viejas.com
619-445-5400

**DESCRIPTION:** 25 miles east of San Diego, resort is adjacent to an outlet mall. **GAMING:** slots, live tables, poker room, racebook, bingo. **FOOD & ENTERTAINMENT:** steakhouse, buffet, cafe, coffee bar, lounge. Summer concerts in the park, live entertainment in the lounge. **LODGING:** Viejas Hotel. **CAMPING:** Free overnight RV parking in Lot 11, east of the casino, 24-hour stay limit. Shuttle to casino. Nearby Ma-Tar-Awa Campground (at 619-445-3276) has free shuttle service to the casino. **DIRECTIONS:** From I-8 exit 33 (Alpine Blvd/Willows Rd) take Willows Rd north for 1.5 miles.

# Bishop

### Paiute Palace Casino
2742 N Sierra Hwy (US-395)
Bishop, CA 93514

www.paiutepalace.com
760-873-4150 • 888-372-4883

**DESCRIPTION:** Casino at foot of the Eastern Sierras, on US-395. **GAMING:** 24/7, slots, table games, poker room, tournaments. **FOOD & ENTERTAINMENT:** restaurant. Convenience store; 24-hour gas station. **LODGING:** There is no hotel at this location. **CAMPING:** Dry camping, $10 per day, register at Players Club for parking permit. Shuttle service. Well-lit RV lot, no hookups & no dump. Water is available. **DIRECTIONS:** The casino is located directly on the southbound side of US-395, near the junction of US-6, on the north end of Bishop.

# Blue Lake

### Blue Lake Casino Hotel
777 Casino Way
Blue Lake, CA 95525

www.bluelakecasino.com
877-252-2946

**DESCRIPTION:** Casino resort on the Redwoods Coast, north of Eureka. **GAMING:** slots, gaming tables, poker room, non-smoking areas. **FOOD & ENTERTAINMENT:** fine dining, casual cafe, pub & sports bar, entertainment in the lounge. Resort hosts seasonal festivals, expos. **LODGING:** Luxury hotel. **CAMPING:** Secure RV lot located next to the gas station, walking distance to casino. Convenience store. Two free nights RV stay for casino players. No hookups, dump station, air, water & supplies. **DIRECTIONS:** From US-101 exit 716A, take CA-299 east for 5.4 miles to the Blue Lake exit.

## Brooks

### Cache Creek Casino Resort
*14455 State Hwy 16*
*Brooks, CA 95606*

www.cachecreek.com
530-796-3118 • 888-772-2243

**DESCRIPTION:** Casino resort in Northern California's Capay Valley. **GAMING:** slots, gaming tables, high stakes table area, baccarat, non-smoking slots area. **FOOD & ENTERTAINMENT:** steakhouse, buffet, Asian, cafe, deli, coffee shop, sports pub, grill. Entertainment weekends. **LODGING:** Luxury hotel, golf course, Mini mart/gas station. **CAMPING:** Surface parking for RVs, follow the road toward the hill past the mini mart to the bus/RV lot. Free overnight parking OK, no hookups. **DIRECTIONS:** From I-505 exit 21 follow CA-16 west 12.5 miles. The casino is on the right in Brooks.

## Cabazon

### Morongo Casino Resort & Spa
*49500 Seminole Dr*
*Cabazon, CA 92230*

www.morongocasinoresort.com
951-849-3080 • 800-252-4499

**DESCRIPTION:** Casino resort on Morongo Indian Reservation, near I-10. **GAMING:** 24/7, slots & gaming tables; poker room. **FOOD & ENTERTAINMENT:** buffet, fine dining, Mexican & Asian specialties, food court, bar & grill. Headline entertainment weekends, live music in the lounge. **LODGING:** Luxury hotel. **CAMPING:** RV and truck parking next to the bingo hall. Overnight RV parking permitted, free, no hookups. **DIRECTIONS:** From I-10 at exit 144, the casino can be seen from the interstate. Coming from the east on I-10, take the Cabazon/Main St. exit, go north, then west on Seminole Dr. Coming from the west, exit at Apache Trail, then north to Seminole Dr., then east to the casino.

## Campo

### Golden Acorn Casino
*1800 Golden Acorn Way*
*Campo, CA 91906*

www.goldenacorncasino.com
619-938-6000

**DESCRIPTION:** Popular truck stop 40 miles east of San Diego alongside Interstate 8. **GAMING:** open 24/7, slots, live action gaming tables, bingo. **FOOD & ENTERTAINMENT:** restaurant, deli, bar. Convenience store. **LODGING:** There is no hotel at this location. **CAMPING:** Ample parking for RVs. Free overnight dry camping permitted. **DIRECTIONS:** At I-8 exit 61, casino is visible from the interstate.

## Coachella

### Augustine Casino
*84-001 Ave 54*
*Coachella, CA 92236*

www.augustinecasino.com
760-391-9500

**DESCRIPTION:** Cozy 24-hour casino, five miles from I-10, where the locals play. **GAMING:** slots, gaming tables, non-smoking slots area. **FOOD & ENTERTAINMENT:** Cafe 54, buffet or menu service, casual bar & grill, lounge. **LODGING:** There is no hotel at this location. **CAMPING:** RV parking, east side of the lot, sections E7 and E9. Free overnight parking OK. **DIRECTIONS:** From 1-10, exit 146, south on Dillon Rd for 1.5 miles, south on Van Buren St for 3 miles to the casino (corner of Van Buren & Avenue 54).

### Spotlight 29 Casino
*46-200 Harrison Pl*
*Coachella, CA 92236*

www.spotlight29.com
760-775-5566

**DESCRIPTION:** Casino, hosted by 29 Palms Band of Indians, located next to the interstate. **GAMING:** open 24 hours, slots, live gaming tables, poker room, non-smoking section. **FOOD & ENTERTAINMENT:** steakhouse, buffet, entertainment in the bars. Shows on weekends. **LODGING:** There is no hotel at this location. **CAMPING:** RV parking is next to the truck parking. Overnight is OK, stay limit 24 hours. **DIRECTIONS:** The casino is 130 miles east of Los Angeles. From I-10 exit 146 (Dillon Rd/Coachilla), the casino can be seen from the eastbound lanes of the interstate.

## Coarsegold

### Chukchansi Gold Resort & Casino
*711 Lucky Ln*
*Coarsegold, CA 93614*

www.chukchansigold.com
559-692-5200 • 866-794-6946

**DESCRIPTION:** Casino in the Sierra foothills, 20 miles from Yosemite National Park's southern entrance. **GAMING:** 24/7, slots, gaming tables, poker room. **FOOD & ENTERTAINMENT:** buffet, cafe, noodle bar, steakhouse, diner, bakery. Live concerts, shows. Free lounge entertainment. **LODGING:** Hotel, amenities. **CAMPING:** Designated area for RV parking is the back far-left corner of the lot. Overnight parking permitted. No hookups. Notify Security if staying overnight. **DIRECTIONS:** From CA-99 exit 131 take CA-41 north for 36.3 miles then east on Lucky Lane .7 mile.

## Colusa

### Colusa Casino Resort
*3770 Hwy 45*
*Colusa, CA 95932*

www.colusacasino.com
530-458-8844

**DESCRIPTION:** Casino resort 75 miles north of Sacramento on Wintun Reservation. **GAMING:** 24/7, slots, live table games, keno, high stakes bingo. Food and Entertainment: fine dining, buffet, grill, snack bar & lounge. **LODGING:** Lodge rooms, amenities. **CAMPING:** RV parking lot is behind the casino, no hookups. Free overnight parking is permitted. **DIRECTIONS:** From I-5 Williams exit 578, take CA-20 east 8.4 miles, then north on CA-45 for 3.1 miles.

## Corning

### Rolling Hills Casino
*2655 Everett Freeman Way*
*Corning, CA 96021*

www.rollinghillscasino.com
530-528-3500 • 530-528-3586 (RV Reservations)

**DESCRIPTION:** The resort includes a casino, Lodge, Inn, RV Park, Travelers Center & golf course. **GAMING:** slots, live-action gaming tables, separate non-smoking areas. **FOOD & ENTERTAINMENT:** buffet, steakhouse, lounge, coffeehouse. Live shows in the event center; golf course. **LODGING:** Inn and Lodge, amenities. **CAMPING:** 72 full-hookup, extra long pull-thru sites, Wi-Fi access, easy walk to casino & golf course. RV Park registration at the Travelers Center; RV host on site. Laundry, pet day care available. Free overnight parking is also permitted in the front lot. **DIRECTIONS:** Located about 115 miles north of Sacramento. From I-5 exit 628 in Corning (at Liberal Ave), Rolling Hills is visible from the southbound lanes of the interstate.

## Crescent City

### Elk Valley Casino
*2500 Howland Hill Rd*
*Crescent City, CA 95531*

www.elkvalleycasino.com
707-464-1020 • 888-574-2744

**DESCRIPTION:** Along California coastline on the edge of Redwood National Forest. **GAMING:** Small 24-hour casino, slots, blackjack tables, poker room, bingo four days a week. **FOOD & ENTERTAINMENT:** bar & grill, open daily, morning till night. **LODGING:** There is no hotel at this location. **CAMPING:** Free dry camping in the gravel lot, no hookups, 2 night stay limit. Register with Security at the front door of the casino upon arrival. **DIRECTIONS:** From US-101 south end of Crescent City, go north on Humboldt Rd 1.5 miles then east at Howland Hill Rd.

## El Cajon

### Sycuan Casino
*5469 Casino Way*
*El Cajon, CA 92019*

www.sycuan.com
619-445-6002 • 800-279-2826

**DESCRIPTION:** A two-story casino 10 miles east of San Diego. **GAMING:** open 24/7: slots, pit/gaming tables, bingo, large non-smoking area for slots & tables with separate entrance. **FOOD & ENTERTAINMENT:** restaurant, buffet, deli, grill, sports bar & snack bar. Live entertainment. **LODGING:** Hotel, amenities. **CAMPING:** RVs should park behind the casino building. Free overnight parking is permitted. Obtain a parking permit from Security if you plan to stay longer than 24 hours. **DIRECTIONS:** From I-8 El Cajon/Second St exit, south on Second and left on Washington for one mile. The street name changes to Dehesa, proceed for six more miles to the casino.

## Friant

### Table Mountain Casino
*8184 Table Mountain Rd*
*Friant, CA 93626*

www.tmcasino.com
559-822-7777

**DESCRIPTION:** Friendly casino in California Central Valley. **GAMING:** open 24-hours, slots, gaming tables, nine-table poker room, bingo. **FOOD & ENTERTAINMENT:** buffet, restaurant, 24-hour cafe. Ticketed concerts at event center. **LODGING:** No hotel at this location. **CAMPING:** Free overnight RV parking on the dirt lot, west side of the casino. Notify Security if staying overnight. **DIRECTIONS:** From CA-99 exit 131 take CA-41 north for 9.9 miles, then exit 135 to Friant Rd east 11.2 miles, continue on Millerton Rd 4.4 miles then north on Table Mountain Rd .2 mile.

## Indio

### Fantasy Springs Resort Casino
*84-245 Indio Springs Dr*
*Indio, CA 92203*

www.fantasyspringsresort.com
760-345-2450

**DESCRIPTION:** Casino destination resort in Palm Springs Valley. **GAMING:** open 24/7, slots, table games, poker room, off track betting, bingo. **FOOD & ENTERTAINMENT:** Six restaurants, casual & fine dining, 3 lounges, coffee bar. Special events weekly, comedy club, bowling alley, golf course. **LODGING:** Luxury hotel. **CAMPING:** RV parking is in the north lot, free overnight permitted for self-contained vehicles. **DIRECTIONS:** 125 miles east of Los Angeles, just off I-10 at exit 144. Casino is visible from the interstate.

## Jackson

### Jackson Rancheria Casino Resort
*12222 New York Ranch Rd*
*Jackson, CA 95642*

www.jacksoncasino.com
800-822-9466 • RV Park: 209-223-8358

**DESCRIPTION:** Resort on the Miwuk Reservation in foothills of the Sierras. **GAMING:** 24/7, slots, video poker, gaming tables, poker room, non-smoking areas. **FOOD & ENTERTAINMENT:** fine dining, casual buffet, grill, cafe & bakery, coffee bar. Ticketed showroom events, summer concerts. Free live music in lounge. **LODGING:** Hotel & amenities. **CAMPING:** Modern RV Park has a pool, recreation building, Wi-Fi throughout. Shuttle to the casino. If staying overnight, RVs are required to check into the RV Park. (Day use only RV parking in Lot 5.) **DIRECTIONS:** From CA-99 exit 254A, take CA-88 (steep grades) north 38 miles, then north on CA-104/Ridge Road 6 miles to New York Ranch Rd south 1.2 miles.

## Lakeport

### Konocti Vista Casino
*2755 Mission Rancheria Rd*
*Lakeport, CA 95453*

www.kvcasino.com
707-262-1900 • RV Park: 877-577-7829

**DESCRIPTION:** On Clear Lake, California's largest natural lake. **GAMING:** slots, video poker, live gaming tables; casino open 8am-2am/24 hours (weekends). **FOOD & ENTERTAINMENT:** Cafe, coffee shop, bar. Music events indoor & outdoor. **LODGING:** Hotel, free Wi-Fi, pool overlooks marina, convenience store, smoke shop. Marina/boat launch, fishing off the dock. **CAMPING:** RV Park, 74 paved full hookup sites, showers, laundry, fitness center. Register at the hotel. RV guests invited to use the pool & other hotel amenities. Limited free RV parking is next to the casino lot, but if staying longer than a day or two, RVers are requested to register at the RV Park. **DIRECTIONS:** From US-101 in Hopland take CA-175 east 17.5 miles, then Soda Bay Rd east 1.8 miles & Mission Rancheria Rd north .5 mile. IMPORTANT NOTE FOR RVs: Highway 175 is NOT recommended for RVs or vehicles with large trailers. It is a narrow, winding mountain road with tight turns. A suggested alternate route is: From US-101 exit 555B (toward Upper Lake Williams) take CA-20 south for 19.5 miles, then take CA-29 south for 11 miles, then CA-281 toward Soda Bay Rd/Clear Lake & stay on US-281/S. Main St for 1.7 miles and turn left onto Mission Rancheria Rd.

## Lakeside

### Barona Resort & Casino
*1932 Wildcat Canyon Rd*
*Lakeside, CA 92040*

www.barona.com
619-443-2300

**DESCRIPTION:** Southern CA luxury resort hosted by Barona Band of Mission Indians. **GAMING:** slots, video poker, video roulette, modified craps, live table games, poker room, off track betting parlor, bingo. **FOOD & ENTERTAINMENT:** buffet, steakhouse, Italian, Mexican & Asian cuisines, cafe, food court, gameside dining. **LODGING:** Hotel, day spa, golf course. **CAMPING:** RVs are welcome. Stop at the gate on arrival, Security will direct you to the designated RV area. No hookups. 72-hour stay limit. **DIRECTIONS:** From I-8 exit 23 go north on Lake Jennings Rd for 2.3 miles, continue on Mapleview St for .5 mile, east on Ashwood St for 1 mile then continue on Wildcat Canyon Road for 5.5 miles to the casino.

## Lemoore

### Tachi Palace Hotel & Casino
*17225 Jersey Ave*
*Lemoore, CA 93245*

www.tachipalace.com
800-942-6886

**DESCRIPTION:** In the heart of California's Central Valley. **GAMING:** 24-hour gaming on five floors, slots, pit/table games, poker room, bingo. **FOOD & ENTERTAINMENT:** buffet, grill, fast food, coffee shop, two lounges. Special events weekly, live entertainment on the casino floor. **LODGING:** Hotel. **CAMPING:** Free overnight parking is permitted for self-contained RVs in Lot 3. **DIRECTIONS:** From I-5 exit 309, go north on CA-41 for 20.7 miles, then east on Jersey Ave for 2.8 miles to the casino.

## Lincoln

### Thunder Valley Casino Resort
*1200 Athens Ave*
*Lincoln, CA 95648*

www.thundervalleyresort.com
916-408-7777

**DESCRIPTION:** Vegas-style casino near Sacramento. **GAMING:** slots, video poker, live action gaming tables, poker room, high limit area, bingo. **FOOD & ENTERTAINMENT:** buffet, steakhouse, cafe, food court, lounge. Shows in outdoor amphitheater. **LODGING:** Luxury hotel. **CAMPING:** RV parking in the designated lot for large vehicles across the street from the casino; overnight parking permitted, 72-hour stay limit, walking distance to the casino. **DIRECTIONS:** From I-80E exit 106, take CA-65 N toward Lincoln/Marysville. Take exit 311 for Sunset Blvd, follow signs to the casino.

## Loleta

### Bear River Casino Hotel
*11 Bear Paws Way*
*Loleta, CA 95551*

www.bearrivercasino.com
707-733-9644

**DESCRIPTION:** Friendly casino near Redwood National Park. **GAMING:** 24 hours, slots, live action gaming tables. Pump & Play smoke-free, alcohol-free, slots-only casino at the convenience store/gas station on property. **FOOD & ENTERTAINMENT:** restaurant, fast food, lounge. Ticketed events in the ballroom. Resort hosts seasonal fairs & festivals. **LODGING:** Hotel. **CAMPING:** Free overnight RV parking is in the top section of the lot. Pull in, then register with security and get a players card at the casino. **DIRECTIONS:** From US-101 exit 692 (Fernbridge/Ferndale), turn left on to Singley Rd. Follow signs.

## Middletown

### Twin Pine Casino & Hotel
*22223 CA29 at Rancheria Rd*
*Middletown, CA 95461*

www.twinpine.com
707-987-0197

**DESCRIPTION:** Casino resort at the northern gateway to Napa Valley. **GAMING:** 24/7, slots, live gaming tables. **FOOD & ENTERTAINMENT:** restaurant, fast food, bar & lounge, wine tastings. Free live lounge entertainment. Ticketed shows monthly. **LODGING:** Hotel rooms & suites. **CAMPING:** Free overnight RV parking on the perimeter of the lot mid-week only; NO RV parking on weekends due to space constraints. **DIRECTIONS:** From I-5 in Williams, CA-20 toward Clear Lake for about 36 miles, then CA-53 for 7 miles and CA-53/CA-29 for 15 miles.

## Nice

### Robinson Rancheria Resort & Casino
*1545 Hwy 20*
*Nice, CA 95464*

www.rrrc.com
707-262-4000

**DESCRIPTION:** Casino resort on Clear Lake north shore, hosted by the Pomo Indians. **GAMING:** open 24/7, slots, live gaming tables, bingo, smoke-free area. **FOOD & ENTERTAINMENT:** Grill, sports bar & snack bar. Weekend events. **LODGING:** Luxury hotel. **CAMPING:** Free overnight parking for RVs is permitted at the back of the lot or along the fence line. Please check in with Security; 48-hour stay limit. **DIRECTIONS:** From US-101 north of Ukiah, CA-20 east 21.8 miles toward Upper Lake/Williams. Robinson Rancheria is on the left as you enter Nice.

## Oroville

### Feather Falls Casino & Lodge
*3 Alverda Dr*
*Oroville, CA 95966*

www.featherfallscasino.com
530-533-3885 • RV Park: 530-533-9020

**DESCRIPTION:** Destination resort includes casino, hotel and RV Park. **GAMING:** 24/7, slots, blackjack tables, poker room. **FOOD & ENTERTAINMENT:** buffet open morning to night, restaurant serves lunch & dinner, live music, shows on weekends. **LODGING:** Lodge rooms/suites. **CAMPING:** KOA RV Park has 43 full hookup spaces, group meeting hall, store, gift shop, laundry. If staying overnight, RVs are asked to register at the RV Park. **DIRECTIONS:** From Marysville, take CA-70 north for 22.7 miles to Ophir Road, then three miles east on Ophir Road.

### Gold Country Casino & Hotel
*4020 Olive Hwy*
*Oroville, CA 95966*

www.goldcountrycasino.com
800-334-9400 • RV Park: 866-991-5060

**DESCRIPTION:** North of Sacramento, popular casino among locals. **GAMING:** 24/7, slots, live-action gaming tables, bingo. **FOOD & ENTERTAINMENT:** Lounge bar, buffet, cafe, espresso bar, snack bar. Events in The Showroom. Live music & dancing at the lounge & Piano Bar. **LODGING:** Luxury hotel, bowling center, gift shop. **CAMPING:** Berry Creek RV Park, adjacent to the casino, has 77 modern full-hookup sites, shuttle service, free CATV & Wi-Fi, pool, mini-mart, laundry, gas station. RVs staying overnight are required to check into the RV Park. **DIRECTIONS:** From CA-99 in Oroville Junction, east on CA-162 (Oroville Dam Rd & Olive Hwy) 10.4 miles.

# Pala

### Pala Casino & Spa Resort
*11154 Hwy 76*
*Pala, CA 92059*

www.palacasino.com
760-510-5100 • 877-946-7252
RV Resort: 844-472-5278 / rvresort@palacasino.com

**DESCRIPTION:** Premier resort in Northern San Diego County hosted by Pala Indian Reservation. **GAMING:** 24/7, slots, pit/gaming tables, poker room. **FOOD & ENTERTAINMENT:** buffet, steakhouse, noodles, cafe, deli, pizzeria, coffeehouse, lounge. Shows at Events Center & Starlight Theater. Free lounge entertainment. **LODGING:** Luxury hotel, retail shopping. Pala Nature Trail. **CAMPING:** 10-acre RV Resort has 100 full-service sites, free Wi-Fi, cable TV, heated swimming pool, 2 spas, many indoor/outdoor amenities, clubhouse, fenced dog park, shuttle to casino. Daytime parking only in the west lot at the casino. If staying overnight, must check in at the RV Park. **DIRECTIONS:** Located 35 miles northeast of San Diego, from I-15 exit 46 at SR-76 (Pala/Oceanside). Take SR-76 east for five miles to the casino.

# Pauma Valley

### Casino Pauma
*777 Pauma Reservation Rd*
*Pauma Valley, CA 92061*

www.casinopauma.com
877-687-2862

**DESCRIPTION:** Charming Indian casino overlooking the Palamar Mountains north of San Diego. **GAMING:** 24/7, slots, gaming tables, poker room. **FOOD & ENTERTAINMENT:** buffet, cafe, deli & pizzeria. Live lounge entertainment. Shows in Pauma Pavilion. **LODGING:** There is no hotel at this location. **CAMPING:** Free overnight parking for RVs, walking distance to the casino. Upon arrival, check in to obtain a parking permit from Security at the front door. **DIRECTIONS:** Take I-15, exit 46 to Hwy-76 (Oceanside/Pala exit) east for 12 miles to Pauma Reservation Rd. (Street sign is partially obstructed. Look for Jilburto's Taco Shop on the right and get into the left lane.) Turn left on to Pauma Reservation Rd for a half mile to the casino.

# Placerville

### Red Hawk Casino
*1 Red Hawk Pkwy*
*Placerville, CA 95667*

www.redhawkcasino.com
530-677-7000

**DESCRIPTION:** Casino on Rancheria of the Shingle Springs Band of Miwok Indians near Sacramento. **GAMING:** 24/7, slots, pit/gaming tables, high stakes room, smoke-free lower lever & poker room. **FOOD & ENTERTAINMENT:** steakhouse, buffet, cafe, Asian cuisine, coffee shop/snacks, three bars/lounges. Live music in the Stage Bar. **LODGING:** No hotel at this location. **CAMPING:** Free overnight parking available, 24-hour stay limit; check in with Security. **DIRECTIONS:** From Capitol City Freeway in Sacramento, east on US-50 for 36 miles, follow signs.

# Porterville

### Eagle Mountain Casino
*681 S Reservation Rd*
*Porterville, CA 93257*

www.eaglemtncasino.com
800-903-3353

**DESCRIPTION:** Cozy casino in the foothills above Porterville hosted by the Tule River Indian Tribe. **GAMING:** 24/7, slots, live action table games. **FOOD & ENTERTAINMENT:** buffet, steakhouse & food court. Ticketed concerts, shows. **LODGING:** There is no hotel at this location. **CAMPING:** Free overnight RV parking is permitted near the casino entrance. **DIRECTIONS:** From Hwy-99 exit 76 take CA-190 east for 21.1 miles then south on Road 284 for .5 mile, then east on Indian Reservation Rd.

# Redding

### Win-River Casino
*2100 Redding Rancheria Rd*
*Redding, CA 96001*

www.winriver.com
530-243-3377

DESCRIPTION: Premier Northern CA destination resort seven miles west of I-5. GAMING: 24-hr, slots, live gaming tables, poker room, bingo. FOOD & ENTERTAINMENT: restaurant, pub & grill, cafe, bar, lounge. DJs, live music weekends in the lounge. LODGING: Luxury hotel. CAMPING: 13 RV spaces with electric hookups at level, long concrete pads & BBQ. Maximum stay, 5 days. Register & pay at hotel front desk. RV free parking is day use only with permit. DIRECTIONS: From I-5 exit 667, merge north onto CA-273 for 7.1 miles, then west on Canyon Rd & south on Redding Rancheria Rd for .3 mile.

## Redwood Valley

*Coyote Valley Casino*
*455 BIA Road 228*
*Redwood Valley, CA 95470*

www.coyotevalleycasino.com
707-485-0700

DESCRIPTION: NOTE: New casino expected to open in 2019, just east of the 101 on Coyote Valley Indian Reservation. GAMING: slots, video poker, video keno, live-action gaming tables, poker room. FOOD & ENTERTAINMENT: Food venues include fine and casual dining, fast food. LODGING: New hotel by mid-2019. CAMPING: Call the casino for information about RV parking. DIRECTIONS: Located 5 miles north of Ukiah near US-101 West Road exit 557.

## Salton Sea Beach

*Red Earth Casino*
*3089 Norm Nivar Rd*
*Salton Sea Beach, CA 92274*

www.redearthcasino.com
760-395-1200

DESCRIPTION: Small, friendly casino at a travel center in the Coachella Valley. GAMING: 24-hour Vegas-style slots only. Food: restaurant & bar. Convenience store & gas station. LODGING: There is no hotel at this location. CAMPING: Free overnight parking for RVs, large paved lot south of the casino, 3-day limit. Must register with Security upon arrival. Free fresh water & fee-pay dump station at travel center. DIRECTIONS: From I-10 exit 146 (Dillon Rd) exit toward Coachella/CA-86 South. Take CA-86 south for about 27 miles.

## San Jacinto

*Soboba Casino*
*23333 Soboba Rd*
*San Jacinto, CA 92583*

www.soboba.com
951-665-1000 • 866-476-2622

DESCRIPTION: NOTE: By mid-2019 the casino will be moved to a new location at the corner of Lake Park Dr. & Soboba Rd, a few miles away from the address listed here. GAMING: 24/7, slots, video poker, table games, poker room. FOOD & ENTERTAINMENT: Various dining venues, lounge, bar. LODGING: Luxury hotel. CAMPING: RVs should check in with Security on arrival for parking information. DIRECTIONS: 90 miles east of Los Angeles. From I-215 exit 22 take Ramona Expressway east for 30 miles to Lake Park Dr. Turn left to the stop sign, then right on Soboba Road.

## Smith River

*Lucky 7 Casino*
*350 N Indian Rd*
*Smith River, CA 95567*

www.lucky7casino.com
707-487-7777

DESCRIPTION: Surrounded by natural beauty, near Oregon state line. GAMING: slots, blackjack tables, poker room, bingo, non-smoking gaming area. FOOD & ENTERTAINMENT: Full-service restaurant, sports bar. Travel Center has convenience store, low gas prices, 24-hr pumps. LODGING: smoke-free hotel. CAMPING: Designated RV parking behind the gas station, walking distance to casino; overnight parking is permitted. DIRECTIONS: The casino resort is visible from the northbound lanes of the 101 Freeway.

## Susanville

### Diamond Mountain Casino & Hotel

*900 Skyline Dr*
*Susanville, CA 96130*

www.dmcah.com
530-252-1100 • 877-319-8514

DESCRIPTION: Casino in a picturesque town in Northern California. GAMING: slots, gaming tables, non-smoking area, bingo. Open 24/7. FOOD & ENTERTAINMENT: cafe, coffee bar, sports bar & grill. Live shows, special events in the lounge. LODGING: Lodge-style rooms. CAMPING: Free overnight parking available for casino players. Park at the far end of the lot. Please notify Security if you plan to stay overnight. DIRECTIONS: 160 miles northeast of Sacramento on US-395 in Susanville (between Lake Tahoe and Lasson Volcanic Park).

## Temecula

### Pechanga Resort Casino

*45000 Pechanga Pkwy*
*Temecula, CA 92592*

www.pechanga.com
951-693-1819 • RV Park: 877-997-8386

DESCRIPTION: Spacious casino resort in Temecula Valley. GAMING: open 24/7, slots, gaming tables, high limit areas, non-smoking poker room, non-smoking areas on gaming floor. FOOD & ENTERTAINMENT: 11 dining venues, fine & casual dining, quick food. Shows in the theater. Comedy Club live shows weekends, musical guests in the Cabaret. LODGING: Luxury hotel, many amenities. CAMPING: Modern RV Park, 168 full-hookup sites, heated pool, two Jacuzzi spas, recreation room, laundry, gas station, car wash, convenience store. Pechanga can serve as home base for visitors exploring southern California, RV rallies welcome. Shuttle service to casino. Free dry camping is permitted in the lot behind the gas station (for limited stay). DIRECTIONS: From I-15, exit 50 (Indio/Route 79 South), Pechanga Indian Reservation signs are at the exit. Go south on Route 79 for .7 mile, right on Pechanga Parkway for 1.5 miles.

## Trinidad

### Cher-Ae Heights Casino

*27 Scenic Dr*
*Trinidad, CA 95570*

www.cheraeheightscasino.com
707-677-3611

DESCRIPTION: Casino on cliff overlooking Northern CA shore. GAMING: open 24/7, slots, live pit/gaming tables, poker room, bingo six days. FOOD & ENTERTAINMENT: fine dining, quick bites, Seascape venue for fresh seafood. LODGING: There is no hotel at this site. CAMPING: RV dry camping, no hookups. 24-hour shuttle. Check in with Security prior to parking. $20 maintenance fee for every 1-3 day stay. Call Security at 707-599-0124 for information. DIRECTIONS: From US-101 Trinidad exit 728 (Trinidad Beach sign at exit) immediately turn south on to Scenic Drive for one mile. Note: there are steep grades going up to the casino.

## Tuolumne

### Black Oak Casino

*19400 Tuolumne Rd N*
*Tuolumne, CA 95379*

www.blackoakcasino.com
877-747-8777 • RV Park: 209-928-9555

DESCRIPTION: In the Sierra foothills, resort hosted by The Tuolumne Band of Me-Wak Indians. GAMING: open 24/7, slots, keno, gaming tables, large smoke-free slots area. FOOD & ENTERTAINMENT: Nine restaurants: fine & casual dining, weekly themed buffets, cafe, fast food, coffee shop, sports bar & grill. Live regional music in the lounge, bowling center. LODGING: Smoke-free hotel, gift shop features authentic Native American goods & jewelry. CAMPING: Modern RV Park on a hillside just above the casino, 85 full-hookup sites, clubhouse, pool & spa, satellite TV, Wi-Fi, laundry, dog park, shuttle to casino. A good place to stop on the way into Yosemite. DIRECTIONS: 100 miles southeast of Sacramento. From CA-99 exit 233 take CA-219 east 4.8 miles, McHenry Ave north 1.8 mile, Patterson Rd east 3 miles, continue on CA-108 east for 40.6 miles to the Mono Way exit, then

Tuolumne Rd east 6.9 miles.

## Twentynine Palms

### Tortoise Rock Casino

*73829 Baseline Rd*
*Twentynine Palms, CA 92277*

www.tortoiserockcasino.com
760-367-9759

**DESCRIPTION:** Tribal gaming venue near Joshua Tree National Park. **GAMING:** open 24/7, slots, table games. **FOOD & ENTERTAINMENT:** grill open all day, live lounge entertainment weekends. **LODGING:** There is no hotel at this location. **CAMPING:** Free overnight parking for RVs, 72-hour stay limit. Follow signs to designated area. **DIRECTIONS:** From I-10 exit 117 follow SR-62 east for 41.5 miles then go south on Adobe Rd 1 mile.

## Upper Lake

### Running Creek Casino

*635 E Hwy 20*
*Upper Lake, CA 95485*

www.runningcreekcasino.com
707-262-5500

**DESCRIPTION:** Native American casino located on historic Hwy-20 corridor of Upper Lake. **GAMING:** open 24/7, slots & live action gaming tables (from 10am daily.) Slots & blackjack tournaments. Dining & Entertainment: restaurant, on-the-go express and lounge, local entertainment. **LODGING:** No hotel at this location. **CAMPING:** RVs may park on the dirt area of the lot. Up to 72 hours parking is permitted. **DIRECTIONS:** From US-101, take exit 55B for CA-20 East for 19 miles.

## Winterhaven

### Quechan Casino Resort

*525 Algodones Rd*
*Winterhaven, CA 92283*

www.playqcr.com
760-572-3900

**DESCRIPTION:** Mediterranean-themed destination resort with Quechan Tribal influence. **GAMING:** slots, table games, poker room. **FOOD & ENTERTAINMENT:** steakhouse, cafe, food court, sports bar & grill, event center. **LODGING:** Luxury hotel rooms/suites. **CAMPING:** RV area on the dirt lot south of the casino building. Free overnight parking permitted. **DIRECTIONS:** From I-8 exit 166, go south on Los Algodones Rd. for about 1 mile, casino on right.

# Colorado

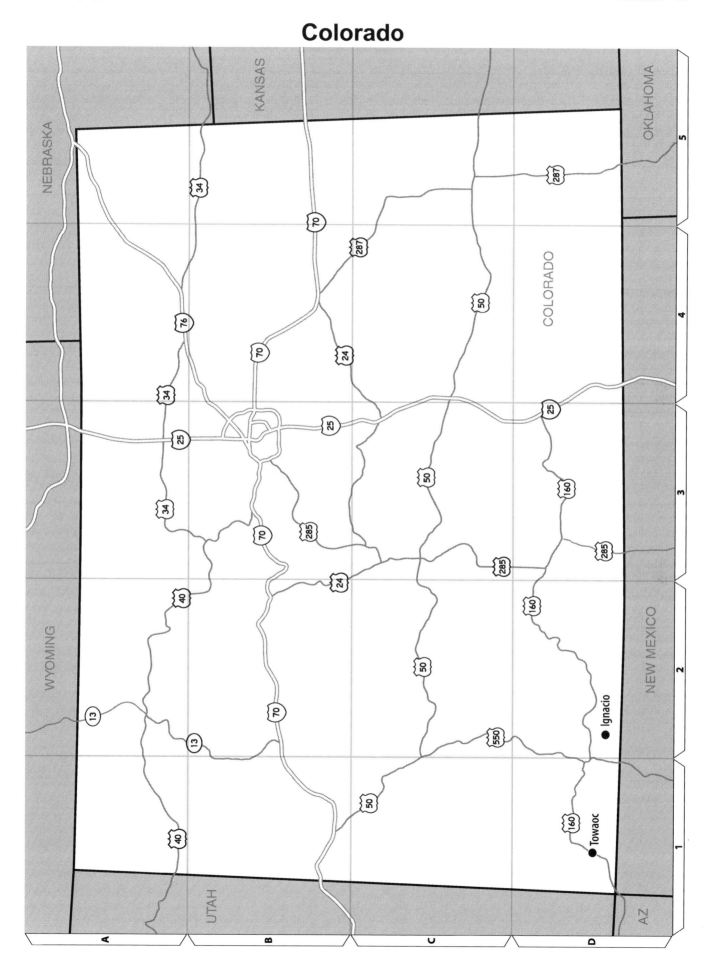

# Colorado

| City | Casino | 🚐 | **P** | 🛏 | 🏌 | 🛡 |
|------|--------|-----|-----|-----|-----|-----|
| Ignacio | Sky Ute Casino Resort | p24 | | x | | |
| Towaoc | Ute Mountain Casino, Hotel & Resort | p76 | x | x | | |

Two friendly Native-American casino resorts, located in southern CO off U.S. Highway 160, have modern RV accommodations. Located near popular tourist destinations including Mesa Verde and Four Corners.

## Ignacio

### Sky Ute Casino Resort
*14324 Hwy 172 N*
*Ignacio, CO 81137*

www.skyutecasino.com
970-563-7777 • 888-842-4180

**DESCRIPTION:** Premier resort surrounded by the beauty of the San Juan mountains. **GAMING:** open 24-hours, slots, pit/gaming tables, non-smoking poker room, bingo, smoke-free gaming areas, high stakes areas. **FOOD & ENTERTAINMENT:** steakhouse, cafe/bistro, grill, quick food, lounge. Concerts in event center, bowling alley. Southern Ute Cultural Center & Museum nearby. **LODGING:** 140 room/suite hotel, pool, fitness center, salon & sap, arcade, miniature golf, business center. **CAMPING:** Modern RV Park, 24 full-hookup sites; no tents or pop-ups. RV guests invited to use hotel amenities. **DIRECTIONS:** From junction US-160 & US-550 (east edge of Durango), go east two miles on US-160 to SR-172, then southeast on SR-172 for 18 miles.

## Towaoc

### Ute Mountain Casino, Hotel & Resort
*3 Weeminuche Dr*
*Towaoc, CO 81334*

www.utemountaincasino.com
970-565-8800 • 800-258-8007
RV Park: 970-565-6544

**DESCRIPTION:** Friendly resort nestled in the shadow of legendary Sleeping Ute Mountain. **GAMING:** 24/7, slots, pit/gaming tables, poker room, live keno, bingo. **FOOD & ENTERTAINMENT:** restaurant, dinner buffet Fridays. Concerts in convention center or outdoor venue. Comedy shows, martial arts, car shows, rodeos and Native American cultural events. Ute Tribal Park tours available. **LODGING:** Southwestern-themed hotel. **CAMPING:** RV Park, 76 level gravel sites, indoor swimming pool, convenience store, walking distance to the casino; shuttle service also provided. Free dry camping for RVs at the travel center south of the casino or on the perimeter of the hotel parking lot. **DIRECTIONS:** From junction US-160 and US-491 in Cortez, travel southwest for 11 miles on US-160/491.

# Connecticut

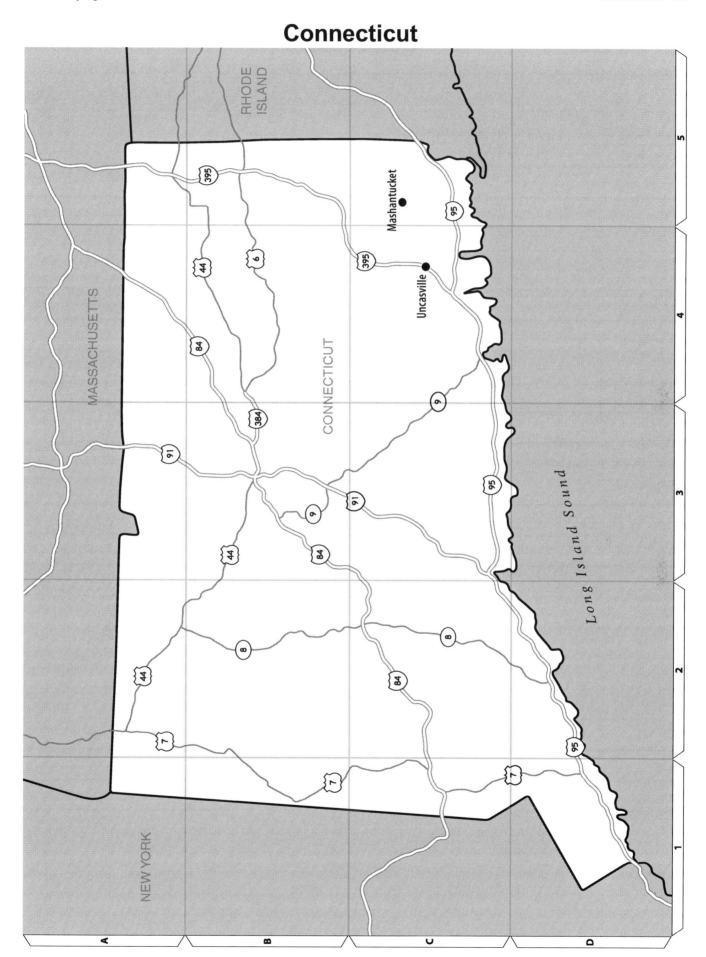

# Connecticut

| City | Casino | 🚐 | 🅿 | 🛏 | 🏌 | 🛡 |
|------|--------|-----|-----|-----|-----|-----|
| Mashantucket | Foxwoods Resort Casino | | x | x | x | 8 |
| Uncasville | Mohegan Sun Casino | | x | x | x | 4 |

Connecticut is home to two spectacular casinos: Foxwoods and Mohegan Sun. Noted worldwide for quality gaming and entertainment, they are located just across the Thames River from one another.

## Mashantucket

### Foxwoods Resort Casino
*350 Trolley Line Blvd*
*Mashantucket, CT 06338*

www.foxwoods.com
860-312-3000

**DESCRIPTION:** Famed Foxwoods, with over 340,000 square feet of gaming space, is one of the 10 largest casinos in the world. It's so big you will want to get a map at the information booth before touring the property. The Mashantucket Pequot Tribe opened Foxwoods in 1992. **GAMING:** slots, pit/table games, East Coast's largest poker room, high-tech race book, keno, non-smoking areas, high stakes bingo. **FOOD & ENTERTAINMENT:** 35 dining venues from gourmet to express. Concerts and shows, comedy club, music and dancing at bars. Golf courses, bowling center. **LODGING:** Four hotels, many amenities. **CAMPING:** From Route 2, RV Parking area is in Lot J, next to the Mobile Gas Station (across from Burger King). The lot is identified for RV parking only, overnight is OK. Dry camping, no hookups, shuttle service. **DIRECTIONS:** From I-95, exit 92, Route 2 west for eight miles to Foxwoods. From I-84, exit 55, Route 2 east to nine miles past Norwich.

## Uncasville

### Mohegan Sun Casino
*1 Mohegan Sun Blvd*
*Uncasville, CT 06382*

www.mohegansun.com
860-862-8000

**DESCRIPTION:** Created in 1996 by the Mohegan Tribe of Connecticut, Mohegan Sun is a lavish casino resort with 350,000 square feet of gaming and home to a spectacular indoor planetarium dome. **GAMING:** Three distinct casinos, slots, pit/table games, poker rooms, pari-mutuel simulcast & smoke-free gaming areas. **FOOD & ENTERTAINMENT:** 29 restaurants, bars and lounges, shopping mall, food court, specialty foods. Free entertainment nightly. Arena & cabaret for special events. **LODGING:** Hotel tower, many amenities, golf course. **CAMPING:** Designated RV parking lot, after you come off Route 2A turn right at the first traffic light and then turn right into the RV lot. Call Security at 860-862-7460 and they will come out to give you a parking permit. Dry camping only, no hookups. 24-hour shuttle service to the casino. **DIRECTIONS:** From I-95 exit 76, north on I-395 to exit 79A (Route 2A East). It is less than one mile to Mohegan Sun Blvd.

# Delaware

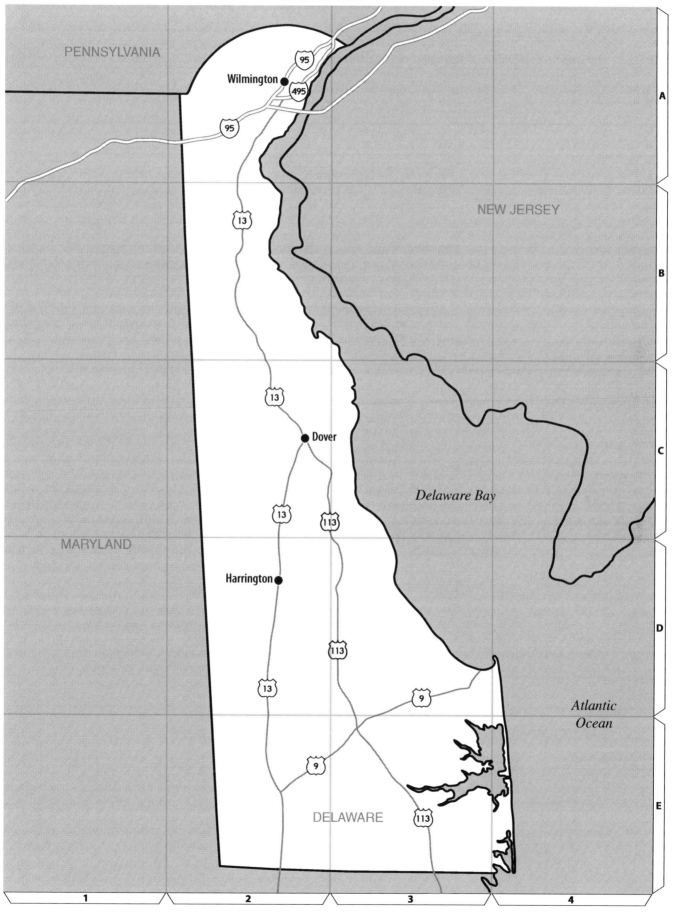

# Delaware

| City | Casino | 🚐 | **P** | 🛏 | 🏌 | 🛡 |
|---|---|---|---|---|---|---|
| Dover | Dover Downs Hotel & Casino | | x | x | | |
| Harrington | Harrington Raceway & Casino | p200 | x | | | |
| Wilmington | Delaware Park Casino | | x | | | 3 |

There are three pari-mutuel facilities in the state with live racing in season. Dover Downs also has NASCAR racing and Harrington is home to the State Fairgrounds and hosts the State Fair each July. All have casinos with slots, pit/table games, simulcasting and sports betting. All casinos are open 24/7 (closed on Easter and Christmas).

## Dover

### Dover Downs Hotel & Casino
*1131 N DuPont Hwy*
*Dover, DE 19901*

www.doverdowns.com
302-674-4600

**DESCRIPTION:** Destination resort in Mid-Delaware. **GAMING:** slots, video poker, live keno, pit/table games, poker room. Live harness racing Nov-Apr, simulcasting year-round. **FOOD & ENTERTAINMENT:** steakhouse, deli, buffet, casual dining, coffee shops. Dover International Speedway (NASCAR) adjacent to Dover Downs. **LODGING:** Hotel. **CAMPING:** RVs should park on the gravel or grassy portion of the casino lot. No hookups, overnight parking permitted for self-contained vehicles. **DIRECTIONS:** Dover Downs is within the city limits of Dover. From SR-1 exit 104 (north of Dover) merge onto Scarborough Rd/US-13 for one-half mile, then south on DuPont Hwy 1.4 miles.

## Harrington

### Harrington Raceway & Casino
*Delaware State Fairgrounds*
*18500 S DuPont Hwy*
*Harrington, DE 19952*

www.harringtonraceway.com
302-398-4920 • RV Park: 302-398-3269

**DESCRIPTION:** Casino and raceway located at the state fairgrounds. **GAMING:** slots, pit/table games, poker room, sports book, daily simulcasting. Live harness racing Apr-Jun, Aug-Oct, "Governor's Day Race" is during Delaware State Fair in July. **FOOD & ENTERTAINMENT:** restaurant, buffet, cafe, lounge, fast food. Snack bar at the track, sandwich shop. **LODGING:** There is no hotel at this location. **CAMPING:** RV Park has several hundred sites, water & electric hookups, central dump. Booked in advance for State Fair, last 2 weeks of July. Open all year; register & pay at administration building. Free RV parking also permitted along the fence where buses park. Overnight parking is OK. **DIRECTIONS:** Located 20 miles south of Dover at the State Fairgrounds on US-13.

## Wilmington

### Delaware Park Casino
*777 Delaware Park Blvd*
*Wilmington, DE 19804*

www.delawarepark.com
302-994-2521 • 800-417-5687

**DESCRIPTION:** Delaware Park combines thoroughbred racing with casino gaming. **GAMING:** slots, live action pit/gaming tables, poker room, daily simulcasting & sports betting. Thoroughbred racing daily, May-Oct. **FOOD & ENTERTAINMENT:** Fine dining, BBQ, pizza, casual cafe, bar & grill, coffee shop. **LODGING:** There is no hotel at this location. **CAMPING:** RVs may park in the bus/truck parking lot. RV overnight stay limit - 24 hours. **DIRECTIONS:** From I-95 exit 4B, take SR-7 north and follow signs to Delaware Park.

# Florida

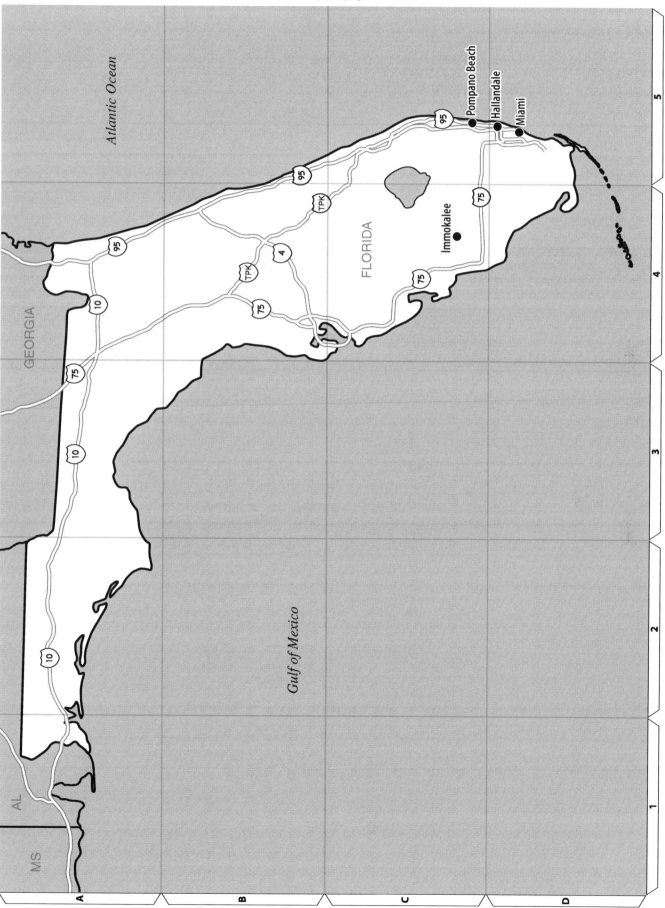

# Florida

| City | Casino | 🚐 | P | 🛏 | 🏌 | 🛡 |
|---|---|---|---|---|---|---|
| Hallandale | Gulfstream Park | | x | | | 2 |
| Immokalee | Seminole Casino Hotel | s6 | x | x | | |
| Miami | Miccosukee Resort & Gaming | | x | x | x | |
| Pompano Beach | Isle Casino Racing Pompano Park | | x | | | 2 |

The majority of Florida's casinos are not RV Friendly, primarily because of space constraints. State-authorized racinos (casinos located at race tracks) operate in Broward and Dade Counties; there are poker rooms at many other tracks. Florida's Indian tribes operate several gaming locations, but Seminole Hard Rock, in Tampa and in Hollywood do not permit RVs on property.

## Hallandale

### Gulfstream Park
*901 S Federal Hwy (US-1)*
*Hallandale, FL 33009*

www.gulfstreampark.com
954-454-7000

DESCRIPTION: Racino combines horse racing with casino gaming and entertainment. GAMING: slots, electronic gaming tables, live-action poker tables, daily simulcasting. Casino open 9am-3am weekdays/ 24hrs (weekends). Live thoroughbred racing Jan-Apr. FOOD & ENTERTAINMENT: clubhouse dining, full-service restaurant, deli. LODGING: There is no hotel at this location. CAMPING: RV parking in the south parking lot (off US-1) at the lower end of the lot, no shuttle. Call ahead to Security for parking authorization. Overnight is OK if the RV owner remains on property. DIRECTIONS: From I-95 exit 18 (Hallandale Beach Blvd) go east to US-1. Follow signs.

## Immokalee

### Seminole Casino Hotel
*506 S 1st St*
*Immokalee, FL 33934*

www.seminoleimmokaleecasino.com
239-658-1313

DESCRIPTION: Friendly, comfortable casino; where the locals play. GAMING: 24-hour slots, live table games, poker room. FOOD & ENTERTAINMENT: deli, noodle house, grill, coffee shop, fresh-baked pastries. Live entertainment weekends. LODGING: Modern hotel. CAMPING: Six free RV spaces with electric hookups available, first come, first-serve. Register at the Security podium before pulling in. DIRECTIONS: From I-75 exit 111, east on Hwy-846 (Immokalee Rd) for 35 miles to the casino.

## Miami

### Miccosukee Resort & Gaming
*500 SW 177th Ave*
*Miami, FL 33194*

www.miccosukee.com
305-925-2555

DESCRIPTION: Hospitable destination resort near southeastern Florida Everglades. GAMING: slots, video poker, table games, high limits gaming area, poker room, high stakes bingo. FOOD & ENTERTAINMENT: fine dining, buffet, 24-hour deli, cafe, snack bar, lounge, golf course; Entertainment center. LODGING: Luxury hotel. CAMPING: RV dry camping area, get a parking pass from Security to display on your vehicle. Overnight parking permitted. DIRECTIONS: From the

Florida Turnpike Homestead Extension exit 25, go west on US-41 for 5.7 miles, turn right, then left into the parking lot. The casino is located on SR-997 just north of US-41 (a major east-west route across south Florida). It is 11 miles north of Homestead.

## Pompano Beach

### *Isle Casino Racing Pompano Park*
*1800 SW Third St*
*Pompano Beach, FL 33069*

www.islepompanopark.com
954-972-2000 • 800-843-4753

**DESCRIPTION:** Isle of Capri location at the Winter Capital of Harness Racing. **GAMING:** Casino hours, 9am-3am/24hrs Fri-Sat, slots, pit/table games, poker room. Harness racing Oct-May, daily racing simulcasting. **FOOD & ENTERTAINMENT:** buffet, steakhouse, deli, Italian restaurant. Entertainment at Farraddays. **LODGING:** There is no hotel at this location. **CAMPING:** Check in with Security to obtain a parking permit. Overnight parking is OK. **DIRECTIONS:** From I-95 exit 36, travel 1.5 miles west, then left on Powerline Rd for .3 mile, then south to Third St.

# Idaho

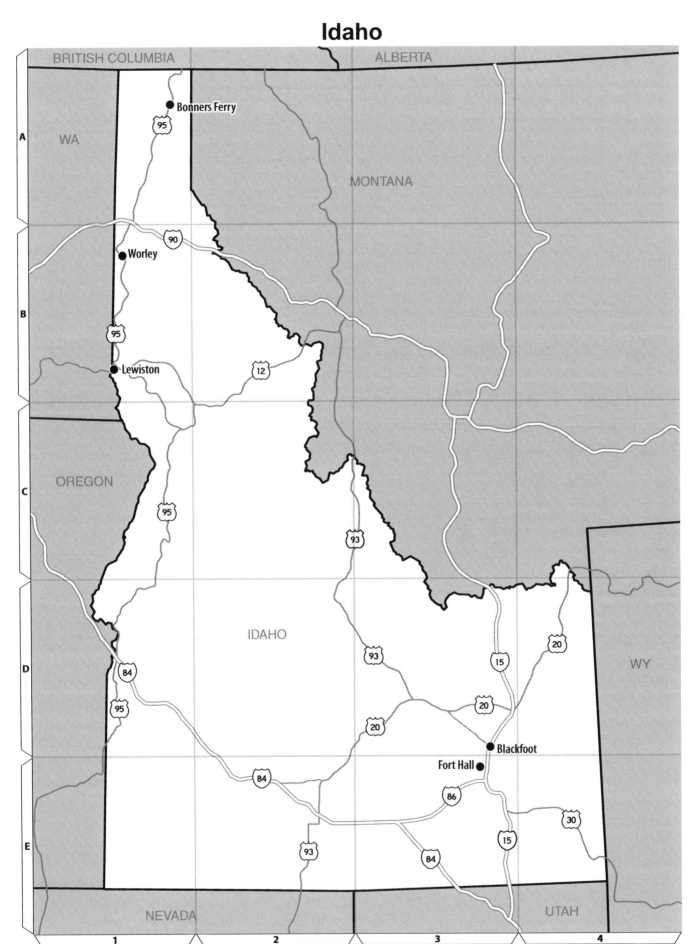

# Idaho

| City | Casino | 🚐 | P | 🛏 | 🚶 | 🛡 |
|------|--------|------|------|------|------|------|
| Blackfoot | Sage Hill Travel Center & Casino | | x | | | 1 |
| Bonners Ferry | Kootenai River Inn Casino & Spa | | x | x | | |
| Fort Hall | Fort Hall Casino & Resort | p37 | x | | | 1 |
| Lewiston | Clearwater River Casino & Hotel | p23 | x | x | | |
| Worley | Coeur D'Alene Casino Resort Hotel | s28 | | x | x | |

Indian casinos in Idaho offer electronic gaming & bingo; live pit/table games prohibited in the state.

## Blackfoot

### Sage Hill Travel Center & Casino
*Interstate 15, Exit 89*
*Blackfoot, ID 83221*

www.shobangaming.com
208-237-8774 Ext.5200 • 208-785-0194

**DESCRIPTION:** Slots-only casino, hosted by the Shoshone Tribe, at a Travel Center next to the interstate. **GAMING:** 100 slots; open 6:30am-2am/5am (Fri-Sat). **FOOD & ENTERTAINMENT:** cafe, convenience store, gas station at Travel Center. **LODGING:** There is no hotel at this location. **CAMPING:** RV parking is available; dry camping overnight is OK. **DIRECTIONS:** Located at exit 89 just off I-15.

## Bonners Ferry

### Kootenai River Inn Casino & Spa
*7169 Plaza St*
*Bonners Ferry, ID 83805*

www.kootenairiverinn.com
208-267-8511 • 800-346-5668

**DESCRIPTION:** Destination resort surrounded by natural beauty of mountains & river. **GAMING:** open 24 hours, slots, video poker, virtual blackjack, non smoking area, bingo. **FOOD & ENTERTAINMENT:** restaurant open daily, morning till night, deli. **LODGING:** Best Western Hotel. **CAMPING:** RV parking at the back of the lot near the fence. Overnight is permitted. **DIRECTIONS:** From I-90 exit 12, travel 76 miles north on US-95 to Bonners Ferry.

## Fort Hall

### Fort Hall Casino & Resort
*Simplot Rd (I-15 at exit 80)*
*Fort Hall, ID 83203*

www.shobangaming.com
208-237-8778 • 800-497-4231

**DESCRIPTION:** Southeast Idaho's only gaming destination. **GAMING:** 24-hour slots, video poker, virtual blackjack, high limit area, and bingo. **FOOD & ENTERTAINMENT:** grill is open daily, morning to night, snack bar at casino. Sports bar in hotel. Event center. **LODGING:** Smoke-free hotel. **CAMPING:** Buffalo Meadows RV Park, 37 full-hookup spaces; RV guests should pull in, then register at the cashier window in the casino. Free dry camping is also permitted on parking lot perimeter. **DIRECTIONS:** The casino is visible from I-15 exit 80.

## Lewiston

### Clearwater River Casino & Hotel
*17500 Nez Perce Rd*
*Lewiston, ID 83501*

www.crcasino.com
208-746-0723 • 877-678-7423
RV Park: 866-719-3885

**DESCRIPTION:** Casino destination resort on the Clearwater River. **GAMING:** 24-hour casino, slots, video poker, electronic blackjack, keno, non-smoking area, off track betting, bingo. **FOOD & ENTERTAINMENT:** bar & grill, 24-hour cafe, lounge. Ticketed touring shows in event center. **LODGING:** Lodge, smoke-free. **CAMPING:** RV Park, 23 full-hookup spaces, outdoor pool, laundry. RV dry camping also permitted near the casino building. **DIRECTIONS:** On US-12/95 about four miles east of Lewiston.

## Worley

*Coeur D'Alene Casino Resort Hotel*
*27068 S Hwy 95*
*Worley, ID 83876*

www.cdacasino.com
800-523-2464
RV Reservations: 800-523-2464

**DESCRIPTION:** Largest casino resort in Idaho. **GAMING:** slots, video poker, electronic blackjack tables, smoke-free area, bingo, OTB room. **FOOD & ENTERTAINMENT:** steakhouse, buffet, grill, cafe, food court, lounge, bar & grill. Free live music in the lounge & bars. Event Center; golf course also has 25-acre practice facility. **LODGING:** Mountain Lodge & Spa Towers. **CAMPING:** 28 spaces, electric hookup, in the east lot, follow signs for RV parking, check-in/pay at Spa Towers front desk. Fee: $20/day includes $15 play cash. RVs must go into the fee-pay spaces - NO free overnight parking for RVs. **DIRECTIONS:** From I-90 exit 12, south on US-95 for 25 miles. Resort is directly on US-95 in Worley.

# Illinois

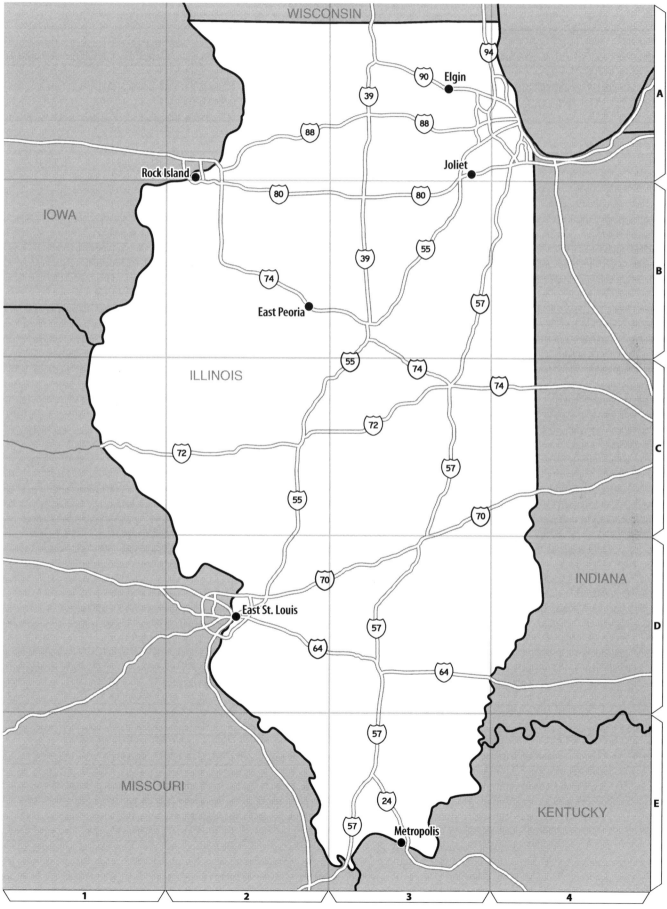

# Illinois

| City | Casino | 🚐 | P | 🛏 | 🏌 | 🛡 |
|------|--------|-----|-----|-----|-----|-----|
| East Peoria | Par-A-Dice Hotel Casino | | x | x | | 1 |
| East St. Louis | Casino Queen | p132 | x | x | | 1 |
| Elgin | Grand Victoria Casino | | x | x | | 6 |
| Joliet | Hollywood Casino | p50 | x | x | | 2 |
| Metropolis | Harrah's Metropolis | | x | x | | 4 |
| Rock Island | Jumer's Casino & Hotel | | x | x | | 1 |

Most Illinois casinos are traditional riverboat style, permanently docked on waterways in the state. Note: Two Chicago metropolitan area casinos are listed in the Indiana section.

## East Peoria

### Par-A-Dice Hotel Casino
*21 Blackjack Blvd*
*East Peoria, IL 61611*

www.paradice.com
309-699-7711

DESCRIPTION: Casino one mile from I-74 with easy on/off from the interstate. GAMING: On four decks: pit/gaming tables, slots. Third deck non-smoking. open 8am–4am/6am (Fri-Sat). FOOD & ENTERTAINMENT: steakhouse, buffet, deli, lounge/ bar. Live entertainment in the bar. LODGING: Hotel. CAMPING: Designated RV spaces along perimeter of the parking lot, walking distance to the casino. Overnight parking permitted for self-contained RVs. DIRECTIONS: From I-74 exit 95B, one mile north on Main St. The casino is on the left.

## East St. Louis

### Casino Queen
*200 S Front St*
*East St. Louis, IL 62201*

www.casinoqueen.com
618-874-5000 • RV Park: 618-874-5000 Ext. 8871

DESCRIPTION: Spectacular views of Gateway Arch & St. Louis skyline across the river. GAMING: slots, video poker, live action pit/table games. Casino hours, 8am-6am daily. FOOD & ENTERTAINMENT: buffet, steakhouse, deli & chips, lounge & nightclub with live local entertainment. For sightseeing in St. Louis, guests can take the Metrolink from a nearby station. LODGING: Hotel rooms/suites. CAMPING: RV Park open Mar-Oct, full-hookup pull-thru sites, Shuttle to casino. Free dry camping is also permitted (24-hour limit) on the gravel parking area east of the casino parking lot. DIRECTIONS: From I-70/I-55 westbound, use exit 2A (3rd Street) or eastbound use exit 1 (4th St) East St Louis, then follow brown riverboat casino signs. From I-255 exit 17B, take SR-15 west, following brown riverboat casino signs.

## Elgin

### Grand Victoria Casino
*250 S Grove Ave*
*Elgin, IL 60120*

www.grandvictoria.com
847-468-7000

DESCRIPTION: Gaming & dining destination on the Fox River, 20 miles west of Chicago. GAMING: slots, pit/table games, high limit room. Casino open 8:30am-6:30am daily. Food and Entertainment: steakhouse, unique buffet, casual burger house, deli, lounge. Summer concert series outdoors. LODGING: There is no hotel at this location. CAMPING: RV dry camping surface lot across from the casino, next to the parking deck, at the back of the lot. Notify Security if you plan to stay overnight. **DIRECTIONS:** From I-90 tollway (milepost 24), take SR-31 south for 2.3 miles to Chicago Ave. Left on Chicago Avenue for .3 mile to South Grove Avenue, then right for .25 mile.

## Joliet

### Hollywood Casino
*777 Hollywood Blvd*
*Joliet, IL 60436*

www.hollywoodcasinojoliet.com
888-436-7737

**DESCRIPTION:** Casino boat near Chicago, docked on the Des Plains River convenient to I-80. **GAMING:** slots, video poker, pit/gaming tables. Casino open 7:30am–5:30am daily. **FOOD & ENTERTAINMENT:** steakhouse, buffet, deli, lounge. Shows at amphitheater. **LODGING:** Hotel, complimentary breakfast, casino shuttle service. **CAMPING:** RV Park has 50 paved sites, electric & water (electric-only in winter), central dump. RV guests are invited to complimentary breakfast at the hotel. Limited overnight parking permitted in the casino lot. **DIRECTIONS:** From I-80 exit 127, south on Hollywood Road for .6 mile to the end, turn left and go east on US-6 for .5 mile to the casino.

## Metropolis

### Harrah's Metropolis
*100 E Front St*
*Metropolis, IL 62960*

www.caesars.com/harrahs-metropolis
618-524-2628

**DESCRIPTION:** Southern Illinois casino resort on the picturesque Ohio River. **GAMING:** slots, pit/table games, poker room. Casino hours daily, 8am–6am. **FOOD & ENTERTAINMENT:** restaurant open morning to night, buffet, express food. **LODGING:** Modern hotel. **CAMPING:** Free RV overnight parking; use the designated lot across from the hotel, follow signage for oversize vehicles, walking distance to the casino. **DIRECTIONS:** From I-24 exit 37, west on US-45 for 3.8 miles to Ferry Street in Metropolis. Turn left on Ferry St and follow to Front St.

## Rock Island

### Jumer's Casino & Hotel
*777 Jumer Dr*
*Milan, IL 61201*

www.jumershotelcasino.com
309-756-4600

**DESCRIPTION:** Vegas-style gaming combined with Midwestern hospitality. **GAMING:** slots, pit/gaming tables, poker room, Casino hours 7am-5am daily. **FOOD & ENTERTAINMENT:** steakhouse, buffet, cafe, sports bar, nightclub. Event Center. **LODGING:** Luxury hotel rooms/suites. **CAMPING:** Check in with Security for parking directions. Overnight parking permitted. **DIRECTIONS:** Located at the intersection of I-280 (at exit 11) and SR-92.

# Indiana

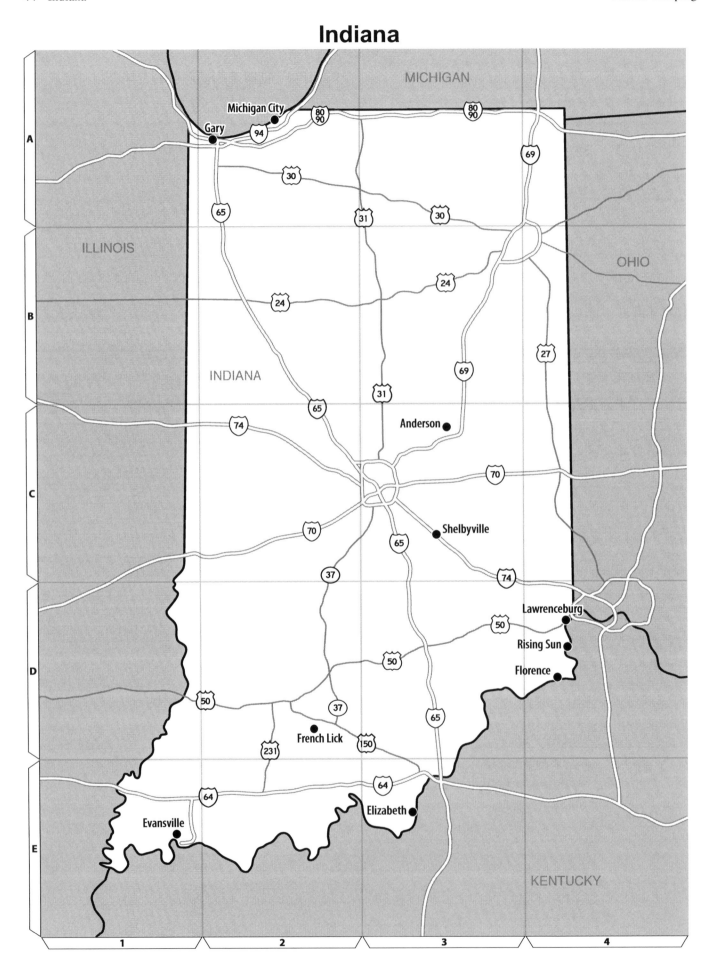

# Indiana

| City | Casino | 🚐 | P | 🛏 | 🏌 | 🛡 |
|------|--------|-----|-----|-----|-----|-----|
| Anderson | Hoosier Park Racing & Casino | | x | | | 2 |
| Elizabeth | Horseshoe Southern Indiana | | x | x | x | 9 |
| Evansville | Tropiecana Evansville | | x | x | | |
| Florence | Belterra Casino Resort | | x | x | x | 9 |
| French Lick | French Lick Resort & Casino | s6 | | x | x | |
| Gary | Majestic Star Casino & Hotel | | | x | | 3 |
| Lawrenceburg | Hollywood Casino | | x | x | | |
| Michigan City | Blue Chip Casino Hotel | | x | x | | |
| Rising Sun | Rising Star Casino Resort | p56 | x | x | x | |
| Shelbyville | Indiana Grand Racing & Casino | | x | | | 1 |

In 1993 the Indiana Riverboat Act approved casino gaming on riverboats in 10 Ohio River or Lake Michigan locations. In 2008, the state's first racinos opened when slots and table play were added at two race tracks in central Indiana. In 2015, riverboats were given an option to move gambling to on-land locations near where the boat had been docked; a few casinos have moved all or part of their gaming off the boats.

## Anderson

### Hoosier Park Racing & Casino
*4500 Dan Patch Cir*
*Anderson, IN 46013*

www.hoosierpark.com
765-642-7223

**DESCRIPTION:** Friendly 24-hour gaming & racing facility. **GAMING:** slots, video poker, electronic blackjack, 3-card poker & roulette, non-smoking area, high limit area. Live standardbred racing Apr-Nov, simulcasting year round. **FOOD & ENTERTAINMENT:** steakhouse, buffet, trackside restaurant, deli, grill, cantina, lounge, bar. Entertainment weekly in the showroom. **LODGING:** No hotel at this location. **CAMPING:** Free dry camping for RVs; overnight OK.

Follow signs for truck & RV parking. **DIRECTIONS:** From I-69 exit 226 take SR-9 north for .7 mile then east on SR-236/E 53rd for .7 mile and north at Dan Patch Circle.

## Elizabeth

### Horseshoe Southern Indiana
*11999 Casino Center Dr*
*Elizabeth, IN 47117*

www.caesars.comhorseshoe-southern-indiana
866-676-7463

**DESCRIPTION:** Destination resort for luxury on-land gaming. **GAMING:** slots, pit/gaming tables, poker room, high limit area. **FOOD & ENTERTAINMENT:** steakhouse, buffet, cafe, casual dining, cafe, quick food, ice cream shop. Ticketed shows in event center, golf course. **LODGING:** Luxury hotel. **CAMPING:** From Hwy-111 southbound, RVs should drive past the parking garages and hotel, cross the bridge, then turn right on Stucky Road to the outdoor lot designated for large vehicles (on the left). Overnight RV parking camping is permitted; no hookups. **DIRECTIONS:** From I-64 exit 123 (New Albany), follow signs to SR-111. Take SR-111 south for 8.5 miles to Horseshoe.

## Evansville

### Tropicana Evansville
*421 NW Riverside Dr*
*Evansville, IN 47708*

www.tropevansville.com
812-433-4000

**DESCRIPTION:** Entertainment complex overlooks scenic Ohio River in southern Indiana. Open 24/7. **GAMING:** modern gaming floor: slots, video poker, pit/gaming tables, poker room. **FOOD & ENTERTAINMENT:** restaurant, buffet, deli, lounge, live entertainment nightly in piano bar. **LODGING:** Hotel, gift shop. **CAMPING:** Free overnight parking for self contained RVs on the surface lot. **DIRECTIONS:** From I-64 exit 25, south on US-41 for about 15 miles to Lloyd Expressway, then west to Fulton Ave and south for three blocks.

## Florence

### Belterra Casino Resort
*777 Belterra Dr*
*Florence, IN 47020*

www.belterracasino.com
812-427-7777

**DESCRIPTION:** Popular resort on Ohio River between Louisville & Cincinnati. **GAMING:** open 24/7, slots, gaming tables, poker room. **FOOD & ENTERTAINMENT:** steak/seafood restaurant, buffet, sports bar & grill, coffee shop, cafe, bar. Ticketed shows, concerts. **LODGING:** Hotel & Inn, golf course. **CAMPING:** RVs may use the large open area parking lot for dry camping; overnight is OK. **DIRECTIONS:** From I-71 in Kentucky, exit 57 (Warsaw/Sparta), follow SR-35 to Warsaw, Kentucky. At US-42 turn left toward the Markland Dam Bridge and turn left on to the bridge. After crossing the bridge, turn left at the stop sign and follow SR-156 to the casino.

## French Lick

### French Lick Resort & Casino
*8670 W State Rd 56*
*French Lick, IN 47432*

www.frenchlick.com
812-936-9300 • 888-936-9360

**DESCRIPTION:** Elegant resort in the hills of Hoosier National Forest. **GAMING:** slots, video poker, pit/table games, poker room, high limit gaming area. **FOOD & ENTERTAINMENT:** steakhouse, family restaurant, bar & grill, pizzeria, coffee shop, deli, clubhouse restaurant. Event Center, classical music, weekends in atrium, golf courses. **LODGING:** Luxury hotel, bowling alley, arcade. **CAMPING:** Six full hook-up sites located behind the casino building near the train depot; $75 per night. Overnight RV guests required to pull into the full-hookup sites. NO free RV parking in the lot. **DIRECTIONS:** From Indianapolis, go south on SR-37 about 98 miles to Paoli, then take SR-56 west for 10 miles. From Louisville, take I-64 west to exit 122, then US-150 west to Paoli, then SR-56 west for 10 miles.

## Gary

### Majestic Star Casino & Hotel
*One Bluffington Harbor Dr*
*Gary, IN 46312*

www.majesticstarcasino.com
888-225-8259

**DESCRIPTION:** Destination resort near Chicago, open 24/7. **GAMING:** Six floors of gaming, slots, pit/table games, poker room, non-smoking level. **FOOD & ENTERTAINMENT:** steakhouse, buffet, noodle bar, quick food, coffee shop, lounge. **LODGING:** Luxury hotel. **CAMPING:** Free parking for self-contained vehicles is permitted in the hotel lot. Contact Security at 219-977-9999 if you plan to stay overnight. **DIRECTIONS:** From I-90 exit 10 (Cline Ave/IN-912) travel north following signs to riverboats.

## Lawrenceburg

### Hollywood Casino
*777 Hollywood Blvd*
*Lawrenceburg, IN 47025*

www.hollywoodindiana.com
888-274-6797

**DESCRIPTION:** Gaming destination resort on the Ohio River west of Cincinnati, open 24/7. **GAMING:** slots, live action pit/table games, poker room. **FOOD & ENTERTAINMENT:** steakhouse, buffet, quick food, grill, coffee shop, bar. Live music weekends. **LODGING:** Hotel connected to the casino. **CAMPING:** Secure parking for oversize vehicles is in the lot north of the casino building across from the Sky Walk garage. Turn right after you enter the resort complex & follow signs. Overnight RV parking is permitted. **DIRECTIONS:** From I-275 west exit 16, take US-50 west. From I-74 exit 164, south on SR-1 for approximately 14 miles to US-50. Follow riverboat signs.

## Michigan City

### Blue Chip Casino Hotel
*777 Blue Chip Dr*
*Michigan City, IN 46360*

www.bluechipcasino.com
219-879-7711

**DESCRIPTION:** Favorite getaway resort for gaming & live entertainment in the Chicago area. **GAMING:** slots, pit/table games, poker room. **FOOD & ENTERTAINMENT:** steakhouse, casual dining, buffet, deli. Concerts in the event center. Live music, shows on weekends in the lounge. **LODGING:** Luxury hotel, retail shops. **CAMPING:** RV parking, northeast section of the lot. Overnight is OK. Shuttle service. **DIRECTIONS:** From I-94 exit 40B, one mile on US-20, then continue 4 miles on E Michigan Blvd to US-12, then right (east) & cross the bridge .3 mile to the casino lot.

## Rising Sun

### Rising Star Casino Resort
*600 Rising Star Dr*
*Rising Sun, IN 47040*

www.risingstarcasino.com
812-438-1234 • RV Park: 800-472-6311

**DESCRIPTION:** Destination resort on picturesque Ohio River, open 24/7. **GAMING:** slots, pit/table games, video poker, video keno, non-smoking area. **FOOD & ENTERTAINMENT:** steakhouse, buffet, pub, quick food. Shows in the theater. Live lounge entertainment,

golf course. **LODGING:** Luxury hotel, indoor pool, whirlpool, sauna, health club. **CAMPING:** Modern, full-service RV Park, 56 full hook-up sites, pavilion, laundry, dog park, bocce ball court, shuffleboard; RV guests have access to indoor pool and other hotel amenities, casino shuttle. RV dry camping permitted in the casino surface lot for limited stay. **DIRECTIONS:** From the Cincinnati area, take I-275 west to exit 16, then west on US-50 for 6.9 miles, then south on SR-56 for 7.8 miles. This takes you through the historic town of Aurora and on a scenic byway along the river. Turn left at Rising Star Drive.

## Shelbyville

### Indiana Grand Racing & Casino
*4300 N Michigan Rd*
*Shelbyville, IN 46176*

www.IndianaGrand.com
877-386-4463

**DESCRIPTION:** Gaming destination for casino and horse racing action, close to Indianapolis. **GAMING:** 24/7, slots, electronic popular table games, automated poker room. Live Thoroughbred & Quarter Horse racing May-Oct, racing simulcasting & OTB. **FOOD & ENTERTAINMENT:** steakhouse, buffet, brew & pub. Free live music weekends at Center Bar. **LODGING:** There is no hotel at this location. **CAMPING:** Free parking is available for RVs; overnight is OK. **DIRECTIONS:** From I-74 exit 109 go east on Fairland Rd .3 mile then north on Michigan Rd .2 mile.

# Iowa

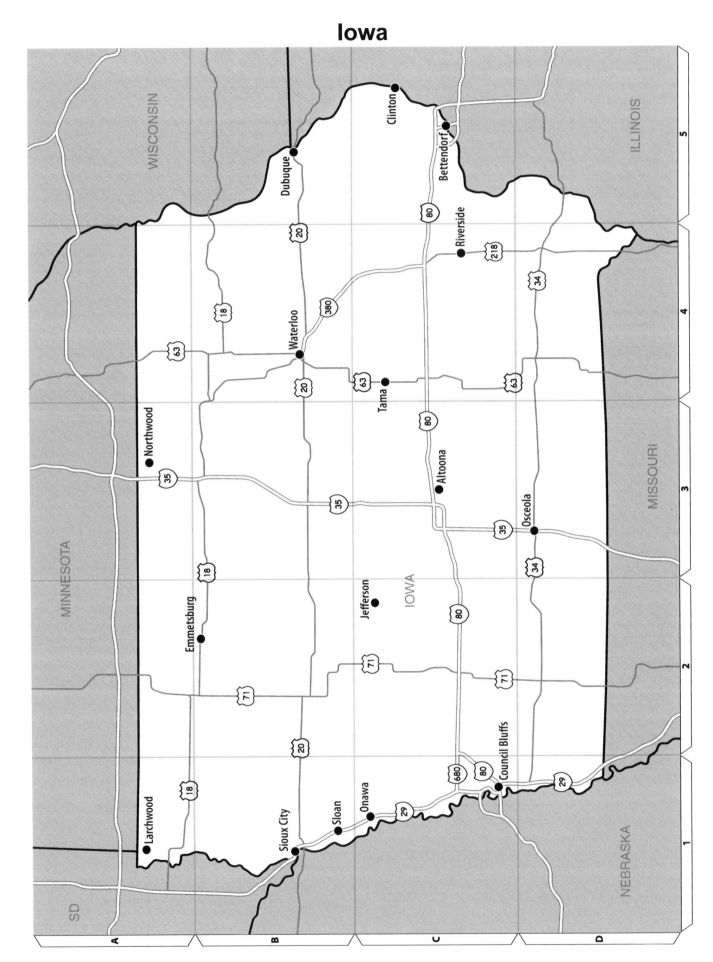

# Iowa

| City | Casino | 🚐 | **P** | 🛏 | 🏌 | 🛡 |
|------|--------|-----|------|-----|-----|-----|
| Altoona | Prairie Meadows | | x | x | | 1 |
| Bettendorf | Isle of Capri Casino | | x | x | | 1 |
| Clinton | Wild Rose Casino & Resort | | x | x | | |
| Council Bluffs | Ameristar Casino Hotel | | x | x | | 1 |
| Council Bluffs | Harrah's Council Bluffs | | x | x | x | 1 |
| Council Bluffs | Horseshoe Council Bluffs | p44 | | x | | 1 |
| Dubuque | Diamond Jo Casino | | x | | | 1 |
| Dubuque | Q Casino | | x | | | 2 |
| Emmetsburg | Wild Rose Casino & Resort | p68 | x | x | | |
| Jefferson | Wild Rose Casino & Resort | | x | x | | |
| Larchwood | Grand Falls Casino & Golf Resort | p15 | | x | | |
| Northwood | Diamond Jo Worth Casino | | x | x | | 1 |
| Onawa | Blackbird Bend Casino | s6 | x | | | 6 |
| Osceola | Lakeside Hotel Casino | p47 | x | x | | 1 |
| Riverside | Riverside Casino & Golf Resort | | x | x | x | |
| Sioux City | Hard Rock Casino & Hotel | | x | x | | 1 |
| Sloan | WinnaVegas Casino Resort | s14 | x | x | | 3 |
| Tama | Meskwaki Bingo, Casino Hotel | p50 | | x | | |
| Waterloo | Isle Casino Hotel | | x | x | | 3 |

Iowa's gaming includes permanently docked riverboats, land-based resorts, Indian casinos and pari-mutuel racinos. All casinos are Vegas-style.

## Altoona

### Prairie Meadows
*1 Prairie Meadows Dr*
*Altoona, IA 50009*

www.prairiemeadows.com
515-967-1000

**DESCRIPTION:** Prairie Meadows is the nation's first racino, casino & live racing combination. Open 24/7. **GAMING:** slots, gaming tables, race book, smoke-free poker room. Live racing (thoroughbred and quarterhorse) Apr-Oct; simulcasting daily. **FOOD**

**& ENTERTAINMENT:** steakhouse, casual dining, cafe, quick food, lounge. Concerts in big stage venue; live lounge entertainment weekends. **LODGING:** Hotel rooms/suites. **CAMPING:** RVs may park in the truck lot; overnight OK if you do not put slides out. Do not extend jacks in the lot. **DIRECTIONS:** Near I-80 exit 142.

## Bettendorf

### Isle of Capri Casino
*1777 Isle Pkwy*
*Bettendorf, IA 52722*

www.islebettendorf.com
610-241-1616

**DESCRIPTION:** A destination resort on the Mississippi

River, near I-74 with easy on/off access. **GAMING:** slots, pit/gaming tables, baccarat, poker room. **FOOD & ENTERTAINMENT:** grille, buffet, quick food, lounge. Touring shows on weekends. **LODGING:** Hotel, gift shop. **CAMPING:** Free RV dry camping is in the east lot; no hookups. Overnight is permitted. **DIRECTIONS:** From I-74 exit 4 (State St/Riverfront), go east on State Street for .4 mile. Turn right at 17th St/George Theunen Drive to the casino complex –or– From I-80 in Illinois take exit 10 to I-74 west for 14 miles. After crossing the Mississippi River, take Iowa exit 4 (Grant St/State St), then east on State St to the George Theunen Bridge.

## Clinton

### Wild Rose Casino & Resort - Clinton
*777 Wild Rose Circle*
*Clinton, IA 52732*

www.wildroseresorts.com
563-243-9000

**DESCRIPTION:** Casino resort on 29 acres in Clinton. **GAMING:** slots, pit/gaming tables (open at 11am). Casino hours 8am-2am/24hrs (Fri&Sat). **FOOD & ENTERTAINMENT:** buffet, bar & grill. Concerts at event center. **LODGING:** Hotel rooms/suites. **CAMPING:** RV parking is permitted at the back of the casino; overnight is OK. **DIRECTIONS:** From I-80 exit 195B take US-61 north 14.9 miles to exit 137, then US-30 east for 16.2 miles and north at Mill Creek Pkwy/ 30th St.

## Council Bluffs

### Ameristar Casino Hotel
*2200 River Rd*
*Council Bluffs, IA 51501*

www.ameristar.com/CouncilBluffs
712-328-8888 • 866-667-3386

**DESCRIPTION:** Ameristar II riverboat casino overlooks Missouri River. **GAMING:** slots, video poker, live pit/ table games, high limit room. **FOOD & ENTERTAINMENT:** buffet, steakhouse, sports bar & grill, quick food. Free live entertainment on weekends. **LODGING:** Hotel. **CAMPING:** RV parking in the north lot or in the truck parking lot. Overnight parking is OK for self-contained RVs. **DIRECTIONS:** From I-80 use exit 1A to I-29 north exit 52/Nebraska Ave. & follow signs to riverboat casino.

### Harrah's Council Bluffs
*One Harrah's Blvd*
*Council Bluffs, IA 51501*

www.caesars.com/harrahs-council-bluffs
712-329-6000

**DESCRIPTION:** Destination resort overlooking Missouri River. **GAMING:** Modern casino in the hotel, slots, popular pit/table games, poker room. **FOOD & ENTERTAINMENT:** buffet, grill, 12th floor dining has spectacular views of downtown Omaha. Live music Fridays. **LODGING:** Hotel. Free shuttle to the nearby Horseshoe for guests who want to casino hop. **CAMPING:** RV parking in the north lot or on the perimeter of the hotel lot, no hookups. Notify Security if you plan to stay overnight. There is a full-service RV Park at the nearby Horseshoe casino. **DIRECTIONS:** Located at I-29 exit 53 (East 9th Ave exit).

### Horseshoe Council Bluffs
*2701 23rd Ave*
*Council Bluffs, IA 51501*

www.caesars.com/horseshoe-council-bluffs
712-329-6415 • RV Park: 712-396-3715

**DESCRIPTION:** Legendary casino destination. **GAMING:** slots, live action pit/table games, poker room with many promotions, keno, non-smoking section. **FOOD & ENTERTAINMENT:** steakhouse, buffet, cafe, free live entertainment in the lounge. **LODGING:** Hilton Garden Inn. **CAMPING:** RV Park, open May-Sep, 44 back-in sites, water & electric hookups, dump station; monthly rates, walking distance to the casino. **DIRECTIONS:** From I-80/I-29 exit 1B, north .5 mile on 24th Street to 23rd Avenue, west on 23rd for .4 mile —or— From I-29 exit 52, follow casino signs. The casino complex is visible from the westbound lanes of I-80.

# Dubuque

### Diamond Jo Casino
*301 Bell St*
*Dubuque, IA 52001*

www.diamondjodubuque.com
563-690-4800 • 800-582-5956

**DESCRIPTION:** Gambling & entertainment complex located in the Port of Dubuque. **GAMING:** open 24/7, slots, live pit/gaming tables, poker room, high limit room. **FOOD & ENTERTAINMENT:** grille, buffet, deli, sports bar, casual bar, bowling center. Live shows four nights a week. **LODGING:** There is no hotel at this location. **CAMPING:** RV parking is available in the lots on the east side and south side of the casino (near River Museum.) Free overnight parking permitted for self-contained vehicles. **DIRECTIONS:** From US-20 Locust Street exit in downtown Dubuque, north on Locust .3 mile to Third St, east on Third for .4 mile, then south to the casino.

### Q Casino
*1855 Greyhound Park Rd*
*Dubuque, IA 52004*

www.qcasinoandhotel.com
563-582-3647

**DESCRIPTION:** Greyhound racetrack & casino overlooking Mississippi River. **GAMING:** slots, live-action pit/gaming tables, poker parlor; open 24/7. Live dog racing May-Oct. **FOOD & ENTERTAINMENT:** buffet, fine dining, quick food, casual dining, lounge. Entertainment venue. **LODGING:** Hilton Garden Inn. **CAMPING:** Parking for oversize vehicles in the south end of the lot, near the river. Free overnight RV parking permitted. **DIRECTIONS:** The casino and entertainment venue are located off Hwy-151/61 at the Dubuque-Wisconsin Bridge. From US-20, exit at Downtown Dubuque to Hwy-151/61 north for 1.2 miles to the Greyhound Park Rd. exit.

# Emmetsburg

### Wild Rose Casino & Resort - Emmetsburg
*777 Main St, US-18*
*Emmetsburg, IA 50536*

www.emmetsburg.wildroseresorts.com
712-852-3400

**DESCRIPTION:** Country resort situated on nine acres in northwest Iowa. **GAMING:** slots, live pit/gaming tables, casino hours 8am-2am/24hrs (Fri-Sat). **FOOD & ENTERTAINMENT:** Irish Pub, casual dining, bar, coffee shop. Entertainment venue. **LODGING:** Hotel. **CAMPING:** RV Park, overlooking the lake, 68 sites, electric & water, central dump. Moderate rates include breakfast. Free parking permitted in the casino lot, limited to 24 hours. **DIRECTIONS:** Located on the east edge of Emmetsburg directly on US-18.

# Jefferson

### Wild Rose Casino & Resort - Jefferson
*777 Wild Rose Dr*
*Jefferson, IA 50129*

www.jefferson.wildroseresorts.com
515-386-7777

**DESCRIPTION:** Friendly small-town casino in Greene County. **GAMING:** slots and live-action gaming tables. Casino hours 8am-2am/24hrs weekends. **FOOD & ENTERTAINMENT:** sports bar and grill open daily, cafe. Live music in casino Thursdays. Ticketed shows, events in Greene Center. **LODGING:** Smoke-free hotel. **CAMPING:** The west parking lot is designated for RV parking. Overnight is permitted, no hookups. **DIRECTIONS:** Located at the intersection of US-30 and Hwy-4 about 70 miles northwest of Des Moines.

# Larchwood

### Grand Falls Casino & Golf Resort
*1415 Grand Falls Blvd*
*Larchwood, IA 51241*

www.grandfallscasinoresort.com
712-777-7777

**DESCRIPTION:** Vegas-inspired resort in picturesque northwestern Iowa. **GAMING:** open 24/7; slots, live action pit/gaming tables, poker room, high limit area. **FOOD & ENTERTAINMENT:** Steak/seafood restaurant, buffet, cafe, quick food. Touring headliner entertainment. Free local shows in the lounge, golf course. **LODGING:** Luxury hotel. **CAMPING:** 15-space RV area at north end of the parking lot, electric & water hookups, central dump. Pull into a space, register & pay at the hotel front desk. Free dry camping is limited to 24hrs, in the casino lot. **DIRECTIONS:** Just east of Sioux Falls, SD. From I-229 exit 6, take Highway 42 east for 10.5 miles. From I-90 exit 406 (in SD) take SD-11 south for 6.4 miles, then east on SD-42 for 4.2 miles.

## Northwood

### Diamond Jo Worth Casino
*777 Diamond Jo Ln*
*Northwood, IA 50459*

www.diamondjoworth.com
641-323-7777

**DESCRIPTION:** Charming casino at The Top of Iowa, next to I-35. **GAMING:** 24/7 casino, slots & gaming tables. **FOOD & ENTERTAINMENT:** Grill, buffet, quick food. Ticketed shows in Event Center. Free live music Fri & Sat night on casino stage. **LODGING:** Country Inn & Suites. **CAMPING:** Free overnight parking permitted at the casino. Dump station at the nearby welcome center. **DIRECTIONS:** Just south of the Iowa/Minnesota border at I-35 exit 214, next to southbound lanes near the Iowa Welcome Center.

## Onawa

### Blackbird Bend Casino
*17214 210th St*
*Onawa, IA 51040*

www.blackbirdbendcasinos.com
844-622-2121

**DESCRIPTION:** Cozy casino hosted by the Omaha Tribe. **GAMING:** slots, live-action gaming tables, electronic roulette. Casino hours: 8am-2am, 24hrs, Fri & Sat. **FOOD & ENTERTAINMENT:** cafe, open daily morning till night, menu service & buffet. **LODGING:** There is no hotel at this location. **CAMPING:** Free overnight parking with electric hookups for RVs in the lot just across from the casino entrance. **DIRECTIONS:** From I-29 exit 112 at Onawa, take Hwy-175 west for 1 mile,

then right onto Dogwood Ave north for 1.6 miles, then left onto County Hwy-K42 east/northeast for 2.4 miles, then left onto 210th St for 1 mile.

## Osceola

### Lakeside Hotel Casino
*777 Casino Dr*
*Osceola, IA 50213*

www.lakesidehotelcasino.com
641-342-9511

**DESCRIPTION:** Friendly casino resort, convenient to I-35 in central Iowa. **GAMING:** 24-hour slots, video poker, keno, pit/tablegames. **FOOD & ENTERTAINMENT:** cafe & buffet, open all day, sports bar. Shows in event center & outdoor amphitheater. **LODGING:** Hotel. **CAMPING:** RV Park, 47 full-hookup sites, free Wi-Fi, open all year, moderately priced. RV check-in at the valet station in the casino lobby; shuttle service. It is requested that RVs use the RV Park, but if you want to dry camp, use the north area of the lot and do not put the jacks down. **DIRECTIONS:** From I-35 exit 34, west for .2 mile on Clay St to the resort.

## Riverside

### Riverside Casino & Golf Resort
*3184 Hwy 22*
*Riverside, IA 52327*

www.riversidecasinoandresort.com
319-648-1234 • 877-677-3456

**DESCRIPTION:** Upscale resort, inspired by Vegas, owned & operated by Iowans. **GAMING:** slots, live action pit/table games, poker room, non-smoking section. **FOOD & ENTERTAINMENT:** fine dining, buffet, diner, express food, coffee shop. Free lounge entertainment, golf course, ticketed shows in the event center. **LODGING:** Luxury hotel. **CAMPING:** Designated area for RVs in the semi's lot, southeast corner of parking lot. Free overnight parking permitted. Walking distance the casino. **DIRECTIONS:** The resort is located just south of Iowa City. From I-80 exit 239A, take US-27/218 south for 15.8 miles to exit 80, then east on SR-22 for 1.3 miles.

## Sioux City

### Hard Rock Casino & Hotel
*111 Third St*
*Sioux City, IA 51101*

www.hardrockcasinosiouxcity.com
712-226-7625

**DESCRIPTION:** Destination resort in historic downtown Sioux City. Open 24 hours. **GAMING:** slots, pit/table games. **FOOD & ENTERTAINMENT:** American grill, cafe, buffet, pub; indoor & outdoor entertainment venues. **LODGING:** Rock 'n Roll-themed hotel. **CAMPING:** RVs should park in the lot south of the casino (across the street) on Third St. Overnight parking is permitted. **DIRECTIONS:** From I-29 exit 147B turn left onto Gordon St (SR-12) and follow to Pearl St; left on Third St to the casino.

## Sloan

### WinnaVegas Casino Resort
*1500 330th St*
*Sloan, IA 51055*

www.winnavegas.com
712-428-9466

**DESCRIPTION:** Friendly getaway resort 20 miles south of Sioux City. **GAMING:** slots, table games, bingo five days a week. **FOOD & ENTERTAINMENT:** restaurant, buffet, concession stand, snack bar, free entertainment at the lounge. Ticketed shows in event center. **LODGING:** Hotel. **CAMPING:** There are 14 pull-thru electric hookup sites available. Check-in & pay at the casino. Free RV dry camping is permitted in the north parking lot, free dump and fresh water supply. **DIRECTIONS:** From I-29 exit 127, west on 330th St. The casino is three miles from the interstate.

## Tama

### Meskwaki Bingo, Casino Hotel
*1504 305th St*
*Tama, IA 52339*

www.meskwaki.com
641-484-2108 • 800-728-4263

**DESCRIPTION:** Friendly Native American destination resort, open 24/7. **GAMING:** slots, live-action pit/table games, live keno, racing simulcast, poker room, bingo every day, high limits gaming section, separate non-smoking slots area. **FOOD & ENTERTAINMENT:** grille, buffet, cafe, bingo concessions, food arcade. Ticketed shows at indoor & outdoor venues. Free lounge entertainment weekends. **LODGING:** Luxury hotel, indoor pool & whirlpool, exercise area, day spa & salon, gift shop. **CAMPING:** 50-space RV Park, electric hookups, central dump, fresh water. RV guests invited to use hotel amenities. Register/pay at hotel front desk. Free overnight parking permitted in the casino lot; please notify Security if staying overnight. **DIRECTIONS:** From I-80 exit 191/Tama, north on US-63 (two-lane) for 22.8 miles to US-30 (traffic light at junction of US-63/30), then west on US-30 4.4 miles. From I-35 exit 111, go 47 miles east on US-30, a major thoroughfare (opens to four lanes in some areas).

## Waterloo

### Isle Casino Hotel
*777 Isle of Capri Blvd*
*Waterloo, IA 50701*

www.waterloo.isleofcapricasinos.com
610-241-1621

**DESCRIPTION:** Tropical-themed casino hotel. Open 24 hours. **GAMING:** slots, video poker, live-action gaming tables, poker room. **FOOD & ENTERTAINMENT:** steakhouse, grill, buffet, sports bar. Live music & dancing in the lounge; concerts/shows in the Ballroom. **LODGING:** Hotel. **CAMPING:** RVs should park on the north side of the lot. Overnight parking is permitted. **DIRECTIONS:** From I-380 exit onto US-20 west. Take exit 71A to merge onto US-218 south for 1.4 miles, then west on Shaulis Rd for .7 mile.

# Kansas

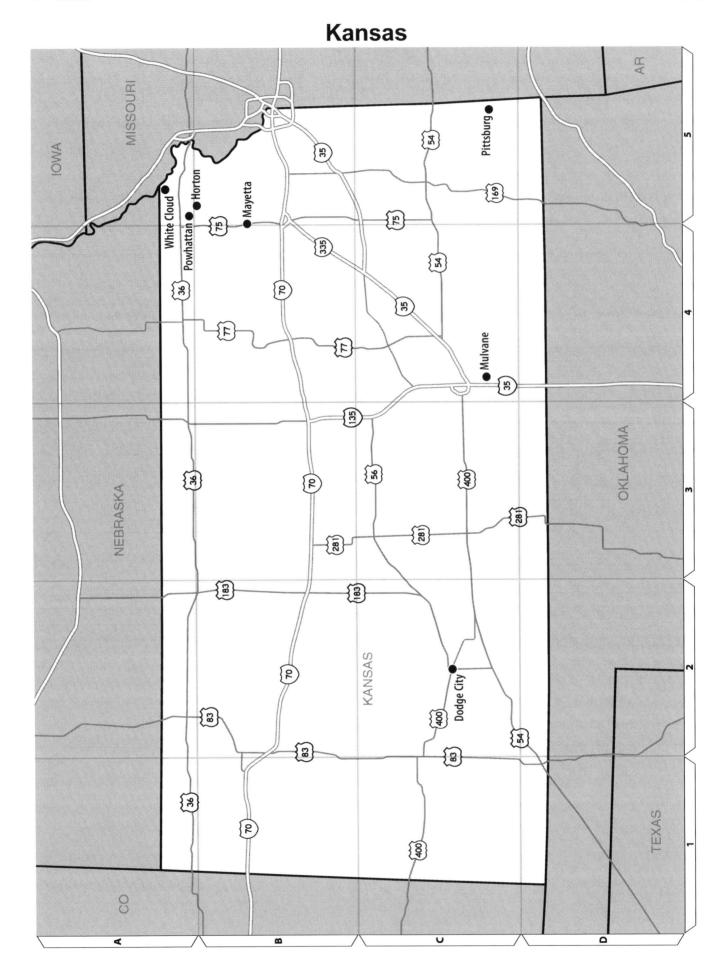

# Kansas

| City | Casino | 🚐 | **P** | 🛏 | 🏌 | 🛡 |
|------|--------|-----|-----|-----|-----|-----|
| Dodge City | Boot Hill Casino & Resort | | x | x | | |
| Horton | Golden Eagle Casino | s6 | x | | | |
| Mayetta | Prairie Band Casino & Resort | p67 | x | x | x | |
| Mulvane | Kansas Star Casino Hotel | | x | x | | 1 |
| Pittsburg | Kansas Crossing Casino & Hotel | | x | x | | |
| Powhattan | Sac & Fox Casino | s10 | x | | x | |
| White Cloud | Casino White Cloud | s6 | x | | | |

Several RV-Friendly Native American casinos are located in northeastern Kansas near US-75. Four other state-owned casinos are at various locations in the state. All casinos are open 24 hours. RV travelers should note that Hollywood Casino in Kansas City does not permit RV parking on the property.

## Dodge City

### Boot Hill Casino & Resort
*4000 W Comanche St*
*Dodge City, KS 63801*

www.boothillcasino.com
620-682-7777

**DESCRIPTION:** In Dodge City, the resort's theme is "Old West-New Entertainment." **GAMING:** slots, pit/table games, poker room. **FOOD & ENTERTAINMENT:** steakhouse, cafe. Free local entertainment weekends. **LODGING:** Hampton Inn & Suites. **CAMPING:** RV dry camping behind the Hampton Inn. Overnight parking permitted for self-contained vehicles. **DIRECTIONS:** Located on the western end of town along US-50 at Comanche St.

## Horton

### Golden Eagle Casino
*1121 Goldfinch Rd*
*Horton, KS 66439*

www.goldeneaglecasino.com
785-486-6601

**DESCRIPTION:** Hosted by the Kickapoo Tribe, the casino is open 24/7. **GAMING:** slots, live pit/gaming tables, poker room, bingo. **FOOD & ENTERTAINMENT:** Restaurant open daily, morning till night. 24-hr snack bar. **LODGING:** There is no hotel at this location. **CAMPING:** Six RV spaces with full hookup on the west side of the parking lot; register/pay at the Players Club. Free overnight dry camping is also allowed; notify Security if staying overnight. **DIRECTIONS:** From I-70 exit 358, go north on US-75 for 42.1 miles to SR-20, east for 4.9 miles; follow casino signs.

## Mayetta

### Prairie Band Casino & Resort
*12305 150th Rd*
*Mayetta, KS 66509*

www.prairieband.com
785-966-7777 • RV Park: 785-966-7778

**DESCRIPTION:** A premier Native American destination resort in the Kansas heartland. **GAMING:** slots, pit/gaming tables, poker room. **FOOD & ENTERTAINMENT:** steakhouse, grill, buffet, sandwich shop. Ticketed shows in the ballroom; golf course. **LODGING:** Hotel rooms/suites, gift shop. **CAMPING:** RV Park, 67 paved, full-hookup pull-thru sites, laundry, free Wi-Fi, cable TV, shuttle service. RVs are also permitted to dry camp at the far end of the casino lot. **DIRECTIONS:** From I-70 exit 358, north on US-75 for 17 miles, then west on 150th Ave for 1.4 miles.

## Mulvane

### Kansas Star Casino Hotel

*777 Kansas Star Dr*
*Mulvane, KS 67110*

www.kansasstarcasino.com
316-719-5000

DESCRIPTION: A south-central Kansas gaming and entertainment destination. GAMING: slots, pit/table games, poker room. FOOD & ENTERTAINMENT: steakhouse, buffet, grill, quick food, two bars. Free entertainment Fridays. Ticketed shows in event center. LODGING: Several hotels nearby. CAMPING: RVs should park on the southeast side of the lot. Overnight permitted for self-contained vehicles. DIRECTIONS: Located at I-35 Exit 33.

## Pittsburg

### Kansas Crossing Casino & Hotel

*1275 S Hwy 69*
*Pittsburg, KS 66762*

www.kansascrossingcasino.com
620-240-4400

DESCRIPTION: Western-themed casino in southeastern Kansas. GAMING: slots, pit/table games, poker room. FOOD & ENTERTAINMENT: casual dining, sports bar. Free entertainment weekends in The Corral. LODGING: Hampton Inn & Suites. CAMPING: RVs should park in the gravel lot on the north end. Overnight parking is permitted. DIRECTIONS: Located at intersection of Highways 60 & 400 in Pittsburg, KS.

## Powhattan

### Sac & Fox Casino

*1322 US Hwy 75*
*Powhattan, KS 66527*

www.sacandfoxcasino.com
785-467-8000

DESCRIPTION: Native American Casino & Travel Center open 24 hours daily. GAMING: slots, live action pit/table games. FOOD & ENTERTAINMENT: buffet, cafe, lounge. LODGING: There is no hotel at this location. CAMPING: Ten RV spaces with electric hookup in the parking lot; register & pay at the gift shop. Central dump & fresh water available for RVs. If not registered for electric hookups, notify Security if you plan to dry camp overnight. DIRECTIONS: From I-70 exit 358, the casino is on the northbound side of US-75, about 43 miles north of Topeka.

## White Cloud

### Casino White Cloud

*777 Jackpot Dr*
*White Cloud, KS 66094*

www.casinowhitecloud.org
785-595-3430

DESCRIPTION: Charming Indian casino surrounded by farmland in northeast corner of Kansas. GAMING: slots, live gaming tables, bingo six days a week. Casino open 9am-1am/3am (Fri-Sat). FOOD & ENTERTAINMENT: Restaurant is open daily morning-night. LODGING: Four country cabins near the casino available for rent. CAMPING: 6 RV sites (water & electric) adjacent to the parking lot. Dump station available. Register & pay in the casino. DIRECTIONS: From I-70 exit 358, go north on US-75 for 54.4 miles, then east on US-36 for 20.2 miles, north on Timber Rd 1 mile, east on 240th St .5 mile, north on Thrasher Rd 5 miles, west on 290th St .5 mile, continue on Timber Rd 2 miles, then east on 310th St .6 mile. A shorter route out of St. Joseph, Missouri, is to take US-36 west for 16.6 miles then SR-7 north 34 miles.

# Louisiana

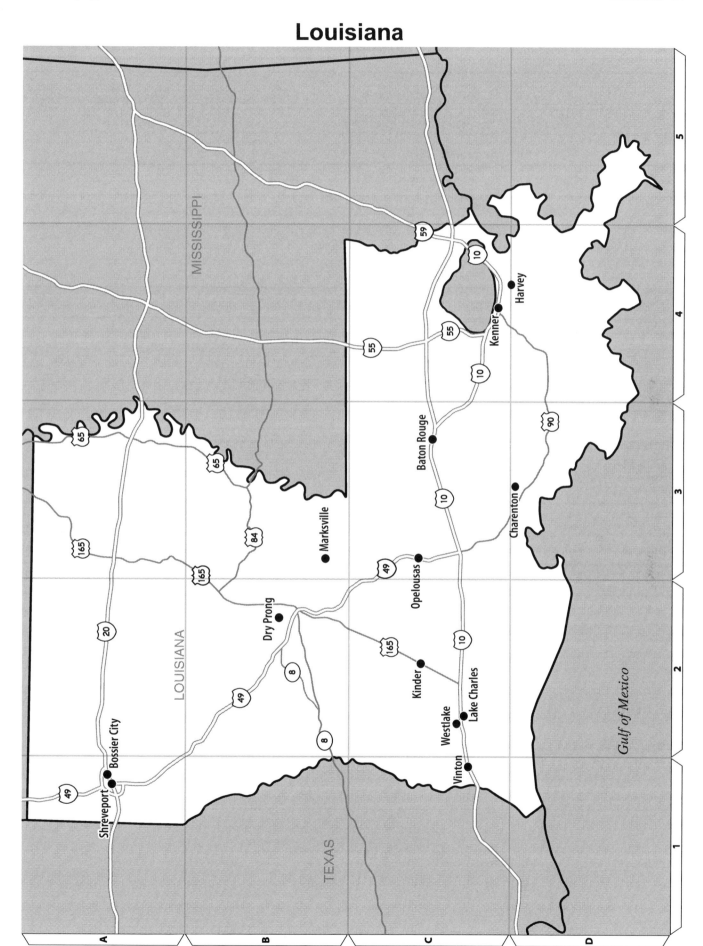

# Louisiana

| City | Casino | 🚐 | P | 🛏 | 🏌 | 🛡 |
|---|---|---|---|---|---|---|
| Baton Rouge | Hollywood Casino | | x | | | 1 |
| Baton Rouge | L' Auberge Casino Hotel | | x | x | | 2 |
| Bossier City | DiamondJacks Casino Resort | p32 | | x | | 1 |
| Bossier City | Harrah's Louisiana Downs | | x | x | | 1 |
| Bossier City | Horseshoe Bossier City | | x | x | | 1 |
| Charenton | Cypress Bayou Casino Hotel | p11 | | x | | |
| Dry Prong | Jena Choctaw Pines Casino | | x | | | |
| Harvey | Boomtown Casino - New Orleans | | x | x | | |
| Kenner | Treasure Chest Casino | | x | | | 2 |
| Kinder | Coushatta Casino Resort | p100 | x | x | x | |
| Lake Charles | Golden Nugget Casino Resort & Hotel | | x | x | x | 2 |
| Lake Charles | L' Auberge Casino Resort | | x | x | x | 1 |
| Marksville | Paragon Casino Resort | p200 | x | x | x | |
| Opelousas | Evangeline Downs Racetrack, Casino & Hotel | | x | x | | 1 |
| Shreveport | Eldorado Resort Casino | | | x | | 1 |
| Shreveport | Sam's Town Hotel & Casino | | x | x | | 1 |
| Vinton | Delta Downs Racetrack, Casino & Hotel | | x | x | | 3 |
| Westlake | Isle of Capri Casino Hotel - Lake Charles | s8 | x | x | | 1 |

Louisiana has a variety of casino styles – riverboats, land-based and racinos (casinos at race tracks). Most casinos in Louisiana are open 24/7. Small video poker rooms may be found at some truck stops and convenience stores throughout the state.

## Baton Rouge

### Hollywood Casino
*1717 River Rd N*
*Baton Rouge, LA 70802*

www.hollywoodbr.com
225-709-7777

**DESCRIPTION:** Hollywood-themed casino riverboat docked on the Mississippi River. **GAMING:** slots, video poker, pit/gaming tables, poker room, separate high limit area. **FOOD & ENTERTAINMENT:** steakhouse, buffet (overlooking river), grille, deli, lounge.

**LODGING:** There is no hotel at this location. **CAMPING:** Free dry camping area at the back of the lot, next to the red barn. Must obtain a parking pass from Security. Courtesy shuttle to casino. **DIRECTIONS:** From I-10 exit 155B to I-110, exit at North St (exit 1D). This is an exit ramp from the left lane! Take North St for .6 mile, then right on River Rd to the casino on the left.

### L'Auberge Casino Hotel - Baton Rouge
*14777 River Rd*
*Baton Rouge, LA 70820*

www.lbatonrouge.com
225-215-7777

**DESCRIPTION:** Elegant casino hotel on the banks of the Mississippi River. **GAMING:** slots, live-action gaming tables, poker room. Casino is in the hotel. **FOOD &**

**ENTERTAINMENT:** Four restaurants, fine dining to casual fare, bar. Ticketed shows in the event center. Live music in the lounge. **LODGING:** Three-star hotel. **CAMPING:** Free parking for RV's on the far side of the lot. Inform Security if you plan to stay overnight. **DIRECTIONS:** From I-10 east take exit 162A onto Bluebonnet. Right on LA-30, N. Nicholson Dr, then left onto L'Auberge Crossing Dr.

## Bossier City

### *DiamondJacks Casino & Resort*
*711 Diamondjacks Blvd*
*Bossier City, LA 71111*

www.diamondjacks.com
318-678-7777 • RV Park: 318-678-7661

**DESCRIPTION:** Casual casino on the banks of the Red River, convenient to I-20. **GAMING:** slots, video poker, gaming tables. **FOOD & ENTERTAINMENT:** buffet, steakhouse, grill, sports bar with free live local entertainment. Ticketed shows in Legends Theater. **LODGING:** Hotel rooms on 12 floors, arcade, gift shop. **CAMPING:** RV Park open all year, 32 level paved, full hookup sites, laundry. Free parking is available in the front lot, only when the RV Park is full. **DIRECTIONS:** From I-20 take exit 20A to Diamondjacks Blvd.

### *Harrah's Louisiana Downs*
*8000 E Texas St*
*Bossier City, LA 71111*

www.caesars.com/harrahs-louisiana-downs
318-742-5555

**DESCRIPTION:** Premier racino combines a casino with live horse racing. **GAMING:** 24-hour casino, slots & video poker. Thoroughbred racing May-Sep, Quarterhorse racing Jan-Mar, daily simulcasting. **FOOD & ENTERTAINMENT:** Clubhouse dining at the track, buffet, deli, cafe, casual dining, quick food. **LODGING:** Spring Hill studio-style rooms. **CAMPING:** Overnight parking is permitted for self-contained RVs in the section designated for trucks & oversize vehicles. **DIRECTIONS:** Louisiana Downs just off I-20 at exit 26; can be seen from the westbound lanes of the interstate.

### *Horseshoe Bossier City*
*711 Horseshoe Blvd*
*Bossier City, LA 71111*

www.caesars.com/horseshoe-bossier-city
318-742-0711

**DESCRIPTION:** Upscale destination resort. **GAMING:** slots, pit/gaming tables, poker room with full tournament schedule. **FOOD & ENTERTAINMENT:** steakhouse, buffet, Asian restaurant, noodle bar, burger bar. Live music in bars & lounges. Headline shows at Riverdome. **LODGING:** Hotel suites, retail shopping concourse, boutique shops. Unique display in lobby shows one million dollars in $100 bills. **CAMPING:** Overnight RV parking permitted in designated areas (1st or 2nd surface lot). **DIRECTIONS:** From I-20 exit 19B, go north .2 mile to the casino.

## Charenton

### *Cypress Bayou Casino Hotel*
*832 Martin Luther King Rd*
*Charenton, LA 70523*

www.cypressbayou.com
337-923-7284 • RV Park: 800-284-4386

**DESCRIPTION:** Full-service Native American casino destination resort in south-central Louisiana. **GAMING:** slots, video poker, pit/table games, high-stakes bingo, non-smoking slots area. **FOOD & ENTERTAINMENT:** steakhouse, Asian dining, cantina, quick food, coffee shop. Live lounge music, night club shows on Fri & Sat. Ticketed events at The Pavilion. Chitimacha Tribe of Louisiana Museum open Tue-Sat. **LODGING:** Contemporary-style hotel, business center. **CAMPING:** RV Park, 30 full-hookup sites, walking path, boat launch, playground, Trading Post open daily. Shuttle service. **DIRECTIONS:** From I-10 exit 103A, take US-90 east (along future I-49 corridor) 42.5 miles to SR-83, then east on SR-83 and left on SR-182 for .5 mile. Turn right onto Ralph Darden Memorial Pkwy for two miles to the resort.

## Dry Prong

### *Jena Choctaw Pines Casino*
*149 Chahta Trails*

*Dry Prong, LA 71423*

www.jenachoctawpinescasino.com
318-648-7773

**DESCRIPTION:** Cozy Native American casino located just north of Alexandria. **GAMING:** open 24/7 with slots & poker room. **FOOD & ENTERTAINMENT:** buffet, sports bar, live entertainment. **LODGING:** No hotel at this location. **CAMPING:** RV parking is available; overnight OK. **DIRECTIONS:** From I-49 take exit 84 to US-167N/LA-28 Pineville Expy. Follow US-167 north for about 12 miles.

## Harvey

### Boomtown Casino - New Orleans
*4132 Peters Rd*
*Harvey, LA 70058*

www.boomtownneworleans.com
504-366-7711

**DESCRIPTION:** Friendly neighborhood casino near New Orleans. **GAMING:** slots, video poker, pit/gaming tables, poker room, separate non-smoking slots area. **FOOD & ENTERTAINMENT:** steakhouse, Asian dining, bayou buffet, quick food. Live nightclub entertainment, dance floor. **LODGING:** Hotel. **CAMPING:** RV dry camping in southeast corner of the lot; overnight OK, courtesy shuttle. **DIRECTIONS:** About 12 miles from interstate. From I-10 eastbound, take exit 234B. From I-10 westbound, take exit 234C. Cross the bridge and continue on elevated Westbank Expressway (US-90 West Business Route) for six miles. Exit at Manhattan Blvd – exit 6. Continue on ground-level Westbank Expressway middle lane (do not enter tunnel). Follow the blue casino signs. The expressway ends at Peters Road. Turn left and follow Peters Road for 4.5 miles.

## Kenner

### Treasure Chest Casino
*5050 Williams Blvd*
*Kenner, LA 70065*

www.treasurechestcasino.com
504-443-8000

**DESCRIPTION:** Paddle wheeler docked on Lake Pontchartrain in Kenner, suburb of New Orleans. **GAMING:** slots, pit/table games (open 10am), non-smoking area. **FOOD & ENTERTAINMENT:** buffet, cafe. Local, regional entertainment in the lounge. **LODGING:** Hilton Garden Inn, shuttle service. **CAMPING:** RVs should use the Hilton Garden hotel lot, across from the casino; use the section of the lot along Williams Blvd. Overnight is permitted. **DIRECTIONS:** From I-10 exit 223, north on Williams Blvd (SR-49) for 1.5 miles to the casino on the shores of Lake Pontchartrain.

## Kinder

### Coushatta Casino Resort
*777 Coushatta Dr*
*Kinder, LA 70648*

www.coushattacasinoresort.com
800-584-7263

**DESCRIPTION:** Large Native-American casino destination resort. **GAMING:** slots, video poker, pit/table games, poker room, high stakes gaming, bingo, off track betting, non-smoking area. **FOOD & ENTERTAINMENT:** Eight restaurants, fine or casual dining, quick food, coffee shop. Live lounge entertainment. Ticketed shows in the pavilion, golf course. **LODGING:** Two hotels, Inn. **CAMPING:** Red Shoes RV Park, 100 paved, full hookup sites, 100 chalets surrounding a two-acre lake, heated outdoor pool, dog park, many other amenities. Shuttle service throughout the resort. Free overnight parking for RVs on the service road near the RV Park entrance or on the perimeter of the parking lot (space permitted). **DIRECTIONS:** From I-10 exit 44, go north 23 miles on US-165 to the resort located five miles north of Kinder.

## Lake Charles

### Golden Nugget Casino Resort & Hotel
*2550 Golden Nugget Blvd*
*Lake Charles, LA 70601*

www.goldennuggetlc.com
337-508-7777

**DESCRIPTION:** Large Vegas-style gaming resort.

GAMING: slots, video poker, pit/table games, poker room and high limits room. FOOD & ENTERTAINMENT: Ten restaurants fine dining, buffet, casual dining, quick food, several bars and lounges, golf course, marina. Ticketed events weekends in the showroom. LODGING: Two hotel towers. CAMPING: RV parking is allowed Monday thru Thursday; overnight OK. NO RV parking on the weekends. DIRECTIONS: From I-10 exit 25 follow I-210 to exit 4 and follow signs to the casino.

### L'Auberge Casino Resort
*777 Ave L'Auberge*
*Lake Charles, LA 70601*

www.llakecharles.com
377-395-7777

DESCRIPTION: Texas Hill Country-themed resort. GAMING: slots, pit/table games, poker room. FOOD & ENTERTAINMENT: Eight dining venues, fine dining to casual, lounges & bars. Live entertainment weekends. Golf course. LODGING: Luxury hotel. CAMPING: Free overnight RV parking available, Monday-Thursday in the lot between sections G & H; weekends RVs should park alongside the roadway coming into the resort. DIRECTIONS: From I-10 exit 25, take the I-210 Loop to exit 4 then north on Nelson Road for .5 mile, left into the resort.

## Marksville

### Paragon Casino Resort
*711 Paragon Pl – Hwy 1*
*Marksville, LA 71351*

www.paragoncasinoresort.com
800-946-1946

DESCRIPTION: Destination resort, the first land-based casino in Louisiana. GAMING: slots, video poker, pit/table games, poker room, keno, race book, high denomination slot & table play, non-smoking area. FOOD & ENTERTAINMENT: steakhouse, oyster bar, diner, buffet, lounge, golf course, cinema. Ticketed events in the showroom. LODGING: Hotel, retail shops. CAMPING: RV Park, 200 paved pull-thru full-hookup sites, cabins, pool, laundry, horseshoes, volleyball,

guest lodge. Free shuttle service throughout the resort. Limited free overnight RV parking permitted in the gravel bus parking lot. DIRECTIONS: From I-49 exit 80 in Alexandria, take US-71 south for 4.5 miles, SR-3170 east for 5.5 miles then SR-1 south for about 18 miles to the resort on the right.

## Opelousas

### Evangeline Downs Racetrack, Casino & Hotel
*2235 Creswell Lane Extension*
*Opelousas, LA 70570*

www.evangelinedowns.com
866-472-2466

DESCRIPTION: Popular racino, horse racing & slots at one location. GAMING: slots, video poker. Live Quarterhorse racing spring & fall, Thoroughbred racing in summer, simulcasting, OTB year round. FOOD & ENTERTAINMENT: steakhouse, buffet, cafe, lounge, live entertainment. Event Center. LODGING: Quaint hotel. CAMPING: RVs should park in the north lot, no hookups, overnight is OK. DIRECTIONS: From I-49 exit 18, east 1 mile on Creswell Ln. Entrance is on left just past Walmart.

## Shreveport

### Eldorado Resort Casino
*451 Clyde Fant Pkwy*
*Shreveport, LA 71101*

www.eldoradoshreveport.com
877-602-0711

DESCRIPTION: Eldorado's timeless luxury in downtown Shreveport. GAMING: slots, video poker, pit/table games, poker room, high limits area, weekly tournaments. FOOD & ENTERTAINMENT: buffet, steakhouse, noodle bar, cafe. Live shows, dancing in the lounge. LODGING: Hotel rooms/suites. CAMPING: RV parking is available in the large-vehicle lot directly across the street from the hotel. Overnight parking permitted. DIRECTIONS: From I-20 exit 19A, Spring St, go north to Milam St, right on Milam to Clyde Fant Pkwy.

### Sam's Town Hotel & Casino

*315 Clyde Fant Pkwy*
*Shreveport, LA 71101*

www.samstownshreveport.com
318-424-7777

**DESCRIPTION:** Casino resort overlooking Red River in downtown Shreveport. **GAMING:** slots, pit/gaming tables. **FOOD & ENTERTAINMENT:** steakhouse, buffet, café, quick food. Live local & regional entertainment in the lounge. **LODGING:** Hotel. **CAMPING:** RV parking in the lot across from the parking garage, overnight is permitted. **DIRECTIONS:** From I-20 exit 19A, Spring St, go north 4 blocks, turn right on Fannin, east to the casino.

## Vinton

### Delta Downs Racetrack, Casino & Hotel

*2717 Delta Downs Dr*
*Vinton, LA 70668*

www.deltadowns.com
337-589-7441

**DESCRIPTION:** Racino near the Texas state line, live horse racing & slots. **GAMING:** slots, video poker, roomy gaming floor. Live Thoroughbred racing Oct-Mar; Quarterhorse racing Apr-Jul. Daily simulcasting. **FOOD & ENTERTAINMENT:** Trackside fine dining, buffet, grille, quick food. Live lounge entertainment. **LODGING:** Hotel. **CAMPING:** RV parking lot east of the hotel, follow signs. Overnight parking permitted. **DIRECTIONS:** From I-10 exit 4 or exit 7, follow signs. Racetrack on CR-3063 (3 miles from I-10).

## Westlake

### Isle of Capri Casino Hotel - Lake Charles

*100 Westlake Ave*
*Westlake, LA 70669*

www.lake-charles.isleofcapricasinos.com
337-430-0711

**DESCRIPTION:** Isle of Capri resort can be seen from the interstate; easy on/off access. **GAMING:** slots, pit/gaming tables, poker room. **FOOD & ENTERTAINMENT:** buffet, bar & grill, quick food. Live lounge entertainment. **LODGING:** Hotel. **CAMPING:** Eight RV spaces with electric hookups adjacent to the hotel, free Wi-Fi. Spaces are tight, no room to extend slideouts. Register & pay at the hotel front desk. Advance reservations suggested. Free overnight RV parking is also available in the parking lot on north side along the fence by the I-10 bridge. **DIRECTIONS:** From I-10 exit 27; Isle of Capri can be seen from the eastbound lanes. Follow the green casino signs.

# Maine

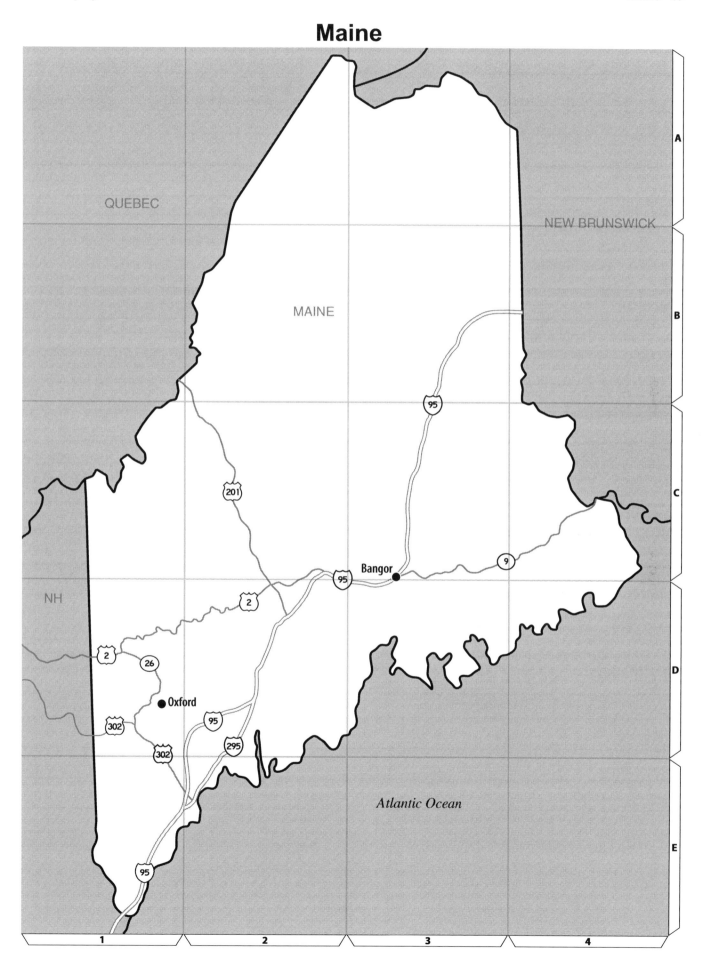

# Maine

| City | Casino | 🚐 | 🅿 | 🛏 | 🏌 | 🛡 |
|------|--------|-----|-----|-----|-----|-----|
| Bangor | Hollywood Casino Hotel & Raceway | p5 | | x | | 2 |
| Oxford | Oxford Casino & Hotel | | x | | | |

Maine has two casino locations: Hollywood Casino Hotel in downtown Bangor, across from the raceway in historic Bass Park, and the Oxford Casino, located a half hour from Portland.

## Bangor

### Hollywood Casino Hotel & Raceway
*500 Main St*
*Bangor, ME 04401*

www.hollywoodcasinobangor.com
207-561 6100

**DESCRIPTION:** Premier racino combining live racing with casino gaming. **GAMING:** Open 8am-3am daily, slots, live-action pit/table games, racebook, poker room. Harness racing May-Nov; simulcasting & OTB noon-midnight. **FOOD & ENTERTAINMENT:** buffet, snack bar, bar & grill. Quick food at the track. Live entertainment in the lounge. **LODGING:** Hotel rooms/suites. **CAMPING:** RV park at the raceway, across the street from the casino hotel, is the only option for RV parking. Must call the casino in advance to arrange for parking. (Casino does not have surface parking.) **DIRECTIONS:** From I-95 exit 182A, take I-395 E/ME-15 South for 1.3 miles to exit 3, then US-1A east .5 mile, merge onto Main St .2 mile.

## Oxford

### Oxford Casino & Hotel
*777 Casino Way*
*Oxford, ME 04270*

www.oxfordcasino.com
207-539-6700

**DESCRIPTION:** Small casino/hotel in southern Maine, open 24/7. **GAMING:** slots, gaming tables. **FOOD & ENTERTAINMENT:** Pub-style restaurant, grille, express food. **LODGING:** Modern hotel rooms. **CAMPING:** Designated parking section for oversize vehicles. Stays are limited to 24 hours. **DIRECTIONS:** From Maine Turnpike exit 63, drive 17 miles north on Route 26 to the casino.

# Maryland

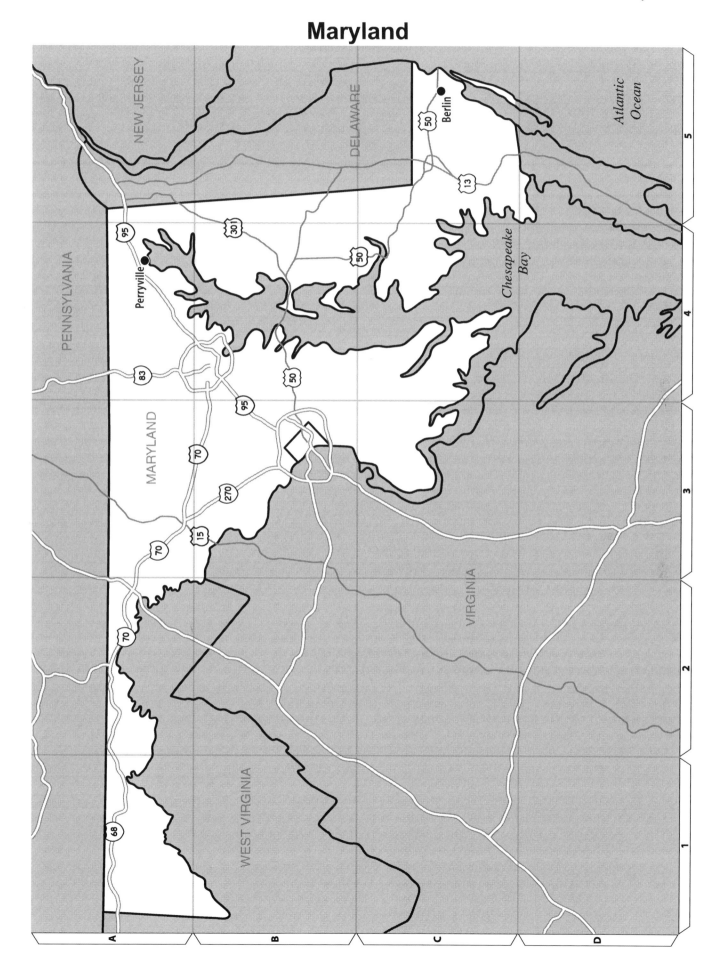

# Maryland

| City | Casino | ![RV] | ![P] | ![Lodging] | ![Golf] | ![Shield] |
|------|--------|-------|------|------------|---------|-----------|
| Berlin | Ocean Downs Casino | | x | | | |
| Perryville | Hollywood Casino | | x | | | 1 |

Two of Maryland's casinos are listed below. The state's only racino also features live harness racing in summer. Hollywood Casino is convenient to Interstate 95 in Perryville. Both facilities are RV-friendly.

## Berlin

### Ocean Downs Casino
*10218 Racetrack Rd*
*Berlin, MD 21811*

www.oceandowns.com
410-641-0600

**DESCRIPTION:** Maryland's only racino combines live racing with casino games. **GAMING:** slots, video poker, live action gaming tables, OTB. Casino hours 8am-4am daily/24hrs on weekends. Live harness racing Jun-Aug, simulcasting daily. **FOOD & ENTERTAINMENT:** Eatery & bar open daily, casual dining trackside in racing season. **LODGING:** There is no hotel at this location. **CAMPING:** Parking available for RVs. Please check-in with Security or the casino manager if you want to stay overnight. **DIRECTIONS:** From I-95 exit 19A take US-50 east toward Ocean City (approximately 90 miles) then north on Racetrack Road to the casino.

## Perryville

### Hollywood Casino
*1201 Chesapeake Overlook Pkwy (Turnpike Dr)*
*Perryville, MD 21903*

www.hollywoodcasinoperrysville.com
410-378-8500

**DESCRIPTION:** A Hollywood-themed casino, just off I-95 at exit 93. **GAMING:** slots, live gaming tables, video poker, electronic table games, open 24/7. **FOOD & ENTERTAINMENT:** bar & grill open every day, quick bites. Free live entertainment. **LODGING:** There is no hotel at this location. **CAMPING:** Park on perimeter of the surface lot near the truck area, overnight RV dry camping permitted, no hookups; notify Security if staying overnight. **DIRECTIONS:** From I-95 exit 93 turn right onto MD-222 toward Perryville for .3 mile.

# Michigan

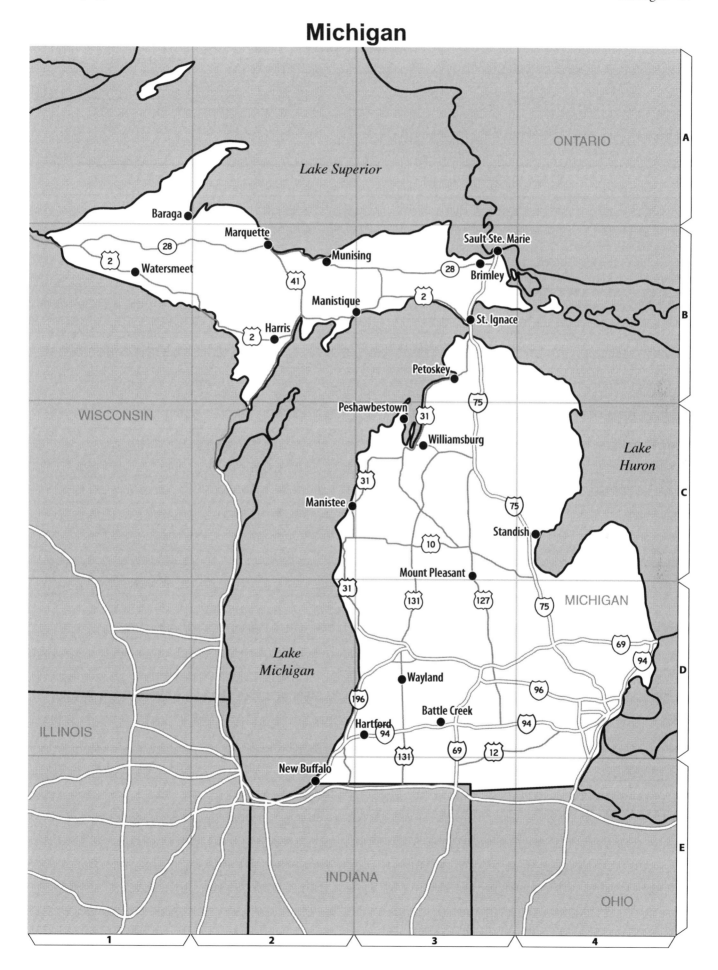

# Michigan

| City | Casino | 🚐 | P | 🛏 | 🏌 | 🛡 |
|------|--------|------|------|------|------|------|
| Baraga | Ojibwa Casino | p12 | | x | | |
| Battle Creek | Firekeepers Casino Hotel | s6 | x | x | | 1 |
| Brimley | Bay Mills Resort & Casino | p117 | | x | x | |
| Brimley | Kings Club Casino | | | | | |
| Harris | Island Resort Casino | p42 | x | x | | |
| Hartford | Four Winds | | x | | | 4 |
| Manistee | Little River Casino Resort | p95 | x | x | | |
| Manistique | Kewadin Casino | s10 | x | | | |
| Marquette | Ojibwa Casino II | | x | | | |
| Mount Pleasant | Soaring Eagle Casino & Resort | | x | x | x | |
| Munising | Kewadin Casino - Christmas | s5 | x | | | |
| New Buffalo | Four Winds Casino Resort | | x | x | | 1 |
| Peshawbestown | Leelanau Sands Casino & Lodge | s15 | x | x | | |
| Petoskey | Odawa Casino Resort | | x | x | | |
| Saint Ignace | Kewadin Shores Hotel & Casino | s21 | x | x | | 2 |
| Sault Ste. Marie | Kewadin Casino | p64 | x | x | | 4 |
| Standish | Saganing Eagles Landing Casino | p50 | | | | 7 |
| Watersmeet | Northern Waters Casino Resort | p14 | | x | x | |
| Wayland | Gun Lake Casino | | x | | | |
| Williamsburg | Turtle Creek Casino & Hotel | | x | x | | |

Michigan is known as "The Great Lakes State" where residents and visitors can enjoy 3,200 miles of Great Lakes shoreline. There are 20 Indian casinos listed in this section – nine in the Upper Peninsula, where outdoor non-gaming activities abound all year, and 11 are located in central Michigan.

## Baraga

### Ojibwa Casino
*16449 Michigan Ave*
*Baraga, MI 49908*

www.ojibwacasino.com
906-353-6333

**DESCRIPTION:** Near Sandpoint Lighthouse on Keneenaw Bay in the Upper Peninsula. **GAMING:** open 24 hours, slots, pit/table games (open noon daily), bingo. **FOOD & ENTERTAINMENT:** restaurant, sports bar & grill, bowling alleys. **LODGING:** Motel. **CAMPING:** 12 full hookup RV spaces, first come/first served, May-Nov. Register and pay at the hotel. **DIRECTIONS:** From US-41 in Baraga, one mile west on M-38.

## Battle Creek

### Firekeepers Casino Hotel
*11177 E Michigan Ave*
*Battle Creek, MI 49014*

www.firekeeperscasino.com
269-660-5722 • 877-352-8777

**DESCRIPTION:** Large gaming destination resort in

southern Michigan. **GAMING:** 24/7, slots, video poker, keno, pit/table games, smoke-free poker room, bingo, high limit lounge. **FOOD & ENTERTAINMENT:** fine dining, casual buffet, cafe, quick food, three bars, lounge. Ticketed shows weekends. **LODGING:** Luxury hotel. **CAMPING:** Spaces with RV hookups are available at the Pit Stop Gas Station on casino property. Pull in and pay at the gas station. Free overnight parking is also permitted in the casino parking lot, please check-in with Security if you plan to stay overnight. **DIRECTIONS:** From I-94 take exit 104 toward 11 Mile Rd. Turn left at 11 Mile Road for .3 mile then left onto E Michigan Ave for .7 mile.

## Brimley

This resort includes two affiliated casinos – Bay Mills and Kings Club. The Bay Mills Native American Reservation on the UP north shore is noted for its captivating views and rich Native American history. The two casinos are located four miles from one another and a free shuttle operates between them.

### Bay Mills Resort & Casino
*11386 W Lakeshore Dr*
*Brimley, MI 49715*

www.baymillscasinos.com
888-422-9645

**DESCRIPTION:** Waterfront resort includes casino, hotel, RV Park & golf course. **GAMING:** open 24hrs, slots, live-action gaming tables & poker room (from 10am daily). **FOOD & ENTERTAINMENT:** fine dining, casual, cafe. **LODGING:** Waterfront hotel, gift shop, golf course. **CAMPING:** RV Park, 117 sites, water & electric, some full hookup, some pull thrus. Open May-Oct. Walking distance to casino. **DIRECTIONS:** From I-75 exit 386, west on M-28 for 7.7 miles, then north into Brimley on M-24 for 2.5 miles & west on Lakeshore Dr. for 2 miles.

### Kings Club Casino
*12140 W Lakeshore Dr*
*Brimley, MI 49715*

www.baymillscasinos.com
906-248-3227

**DESCRIPTION:** Small slots-only casino affiliated with

Bay Mills. **GAMING:** Open 10am-midnight/2:30am weekends, slots only. **FOOD & ENTERTAINMENT:** Cafe open daily. **LODGING:** Hotel is at Bay Mills location. Shuttle service between the two casinos. **CAMPING:** RV Park at Bay Mills. **DIRECTIONS:** From I-75 exit 386, west on M-28 for 7.7 miles, then north into Brimley on M-22 for 2.5 miles and west on Lakeshore Dr for 4.3 miles.

## Harris

### Island Resort Casino
*W 399 Hwys 2 & 41*
*Harris, MI 49845*

www.islandresortandcasino.com
800-682-6040

**DESCRIPTION:** In Upper Peninsula near Lake Michigan north shore. **GAMING:** 24-hr slots, pit/table games (open 10am), poker room, bingo every day. **FOOD & ENTERTAINMENT:** steakhouse, casual dining, grill, subs & pizza, sports bar, custard shop. Free lounge entertainment. Ticketed events in Showroom. **LODGING:** Luxury guest rooms/suites, indoor pool, spa, golf. **CAMPING:** RV Park, 42 full hookup sites, open May-Nov. RV guests may use amenities at the hotel. Shuttle service. Free dry camping permitted on the gravel portion of parking area. **DIRECTIONS:** From Escanaba (on northern shore of Lake Michigan), travel 13 miles west on Hwy-2 & 41 into Harris.

## Hartford

### Four Winds Hartford
*68600 Red Arrow Hwy*
*Hartford, MI 49057*

www.fourwindscasino.com/hartford
866-494-6371

**DESCRIPTION:** Cozy casino near I-94 in southwestern Michigan. **GAMING:** slots, many progressives, live-action pit/table games. Open 24/7. **FOOD & ENTERTAINMENT:** Fast food deli, bar. **LODGING:** There is no hotel at this location. **CAMPING:** The RV lot is near the parking garage. Notify Security if staying overnight. **DIRECTIONS:** From I-94 take exit 41 and follow M-140 north for .7 mile. Turn right on Red Arrow Hwy/E Saint Joseph St for 2.7 miles.

## Manistee

### Little River Casino Resort
*2700 Orchard Hwy*
*Manistee, MI 49660*

www.lrcr.com
231-723-1535 • RV Park: 888-568-2244

**DESCRIPTION:** Charming destination resort near Lake Michigan east shore. **GAMING:** slots, pit/table games, poker room. **FOOD & ENTERTAINMENT:** full-service restaurant, casual buffet, cafe, coffee shop, sports bar & grill, quick food. DJ & dancing in the lounge; ticketed shows in event center. **LODGING:** Hotel rooms/suites, fitness center, indoor pool, sauna & hot tub. **CAMPING:** Modern 95-space RV Park, open Apr-Oct, walking distance to casino, outdoor pavilion. RV guests invited to use hotel amenities. Overnight parking also permitted in the parking lot, no hookups; there is a $5 charge for use of central dump. **DIRECTIONS:** From US-131 (major north/south route) Cadillac exit, take M-55 west to junction US-31, then north for 3.1 miles on US-31. Casino on left.

## Manistique

### Kewadin Casino
*5630W Old US-Hwy2*
*Manistique, MI 49854*

www.kewadinmanistique.com
906-341-5510

**DESCRIPTION:** Vegas-style gaming in hometown atmosphere. **GAMING:** slots, gaming tables, including $3 blackjack. Open 9am-1am/3am Fri-Sat. **FOOD & ENTERTAINMENT:** restaurant & bar. **LODGING:** There is no hotel at this location. **CAMPING:** Free overnight RV parking is available. There are 10 spaces with 20 amp service, west side of the lot, first come, first serve. **DIRECTIONS:** From I-75 exit 344B, west on US-2 for 89 miles. Located west of the Mackinaw Bridge.

## Marquette

### Ojibwa Casino II
*105 Acre Trail*
*Marquette, MI 49855*

www.ojibwacasino.com/Marquette
906-249-4200

**DESCRIPTION:** Friendly casino near Lake Superior. **GAMING:** Open 24 hours, slots, pit/table games. **FOOD & ENTERTAINMENT:** (Expanded facility to be completed by 2019.) Two signature restaurants, quick food, lounge. **LODGING:** New hotel in 2019. **CAMPING:** RV-friendly casino will offer free parking for RVs in 2019 following construction completion. **DIRECTIONS:** About 10.5 miles east of Marquette just off highway M-28 (turn right at Wanda Dr).

## Mount Pleasant

### Soaring Eagle Casino & Resort
*6800 Soaring Eagle Blvd*
*Mount Pleasant, MI 48858*

www.soaringeaglecasino.com
888-732-4537

**DESCRIPTION:** Popular casino destination resort in central Michigan. **GAMING:** slots, pit/table games, poker room, bingo. **FOOD & ENTERTAINMENT:** Seven dining options, fine dining to quick food, lounge. Live entertainment. Ticketed shows-indoor & outdoor venues; golf course, waterpark. **LODGING:** Luxury hotel. **CAMPING:** Large parking area for RV dry camping; overnight OK. Shuttle service. **DIRECTIONS:** From US-127, take M-20 east (Pickard) for 1.2 miles. Turn right onto Leaton Rd & follow signs to the RV parking area across from hotel.

## Munising

### Kewadin Casino - Christmas
*N 7761 Candy Cane Ln*
*Munising, MI 49862*

www.kewadinchristmas.com
906-387-5475 • 800-539-2346

**DESCRIPTION:** Near Lake Superior, casino reflects the charm of the UP. **GAMING:** Open daily 8am–3am, slots, gaming tables including $3 blackjack. **FOOD & ENTERTAINMENT:** Frosty's Pub & Grub open all day, gift shop. **LODGING:** There is no hotel at this location. **CAMPING:** Free overnight parking is available for self-contained RVs. Five parking spaces have electric service, first come, first serve. **DIRECTIONS:** From I-75 exit 386, follow M-28 west for 117 miles.

## New Buffalo

### Four Winds Casino Resort
*11111 Wilson Rd*
*New Buffalo, MI 49117*

www.fourwindscasino.com
866-494-6370

**DESCRIPTION:** Destination resort near Chicago. **GAMING:** slots, live gaming tables, poker room, open 24/7. **FOOD & ENTERTAINMENT:** steakhouse, buffet, deli, fast food, four bars & the only Hard Rock Cafe in Southwest Michigan. Ticketed shows in event center. Live shows at Hard Rock Thu-Sun. **LODGING:** Hotel rooms/suites, shopping promenade. **CAMPING:** Overnight RV parking permitted at the east end of the parking lot. **DIRECTIONS:** From I-94 exit 1 take MI-239 south for .2 mile and Wilson Rd east for .3 mile.

## Peshawbestown

### Leelanau Sands Casino & Lodge
*2521 NW Bay Shore Dr*
*Peshawbestown, MI 49682*

www.leelanausandscasino.com
231-534-8100 • 800-922-2946

**DESCRIPTION:** Small casino resort overlooking Grand Traverse Bay. **GAMING:** slots, live-action gaming tables, bingo. Casino open daily 8am (tables 2pm) till 2am. **FOOD & ENTERTAINMENT:** Casul fare at casino. Live entertainment weekends. **LODGING:** Lodge. **CAMPING:** 15 RV spaces with electric hookups across the street from the casino (next to the gas station). Register & pay at the gift shop. Free overnight dry camping is permitted in the large lot north of the gas station. **DIRECTIONS:** From I-75 exit 254 follow M-72 west about 51 miles, then north on M-22 for 18.7 miles.

## Petoskey

### Odawa Casino Resort
*1760 Lears Rd*
*Petoskey, MI 49770*

www.odawacasino.com
877-442-6464

**DESCRIPTION:** 24-hour gaming in Petoskey, Lake Michigan. **GAMING:** slots, live action gaming tables, poker room. **FOOD & ENTERTAINMENT:** fine dining, buffet, cafe, lounge. Entertainment on weekends. **LODGING:** Hotel, about half-mile from casino. **CAMPING:** RV parking lot is near the casino, follow signs. Overnight is OK. **DIRECTIONS:** From I-75 take exit 290 toward Vanderbilt, go north on Old 27/CR-C48 for 2.7 miles, then west on East Thumb Lake Rd/CR-C48 for 12.2 miles. Turn north on US-131 and follow 12.8 miles to Petoskey, then west on Lears Rd for .7 mile. The casino is past Lowes and Walmart at the end of Lears Rd. Follow Odawa signs.

## Saint Ignace

### Kewadin Shores Hotel & Casino
*3015 Mackinac Trail*
*Saint Ignace, MI 49781*

www.kewadinstignace.com
906-643-7071 • 800-539-2346

**DESCRIPTION:** Casino at the gateway to the UP, near Mackinac Bridge. **GAMING:** open 24/7, slots, gaming tables, poker room, keno. **FOOD & ENTERTAINMENT:** Full-service restaurant, sports bar, deli, lounge. **LODGING:** Hotel on Lake Huron, fitness center, pool & whirlpool. **CAMPING:** There are 21 spaces with electric hookups in the parking lot. Register and pay daily fee at the front desk. RV guests may use the hotel pool. Free overnight parking is also permitted. **DIRECTIONS:** From I-75 exit 348, to Mackinac Trail north for 1.4 miles.

## Sault Ste. Marie

### Kewadin Casino
*2186 Shunk Rd*
*Sault Ste. Marie, MI 49783*

www.kewadin.com
906-632-0530 • RV Park: 800-539-2346

**DESCRIPTION:** Resort in Michigan's oldest city and near the world-famous Soo Locks. **GAMING:** slots, pit/

gaming tables, poker room, keno, open 24/7. **Food & Entertainment:** restaurant, deli, lounges with menu service. Entertainment in the theater. Local music, shows in the lounges. **Lodging:** Hotel, fitness center, indoor pool, sauna, spa. **Camping:** 64-space RV Park, open May-Oct, electric hookups, water & dump station. Pull into a site, then go to the hotel to register. RV guests are invited to use amenities at the hotel. Free dry camping is available at the perimeter of the large lot behind the casino building, overnight is permitted. **Directions:** From I-75 exit 392 (before the bridge to Ontario) go east on Three Mile Rd for 2.4 miles then north on Shunk Rd for .9 mile.

## Standish

### Saganing Eagles Landing Casino
2690 Worth Rd
Standish, MI 48658

www.saganing-eagleslanding.com
989-775-5919 • 888-732-4537

**Description:** Friendly casino in east-central Michigan near Saginaw Bay. **Gaming:** 24-hour slots. **Food & Entertainment:** cafe, bar, quick food. Live music on weekends. **Lodging:** Five-story hotel. **Camping:** Modern RV Park, across the street from the casino, 50 sites, electric & water hookups, central dump station, open all year (no water in winter). Register & pay at casino cashier cage. Free shuttle from RV Park to casino and nearby marina. **Directions:** From I-75 exit 188 take US-23 north 2.2 miles then M-13 south 1.6 miles, east on Worth Rd 2.6 miles.

## Watersmeet

### Northern Waters Casino Resort
N 5384 US-45
Watersmeet, MI 49969

www.lvdcasino.com
906-358-4226 • RV Park: 800 895-2505

**Description:** Upper Peninsula casino located just north of Wisconsin border. **Gaming:** open 24 hours, slots, pit/table games, keno. **Food & Entertainment:** restaurant, food court, sports bar, golf course. **Lodging:** Hotel, gift shop. **Camping:** RV Park open May-Nov, 14 sites, electric & water hookups (nearest dump station 2 miles away). Register at the hotel. **Directions:** Located in the western UP, two miles north of the junction of US-2 & US-45.

## Wayland

### Gun Lake Casino
1123 129th Ave
Wayland, MI 49348

www.gunlakecasino.com
269-792-7777

**Description:** A friendly local casino located between Kalamazoo & Grand Rapids. **Gaming:** open 24/7, slots, video poker, live pit/table games, high limit section. **Food & Entertainment:** buffet, café, quick food, bar, live local entertainment in the lounge. **Lodging:** No hotel at this location. **Camping:** Free parking for RVs is in the north lot. If staying overnight get a parking permit at the Rewards Center. **Directions:** Located on US-131 exit 61.

## Williamsburg

### Turtle Creek Casino & Hotel
7741 M-72 E
Williamsburg, MI 49690

www.turtlecreekcasino.com
231-534-8870

**Description:** Destination resort near Grand Traverse Bay. **Gaming:** 24/7 casino, slots, live action gaming tables, poker room, high limit room. **Food & Entertainment:** steakhouse, buffet, deli, coffee shop. Live music, shows weekends in the lounge. **Lodging:** Hotel rooms/suites. **Camping:** Free parking for RVs on the west side of the paved lot during the week & on the field behind the casino on weekends. Overnight is OK. **Directions:** From I-75 follow M-72 west 30 miles.

# Minnesota

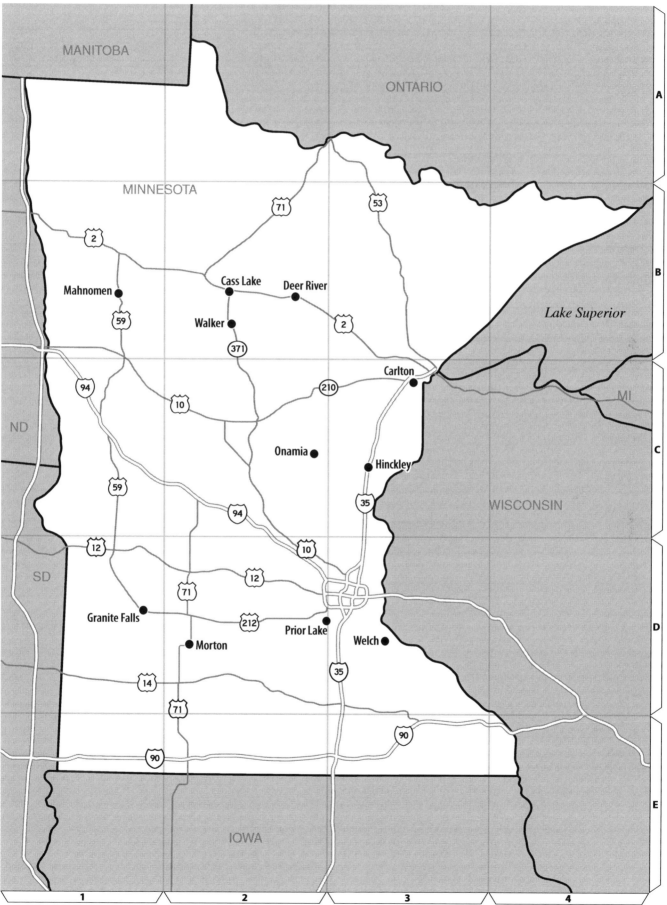

# Minnesota

| City | Casino | 🚐 | 🅿 | 🛏 | 🏌 | 🛡 |
|------|--------|------|------|------|------|------|
| Carlton | Black Bear Casino Resort | | x | x | x | 1 |
| Cass Lake | Palace Casino Hotel | s25 | | x | | |
| Deer River | White Oak Casino | s6 | x | | | |
| Granite Falls | Prairie's Edge Resort Casino | p55 | x | x | | |
| Hinckley | Grand Casino Hinckley | p200 | x | x | x | 1 |
| Mahnomen | Shooting Star Casino | p47 | x | x | | |
| Morton | Jackpot Junction Casino Hotel | p70 | x | x | x | |
| Onamia | Grand Casino Mille Lacs | s12 | x | x | | |
| Prior Lake | Mystic Lake Casino Hotel | p122 | x | x | x | 10 |
| Walker | Northern Lights Casino Hotel | s5 | x | x | | |
| Welch | Treasure Island Resort & Casino | p95 | x | x | | |

Minnesota has had gambling since 1988 when the state's 11 Indian Tribes requested compacts to operate casinos with video games of chance. Later table games, blackjack and poker, were added.

## Carlton

### Black Bear Casino Resort
*1785 MN-210*
*Carlton, MN 55718*

www.blackbearcasinoresort.com
218-878-2327

**DESCRIPTION:** Resort hosted by the Fond du Lac Band of Lake Superior Chippawa. **GAMING:** slots, blackjack tables, bingo daily. **FOOD & ENTERTAINMENT:** steakhouse, buffet, deli, coffee shop. Live local entertainment in the nightclub; ticketed shows in event center, golf course. **LODGING:** Hotel, connected to casino by a skywalk. **CAMPING:** Designated RV spaces in the parking lot behind the casino, overnight parking OK. **DIRECTIONS:** From I-35 exit 235, casino is on the west corner of Hwy-210, visible from southbound lanes of the interstate.

## Cass Lake

### Palace Casino Hotel
*US-2 & Bingo Palace Rd*
*Cass Lake, MN 56633*

www.palacecasinohotel.com
218-335-7000

**DESCRIPTION:** New relocated casino & hotel expected to open in summer 2019. Name changes to Cedar Lakes Casino & Hotel. **GAMING:** 24/7 casino, slots, & tables. **FOOD & ENTERTAINMENT:** Several dining venues, event center. **LODGING:** 100 room hotel. **CAMPING:** RVs should call ahead to verify availability of parking. **DIRECTIONS:** Located on US-2 at 63rd Ave NW, just west of the town of Cass Lake.

## Deer River

### White Oak Casino
*45830 US Hwy 2*
*Deer River, MN 56636*

www.whiteoakcasino.com
218-246-9600

**DESCRIPTION:** Known as the "Best Little Casino in Minnesota," just northwest of Grand Rapids.

**GAMING:** slots, blackjack tables, open 24 hours. **FOOD & ENTERTAINMENT:** cafe open daily, morning till night, bar, gift shop. **LODGING:** There is no hotel at this location. **CAMPING:** About six spaces with free electric hookup in the parking lot, check in & register with Security. Free dry camping is also allowed in the parking lot, both areas walking distance to the casino. **DIRECTIONS:** Casino is directly on US-2, west of Deer River.

## Granite Falls

### Prairie's Edge Resort Casino
5616 Prairie's Edge Ln
Granite Falls, MN 56241

www.prairiesedgecasino.com
320-564-2121

**DESCRIPTION:** Casino getaway resort hosted by the Upper Sioux Community. **GAMING:** Open 24/7, slots, video poker, smoke-free slots areas, blackjack & poker tables (open 10AM). **FOOD & ENTERTAINMENT:** buffet, deli, lounge. Comedy club, event center. **LODGING:** Hotel rooms/suites. **CAMPING:** Modern RV Park, 55 full-hookup spaces, some pull thrus, closed in winter. Free overnight RV parking is also permitted in the parking lot. Convenience store nearby. **DIRECTIONS:** From town center, go south on MN-23 for 2.4 miles then southeast on SR-274/CR-44 for 1.2 miles.

## Hinckley

### Grand Casino Hinckley
777 Lady Luck Dr, Hwy 48
Hinckley, MN 55037

www.grandcasinomn.com
320-384-7771

**DESCRIPTION:** Large Midwest casino resort, open 24/7. **GAMING:** slots, live blackjack tables, poker room, bingo. **FOOD & ENTERTAINMENT:** Ten dining options, fine dining to casual & quick food, bar, lounge. Live music & dancing in the lounge. Ticketed shows at indoor & outdoor venues, golf course. **LODGING:** Luxury hotel & two Inns. **CAMPING:** RV Park, 270 full-hookup sites, many amenities, open all winter. Guest lodge with convenience store, 24-hour shuttle.

Free dry camping is also permitted near the back of the parking lot, limit 24 hours. **DIRECTIONS:** From I-35 exit 183, east on SR-48 for one mile to the resort.

## Mahnomen

### Shooting Star Casino
777 Casino Rd
Mahnomen, MN 56557

www.starcasino.com
800-453-7827

**DESCRIPTION:** Gaming & entertainment hosted by White Earth Nation. **GAMING:** slots, blackjack, poker tables, bingo, non-smoking gaming area, open 24/7. **FOOD & ENTERTAINMENT:** fine dining, buffet, casual & quick food, lounge with live entertainment. Ticketed shows in event center. **LODGING:** Luxury hotel, day spa, indoor heated pool, hot tub, fitness room. **CAMPING:** 47-site RV Park, full hookups, open May–Oct. RV guests may use amenities at the hotel. Free overnight parking for RVs is permitted in the overfill lot designated for buses. **DIRECTIONS:** From I-94 exit 50, take US-59 about 75 miles north to Mahnomen.

## Morton

### Jackpot Junction Casino Hotel
39375 County Rd 24
Morton, MN 56270

www.jackpotjunction.com
507-697-8000 • 800-946-2274
RV Park: 800-946-0077

**DESCRIPTION:** Destination resort overlooking the Minnesota River. **GAMING:** slots, blackjack, poker tables, pull tabs, bingo. **FOOD & ENTERTAINMENT:** fine dining, buffet, grill, coffee shop, quick food, bars. Live entertainment in sports bar. Events, shows in exposition center. **LODGING:** Hotel rooms/suites. Business center. **CAMPING:** RV Park with 30 full-hookup sites, open Apr-Oct. Walking distance to the casino. Convenience store nearby. Free dry camping also available, limit 24 hours & must be in the gravel lot; RVs not allowed to park in the regular surface parking area. **DIRECTIONS:** From I-90 exit 73, follow US-71 north about 69 miles to CR-2 for 1.25 miles and CR-24 south .4 mile.

## Onamia

### Grand Casino Mille Lacs
*777 Grand Ave /US-169 N*
*Onamia, MN 56359*

www.grandcasinomn.com
800-626-5825

**DESCRIPTION:** Destination resort on the shore of Lake Mille Lacs, 90 miles north of Twin Cities. **GAMING:** slots, non-smoking slots area, gaming tables, poker room, bingo, pull tabs. **FOOD & ENTERTAINMENT:** 12 food venues, fine & casual dining, quick food, live music bar, ticketed shows in the event center. Nearby Mille Lacs Indian Museum features restored trading post, displays & exhibits. **LODGING:** Luxury hotel. **CAMPING:** 12 electric hookup RV spaces available in the parking lot. Register and pay at the hotel front desk. Free overnight parking allowed on the surface lot. Security will assist. **DIRECTIONS:** From Twin Cities, take I-694 exit 29 to US-169 north. Just past Onamia, US-169 becomes a two-lane road. Stay on US-169 for eight more miles to the casino on the west side of the highway.

## Prior Lake

### Mystic Lake Casino Hotel
*2400 Mystic Lake Blvd NW*
*Prior Lake, MN 55372*

www.mysticlake.com
952-445-9000 • 800-262-7799
RV Park: 952-445-9000

**DESCRIPTION:** Large resort with variety in entertainment & gaming. **GAMING:** At the main casino, slots, blackjack tables, bingo, high stakes card room, non-smoking slots section. Gaming at Little Six (half mile from the main resort) slots, blackjack tables, casual dining, bar. Shuttle buses, 24 hours throughout resort. **FOOD & ENTERTAINMENT:** Seven restaurants, three bars. Ticketed events in the showroom. Free live entertainment on casino stage, golf course; Mall of America nearby. **LODGING:** Luxury hotel. **CAMPING:** Dakotah Meadows Campground, 122 full hookup sites, Tipi rentals, pavilion, fuel center, self-serve RV wash. Free dry camping is in the lower lot, near the RV Park (follow signs for oversize/truck parking), limit 24 hours, no slideouts. Casino shuttle. **DIRECTIONS:** 25 miles southwest of Twin Cities. From I-35 W exit 1, go west on CR-42 for nine miles & 1 mile south on CR-83 — or — From I-494 exit 10, take US-169 south (Townline Road) for 6.5 miles, then CR-18 south for 3.4 miles to CR-42 west for 3 miles to CR-83 (Mystic Lake Dr) for 1 mile.

## Walker

### Northern Lights Casino Hotel
*6800 Y Frontage Rd NW*
*Walker, MN 56484*

www.northernlightscasino.com
218-547-2744

**DESCRIPTION:** Destination resort on the south shore of Lake Leech in north-central Minnesota. **GAMING:** slots, gaming tables, poker room. **FOOD & ENTERTAINMENT:** buffet, restaurant, snack bar. Local entertainment weekends in the lounge, ticketed shows at event center. **LODGING:** Hotel. **CAMPING:** RVs should park in the lot in front of the hotel, walking distance to the casino. Overnight is OK. Electric hookups are available on a first-come, first-serve basis, check in at the Players Club desk. **DIRECTIONS:** Located at the junction of Highways 371 and 200 at Lake Leech (175 miles north of the Twin Cities).

## Welch

### Treasure Island Resort & Casino
*5734 Sturgeon Lake Rd*
*Welch, MN 55089*

www.ticasino.com
651-388-6300 • 800-222-7077
RV Park: 651-267-3060

**DESCRIPTION:** Caribbean-themed resort overlooking the Mississippi River in southeast MN. **GAMING:** open 24 hours, slots, video poker, video roulette, blackjack, poker room, bingo, pull tabs. Smoke-free areas. **FOOD & ENTERTAINMENT:** buffet, full-service restaurant, grill, sub shop, cafe, coffee shop, bar. Free live entertainment in the lounge. Ticketed shows in event center. **LODGING:** Luxury hotel, bowling

center, golf course. Boating and fishing nearby.
**CAMPING:** RV Park, open Apr–Oct, 95 pull-thru sites, full hookups. Dry camping permitted, minimal fee.
**DIRECTIONS:** Resort is 40 miles southeast of the Twin Cities. From I-35 exit 69 follow MN-19 east 9 miles, north on Northfield Blvd 10.8 miles, east on 240th St 11.6 miles, continue on US-61 south 4 miles, then CR-31 east 1 mile, CR-18 north 2.1 miles and east on Sturgeon Lake Rd 1.3 miles.

# Mississippi

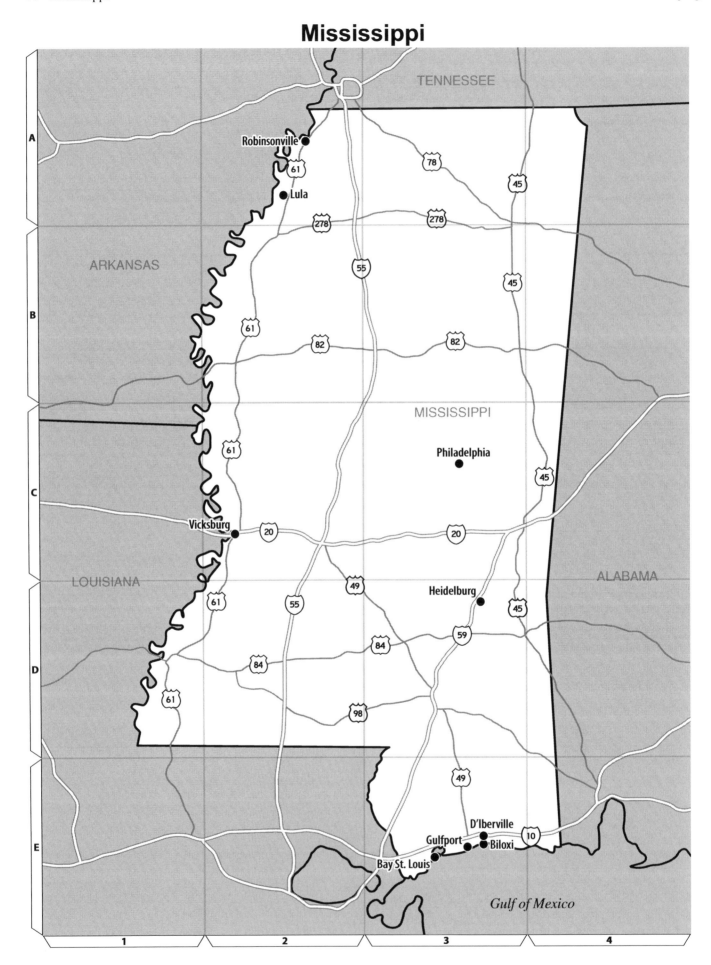

# Mississippi

| City | Casino | 🚐 | 🅿 | 🛏 | 🚶 | 🛡 |
|---|---|---|---|---|---|---|
| Bay St. Louis | Hollywood Casino Gulf Coast | p100 | x | x | x | 9 |
| Bay St. Louis | Silver Slipper Casino | p35 | | | | |
| Biloxi | Beau Rivage Resort & Casino | | x | x | | 4 |
| Biloxi | Boomtown Casino & RV Park | p50 | x | | | 2 |
| Biloxi | Golden Nugget Casino Hotel | | x | x | | 3 |
| Biloxi | Harrah's Gulf Coast | | x | x | x | 3 |
| Biloxi | Palace Casino Resort | | x | x | x | 3 |
| D'Iberville | Scarlet Pearl Casino Resort | | x | | | |
| Gulfport | Island View Casino Resort | | x | x | x | 6 |
| Heidelburg | Bok Homa Casino | | x | | | 9 |
| Lula | Isle of Capri Casino Hotel | p28 | | x | | |
| Philadelphia | Pearl River Resort | | x | x | x | |
| Robinsonville | Gold Strike Casino Resort | | | x | | |
| Robinsonville | Hollywood Casino | p123 | x | x | x | |
| Robinsonville | Horseshoe Tunica | | x | x | | |
| Robinsonville | Resorts Casino | | x | x | x | |
| Robinsonville | Sam's Town Hotel & Gambling Hall | p100 | x | x | | |
| Robinsonville | Tunica Roadhouse Casino & Hotel | | | x | | |
| Vicksburg | Ameristar Casino Hotel | p67 | | x | | 1 |

Mississippi is known as the Casino Capitol of the South. Casinos in the state are Vegas-style and most are open 24/7.

## Bay St. Louis

### *Hollywood Casino Gulf Coast*
*711 Hollywood Blvd*
*Bay St. Louis, MS 39520*

www.hollywoodcasinobsl.com
228-467-9257 • 866-758-2591

**DESCRIPTION:** Charming destination resort for a getaway by the Bay. **GAMING:** slots, video poker, pit/table games, poker room, open 24/7. **FOOD & ENTERTAINMENT:** steakhouse, buffet, grill, lounge. Live entertainment weekends at the bar. **LODGING:** Luxury hotel, gift shop. Marina adjacent to resort, electric & water. **CAMPING:** 100-site RV Park, full-hookups, 24-hour shuttle; limited free overnight RV parking permitted in the lot. **DIRECTIONS:** From I-10 exit 13, take MS 43/603 toward Bay St. Louis for 6 miles, then left on US-90 east for 2 miles, then left at Blue Meadow for .5 mile, then right at Hollywood Blvd and follow signs.

### *Silver Slipper Casino*
*5000 S Beach Blvd*
*Bay St. Louis, MS 39520*

www.silverslipper-ms.com
866-775-4773 • RV Park: 228-469-2777

**DESCRIPTION:** Land-based casino resort on the beach. **GAMING:** open 24/7, slots, video poker, pit/table games, poker room, high limits area, only live keno parlor on the Gulf Coast. **FOOD & ENTERTAINMENT:** buffet, bar & grille, café. Free entertainment in Stage Bar. **LODGING:** Hotel, beachfront attractions along the coast. **CAMPING:** Waterfront RV Park adjacent to the casino, 35 full-hookup, back-in sites. **DIRECTIONS:** From I-10 westbound exit 13, take MS 43/603 south toward Bay St. Louis for 5.4 miles, then west on US-90 for 4.6 miles, then south on Lakeshore Road for 4.5 miles, then west on South Beach Boulevard to the casino. Eastbound travelers on I-10, use exit 2 and follow signs.

## Biloxi

### Beau Rivage Resort & Casino
*875 Beach Blvd*
*Biloxi, MS 39530*

www.beaurivage.com
888-567-6667

**DESCRIPTION:** MGM luxury resort on Mississippi's Gulf Coast. **GAMING:** slots, video poker, pit/gaming tables, poker room, smoke-free area. **FOOD & ENTERTAINMENT:** dining options include: fine and casual dining, quick food; three bars. Ticketed shows & special events. Live music & dancing in the nightclub. **LODGING:** Luxury hotel, retail shops. **CAMPING:** RVs may park in the lot directly across the street from the resort entrance. Overnight is OK. **DIRECTIONS:** From I-10 exit 46, take I-110 south for 3 miles, then east on Beach Blvd.

### Boomtown Casino & RV Park
*676 Bayview Ave*
*Biloxi, MS 39530*

www.boomtownbiloxi.com
228-435-7000
RV Park Reservations: 800-946-2442

**DESCRIPTION:** Friendly Western-themed casino on Biloxi's Back Bay. **GAMING:** open 24/7, slots, video poker, pit/gaming tables. **FOOD & ENTERTAINMENT:** buffet, steakhouse, grill, bakery. **LODGING:** There is no hotel at this location. **CAMPING:** RV Park on four acres across the street from Boomtown is the only

RV Park connected to a casino in Biloxi. 50 modern full-hookup level concrete pads, Wi-Fi, cable TV, 24 hour security. Free shuttle runs daily. **DIRECTIONS:** From I-10 exit 46A, go south on I-110 for 2 miles to exit 1D (first exit after the bridge), then east on Bayview Ave.

### Golden Nugget Casino Hotel
*151 Beach Blvd*
*Biloxi, MS 39530*

www.goldennugget.com/biloxi
228-435-5400

**DESCRIPTION:** Beach Blvd resort, Gulf side, near the bridge over the bay. **GAMING:** slots, video poker, pit/table games, poker room. **FOOD & ENTERTAINMENT:** Seven dining options, live music lounge, waterfront bar. Ticketed shows in the ballroom. **LODGING:** Hotel rooms/suites. **CAMPING:** Free RV overnight parking permitted in the surface lot by the bridge. **DIRECTIONS:** From I-10 exit 46, take I-110 south to US-90 (Beach Blvd) then east to the Golden Nugget.

### Harrah's Gulf Coast
*280 Beach Blvd*
*Biloxi, MS 39530*

www.caesars.com/harrahs-gulf-coast
228-436-2946 • 800-946-2946

**DESCRIPTION:** Luxury destination resort on the Gulf. **GAMING:** slots, video poker, pit/table games; open 24/7. **FOOD & ENTERTAINMENT:** fine dining, buffet, casual dining, open air bar & restaurant, quick food; several bars/lounges. Live music in the lounge. **LODGING:** Hotel rooms/suites, gift shop, golf course. **CAMPING:** RV parking is on the gravel lot on the west side of the casino. Overnight is OK for casino players. Check in with Security. **DIRECTIONS:** From I-10 exit 46, I-110 south to exit 1A, then east on US-90/Beach Blvd, 2.5 miles.

### Palace Casino Resort
*158 Howard Ave*
*Biloxi, MS 39530*

www.palacecasinoresort.com
228-432-8888

**DESCRIPTION:** Biloxi's only smoke-free resort, located on Cadet Point north of the US-90 bridge. **GAMING:** open 24/7, slots, video poker, pit/table games. **FOOD & ENTERTAINMENT:** steakhouse, buffet, cafe & bakery, grill, poolside bar, lounge, sports bar. **LODGING:** Luxury hotel, golf course. **CAMPING:** RV parking is available in the self-park lot west of the casino. Stop at the hotel front desk to obtain a permit for free overnight parking. **DIRECTIONS:** From I-10 exit 46, take I-110 south 3 miles, then US-90 east to Myrtle Ave, then north to the casino.

## D'Iberville

### Scarlet Pearl Casino Resort
*9380 Central Ave*
*D'Iberville, MS 39540*

www.scarletpearlcasion.com
228-392-1889

**DESCRIPTION:** Back Bay destination resort east of Interstate 110. **GAMING:** slots, pit/table games, poker room, sports book, open 24/7. **FOOD & ENTERTAINMENT:** steakhouse, buffet, noodle bar, cafe, grill. Headline entertainment. **LODGING:** 18-story all-glass hotel tower. **CAMPING:** Parking is available for RVs in the main lot north of the casino, overnight is OK. Please notify security if you plan to stay overnight. **DIRECTIONS:** From I-110 exit 2 follow signs to the resort.

## Gulfport

### Island View Casino Resort
*3300 W Beach Blvd*
*Gulfport, MS 39501*

www.islandviewcasino.com
228-314-2100 • 877-774-8439

**DESCRIPTION:** Popular casino in Gulfport; it's where the locals play. **GAMING:** slots, pit/gaming tables, high limits area, open 24/7. **FOOD & ENTERTAINMENT:** buffet, steakhouse, seafood steamer, grille, cafe, diner. Ticketed shows weekends. Live entertainment at Sunset Bar. **LODGING:** Modern hotel. **CAMPING:** On arrival, check in at hotel front desk to obtain a parking permit. **DIRECTIONS:** From I-10 exit 34, take US-49 south for 4.7 miles to US-90, then west .5 mile.

## Heidelburg

### Bok Homa Casino
*1 Choctaw Rd*
*Heidelburg, MS 39439*

www.bokhomacasino.com
601-663-3851 • 866-447-3275

**DESCRIPTION:** Friendly casino hosted by Mississippi Band of Choctaw Indians. **GAMING:** slots, video poker, blackjack, sports book. **FOOD & ENTERTAINMENT:** Quick Eatery open daily. **LODGING:** There is no hotel at this location. **CAMPING:** Free parking for RVs in the gravel lot; overnight permitted. **DIRECTIONS:** From I-59 exit 99, take US-11N for 6.4 miles. Turn right at East Main St for 1.9 miles, then left at Choctaw Rd for .6 mile.

## Lula

### Isle of Capri Casino Hotel
*777 Isle of Capri Pkwy*
*Lula, MS 38644*

www.lula.isleofcapricasinos.com
610-241-1626 • RV Park: 662-363-4600

**DESCRIPTION:** Caribbean-themed casino getaway resort. **GAMING:** 24/7, slots, gaming tables. **FOOD & ENTERTAINMENT:** buffet, bar & grill, express food. Karaoke Fridays. **LODGING:** Two hotels. **CAMPING:** 28 full hookup RV spaces; register at the hotel front desk. **DIRECTIONS:** Located on the Mississippi River across from Helena, Arkansas. From I-40 in Arkansas take exit 216 at Brinkley and follow US-49 east to the Helena bridge. From US-61 in Mississippi go west on US-49 to the casino.

## Philadelphia

### Pearl River Resort
*13541 Hwy 16 W*
*Philadelphia, MS 39350*

www.pearlriverresort.com
601-650-1234 • 866-447-3275

**DESCRIPTION:** Destination resort hosted by the Mississippi Band of Choctaw Indians. **GAMING:** slots, pit/gaming tables, poker room, sports book, bingo. **FOOD & ENTERTAINMENT:** fine dining, buffet, casual, quick food. Ticketed shows in convention center. Free outdoor musical, laser imagery & fireworks evenings. **LODGING:** Hotel rooms/suites, golf course. **CAMPING:** Free overnight parking for RVs in the Golden Moon east area (truck lot). Call for shuttle to the casino. **DIRECTIONS:** From I-20 exit 109, north on SR-15 for 30 miles to SR-16, then west for 3.8 miles. The resort is 35 miles northwest of Meridian.

## Robinsonville / Tunica Resorts

Tunica County, in northwest Mississippi, is home to multiple resorts and is a popular destination for gaming and shows. The riverfront resorts are nestled near the cotton fields in the fertile Mississippi River Delta, where the weather is mild and pleasant year round. Two major casino hubs to explore include:

On **Casino Center Drive**: Gold Strike, Horseshoe and Tunica Roadhouse within walking distance.

On **Casino Strip Blvd**: Sam's Town, Hollywood Casino and Resorts Casino are in walking distance.

Directions to Tunica County casino area:
- From I-55 in Memphis, Tennessee, take exit 7 to US-61 (a four-lane highway) south for 20 miles.
- From I-55 in Mississippi, take exit 280 (Hernando) to SR-304, then west on 304 (a two-lane scenic route) for 19 miles to US-61.

## Casino Center Drive

### Gold Strike Casino Resort
*1010 Casino Center Dr*
*Tunica, MS 38664*

www.goldstrikemississippi.com
888-245-7829

**DESCRIPTION:** Upscale destination resort. **GAMING:** slots, pit/table games, poker room, high limits area. **FOOD & ENTERTAINMENT:** buffet, steakhouse, cafe,

quick bites, bar & lounge. Ticketed shows in theater; nightclub live entertainment. **LODGING:** Hotel. **CAMPING:** RV parking designated lot east of the Tunica Roadhouse, follow signs. Overnight OK.

### Horseshoe Tunica
*1021 Casino Center Dr*
*Robinsonville, MS 38664*

www.caesars.com/horseshoe-tunica
662-357-5500 • 800-303-7463

**DESCRIPTION:** High-end casino in Harrah's Total Rewards network. **GAMING:** slots, tables, poker room. **FOOD & ENTERTAINMENT:** steakhouse, burger bar, buffet, noodles, cafe. Ticketed shows in the nightclub. **LODGING:** Luxury hotel. **CAMPING:** Follow signs to "truck & RV parking" east side of Tunica Roadhouse. Overnight OK.

### Tunica Roadhouse Casino & Hotel
*1107 Casino Center Dr*
*Robinsonville, MS 38664*

www.tunica-roadhouse.com
662-363-4900

**DESCRIPTION:** Contemporary resort on the river. **GAMING:** slots, video poker, pit/gaming tables, open 24 hours. **FOOD & ENTERTAINMENT:** steakhouse, buffet, cafe, quick bites. Live music Friday & Saturday nights. **LODGING:** Hotel. **CAMPING:** RV parking east of the casino, follow signs. Overnight is OK.

## Casino Strip Blvd

### Sam's Town Hotel & Gambling Hall
*1477 Casino Strip Resorts Blvd*
*Robinsonville, MS 38664*

www.samstowntunica.com
662-363-0711

**DESCRIPTION:** Comfortable destination casino resort. **GAMING:** slots, pit/table games, poker room, sports book. **FOOD & ENTERTAINMENT:** steakhouse, buffet, quick bites. Live entertainment at lounge & river palace. **LODGING:** Hotel rooms/suites. **CAMPING:** RV Park, 100 full-hookup sites, paved park roads with security patrols. Free overnight parking available on the west side of the main lot.

### Hollywood Casino
*1150 Casino Strip Resorts Blvd*
*Robinsonville, MS 38664*

www.hollywoodcasinotunica.com
800-871-0711

**DESCRIPTION:** Hollywood-themed casino destination resort. **GAMING:** slots, video poker, pit/gaming tables, poker room, high limits areas, open 24/7. **FOOD & ENTERTAINMENT:** steakhouse, buffet, grill. Live entertainment in the lounge. **LODGING:** Two hotel towers, gift shop, golf course. **CAMPING:** RV Park, 123 paved sites, full hookups. Dry camping is permitted in the lot behind the hotel.

### Resorts Casino
*1100 Casino Strip Blvd*
*Robinsonville, MS 38664*

www.resortstunica.com
662-363-7777

**DESCRIPTION:** Friendly casino destination resort. **GAMING:** slots, video poker, gaming tables, poker room, keno, open 24/7. **FOOD & ENTERTAINMENT:** steakhouse, buffet, quick food. **LODGING:** Hotel. **CAMPING:** RV free dry camping area behind the casino, follow signs, no hookups, free dump station, fresh water.

## Vicksburg

### Ameristar Casino Hotel
*4116 Washington St*
*Vicksburg, MS 39180*

www.ameristar.com
601-638-1000

**DESCRIPTION:** Riverboat casino docked on the Mississippi River. **GAMING:** slots, pit/gaming tables. **FOOD & ENTERTAINMENT:** steakhouse, buffet, bakery & cafe. Live shows & music in the bar. **LODGING:** Hotel. **CAMPING:** RV Park, 67 paved patio sites, full hookups, heated pool/spa, Wi-Fi, CATV, laundry, casino shuttle. The RV Park is located on the east side of Washington St, a short distance from the casino. **DIRECTIONS:** From I-20 exit 1A exit north onto Washington St.

# Missouri

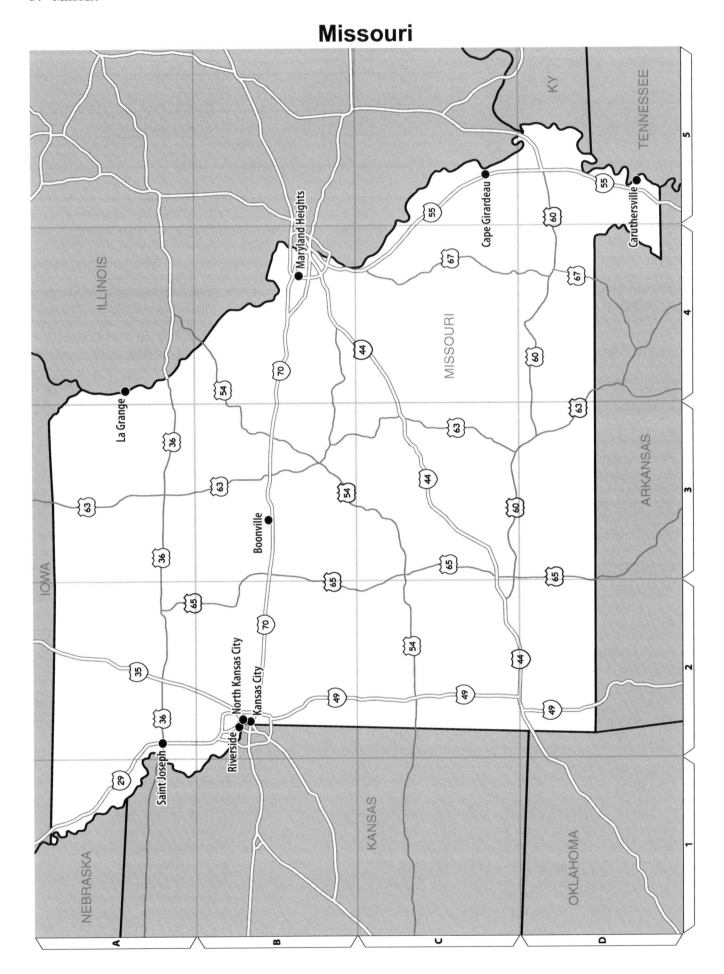

# Missouri

| City | Casino | 🚐 | P | 🛏 | 🏌 | 🛡 |
|------|--------|-----|-----|-----|-----|-----|
| Boonville | Isle of Capri Casino Hotel | | x | x | | 4 |
| Cape Girardeau | Isle of Capri Casino | | x | | | 5 |
| Caruthersville | Lady Luck Casino | p27 | x | | | 6 |
| Kansas City | Ameristar Casino Hotel | | x | x | | 2 |
| La Grange | Mark Twain Casino | p8 | | | | |
| Maryland Heights | Hollywood Casino | | x | x | | 2 |
| North Kansas City | Harrah's North Kansas City | | x | x | | 2 |
| Riverside | Argosy Casino Hotel & Spa | | x | x | | 2 |
| Saint Joseph | St. Jo Frontier Casino | | x | | | 1 |

Voters in Missouri approved riverboat gambling in 1992. Today most casinos are on stationery barges near the water's edge. Hours of operation vary.

## Boonville

### Isle of Capri Casino Hotel
*100 Isle of Capri Blvd*
*Boonville, MO 65233*

www.boonville.isleofcapricasinos.com
660-882-1200 • 800-843-4753

**DESCRIPTION:** Riverboat permanently docked on the Missouri River. **GAMING:** slots, video poker, table games, open: 8am–5am/24hrs (Fri–Sat). **FOOD & ENTERTAINMENT:** buffet, bistro, quick food. **LODGING:** Hotel. **CAMPING:** RV dry camping in the gravel parking lot, overnight OK. **DIRECTIONS:** From I-70 exit 103 (Hwy-B), north 2.8 miles & turn left at the 5th traffic light onto Morgan Street, go .5 mile to casino.

## Cape Girardeau

### Isle of Capri Casino
*777 N. Main St*
*Cape Girardeau, MO 63701*

www.islecape.com
573-730-7777 • 800-843-4753

**DESCRIPTION:** Barge casino docked on Mississippi River. **GAMING:** slots, video poker, pit/table games, poker room. Hours: 8am-4am/24hrs weekends. **FOOD & ENTERTAINMENT:** steakhouse, buffet, quick food. Live entertainment weekends. **LODGING:** No hotel at this location. **CAMPING:** RVs should park on the perimeter of the southwest parking lot. Overnight OK. **DIRECTIONS:** From I-55 exit 96 turn left on William St for 3.5 miles, then left onto S. Main for .8 mile.

## Caruthersville

### Lady Luck Casino
*777 E Third St*
*Caruthersville, MO 63830*

www.caruthersville.isleofcapricasinos.com
573-333-6000 • 800-843-4753

**DESCRIPTION:** Three-deck casino docked on the Mississippi. **GAMING:** slots, pit/table games, first deck smoke free. Open 9am–3am/24hrs (Fri–Sat). **FOOD & ENTERTAINMENT:** bar & grill, express food, pool hall. Live music in the bar. **LODGING:** There is no hotel at this location. **CAMPING:** 27-space full-hookup RV Park, free Wi-Fi, laundry. Check-in & pay at the pavilion. Free dry camping is also permitted, must park along the fence line or in the truck area. **DIRECTIONS:** From I-55, exit 19 (Hayti), east on Hwy-84 for 4.4 miles, then continue straight ahead on 3rd Street for .8 mile.

## Kansas City

### Ameristar Casino Hotel
*3200 N Ameristar Dr*
*Kansas City, MO 64161*

www.ameristar.com
816-414-7000

**DESCRIPTION:** Live-action gaming, dockside on the Missouri River. **GAMING:** 24/7, slots, pit/gaming tables, high limit baccarat pit, poker room. **FOOD & ENTERTAINMENT:** Nine food options, fine & casual dining, sports bar, free live shows. Ticketed events weekends. **LODGING:** Hotel rooms/suites, retail & gift shops. **CAMPING:** Follow signs to the lot for oversized vehicles. Overnight RV parking is permitted. Notify security if staying more than one night. **DIRECTIONS:** From I-435 in MO, exit 55, go east for 1 mile on Rt-210, then south on Ameristar Dr.

## La Grange

### Mark Twain Casino
*104 Pierce St*
*La Grange, MO 63448*

www.marktwaincasinolagrange.com
573-655-4770

**DESCRIPTION:** Hometown casino on the Mississippi River. **GAMING:** slots, pit/table games. Open 8am–2am/4am (Fri–Sat). **FOOD & ENTERTAINMENT:** bistro & grill. **LODGING:** There is no hotel at this location. **CAMPING:** RV Park, open Mar-Oct, 8 sites, electric & water hookups, central dump; check in at Players Club desk. Free overnight parking for RVs is available in the truck lot directly across the street from the casino. **DIRECTIONS:** From I-72 take Hwy 61 north 30 miles to La Grange. The casino is located on the south end of La Grange on Old Hwy 61, now Hwy B.

## Maryland Heights

### Hollywood Casino
*777 Casino Center Dr*
*Maryland Heights, MO 63043*

wwwhollywoodcasinostlouis.com
314-770-8100

**DESCRIPTION:** Dockside gaming in Hollywood-themed resort. Open 24/7. **GAMING:** slots, pit/table games, poker room. **FOOD & ENTERTAINMENT:** steakhouse, buffet, Italian, Asian cusine, grill, bar. Live music Saturdays. **LODGING:** Hotel, gift shop. **CAMPING:** Parking available for RVs; overnight is OK. **DIRECTIONS:** From I-70 exit 231A, south on Earth City Expressway for 1.5 miles to the fourth stoplight, turn right into Hollywood Casino.

## North Kansas City

### Harrah's North Kansas City
*One Riverboat Dr N*
*North Kansas City, MO 64116*

www.caesars.com/harrahs-kansas-city
816-472-7777

**DESCRIPTION:** Casino resort overlooking the Missouri River. **GAMING:** open 24/7, slots, pit/gaming tables, video poker, video keno, poker room, tournaments. **FOOD & ENTERTAINMENT:** steakhouse, buffet, grill, noodle bar, sports bar, coffee house. Ticketed entertainment in the lounge. **LODGING:** Luxury hotel, retail & gift shops. **CAMPING:** Designated RV parking area, drive past the parking garage & follow signage for large vehicle parking; overnight is permitted. **DIRECTIONS:** From I-35 exit 6A, go east on Hwy-210 (Armour Road) for 1.1 miles, then south on Chouteau Trafficway to Harrah's on the right —or— From I-435 exit 55A, go to Hwy-210 west for approximately two miles to Chouteau Trafficway, then south for .25 mile.

## Riverside

### Argosy Casino Hotel & Spa
*777 NW Argosy Pkwy*
*Riverside, MO 64150*

www.argosykansascity.com
816-746-3100

**DESCRIPTION:** Mediterranean-themed destination resort. **GAMING:** open 24/7, slots, video poker, pit/gaming tables, smoke free slots area. **FOOD & ENTERTAINMENT:** steakhouse, deli, buffet and sports bar. **LODGING:** Stylish hotel. **CAMPING:** RVs should use the west end of the lot. Overnight is OK. **DIRECTIONS:** From I-29 exit 3B take I-635 to exit 11, then Hwy 9 and follow signs.

## Saint Joseph

*St. Jo Frontier Casino*
*777 Winners Cir*
*St. Joseph, MO 64501*

www.stjofrontiercasino.com
816-279-5514 • 800-888-2946

**DESCRIPTION:** Cozy local casino docked on Missouri River. **GAMING:** slots, video poker, gaming tables. Open 8am–2am/4am (Fri–Sat). **FOOD & ENTERTAINMENT:** bar & grill, buffet & sports bar, local shows. **LODGING:** There is no hotel at this location. **CAMPING:** Designated area for large vehicles is in the northeast parking lot. Inform Security if you plan to stay overnight. **DIRECTIONS:** From I-29 exit 43, take I-229 north for seven miles to Highland Avenue, exit 7, then west. Located 55 miles north of Kansas City.

# Nevada

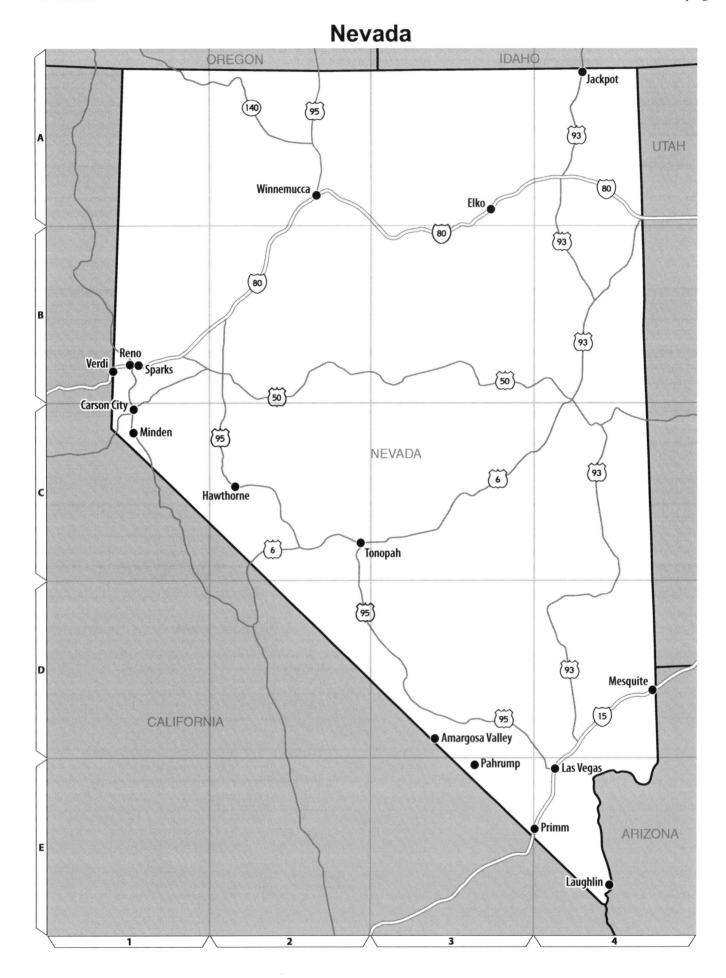

# Nevada

| City | Casino | 🚐 | 🅿 | 🛏 | 🏌 | 🛡 |
|------|--------|-----|-----|-----|-----|-----|
| Amargosa Valley | Longstreet Inn & Casino | p51 | x | x | | |
| Carson City | Carson Nugget | | x | x | | |
| Carson City | Gold Dust West Casino | p48 | | x | | |
| Elko | Commercial Casino | | x | | | 2 |
| Elko | Gold Country Inn, Casino & RV Park | p26 | | x | | 1 |
| Elko | Red Lion Hotel & Casino | | | x | | 1 |
| Elko | Stockmen's Hotel & Casino | | x | x | | 2 |
| Hawthorne | El Capitan Lodge & Casino | | x | x | | |
| Jackpot | Cactus Pete's Resort Casino | p91 | | x | x | |
| Las Vegas | Arizona Charlie's Boulder | p239 | | x | | 2 |
| Las Vegas | Circus Circus Hotel, Casino | p170 | | x | | 1 |
| Las Vegas | Main Street Station Hotel & RV Park | p99 | | x | | 1 |
| Las Vegas | Sam's Town Hotel & Gambling Hall | p500 | | x | | 3 |
| Laughlin | Avi Resort & Casino | p300 | | x | x | |
| Laughlin | Don Laughlin's Riverside Resort | p700 | | x | | |
| Mesquite | CasaBlanca Resort Casino | p45 | x | x | x | 1 |
| Mesquite | Eureka Casino Resort | | x | x | | 1 |
| Mesquite | Virgin River Hotel Casino | | x | x | | 1 |
| Minden | Carson Valley Inn Casino | p60 | | x | | |
| Pahrump | Saddle West Hotel Casino & RV Resort | p80 | | x | | |
| Primm | Primm Valley Casino Resorts | | x | x | | 1 |
| Reno | Bordertown Casino RV Resort | p50 | | | | |
| Reno | Grand Sierra Resort & Casino | p178 | | x | x | 2 |
| Sparks | Alamo Casino & Travel Center | | x | x | | 1 |
| Tonopah | Tonopah Station Casino & Hotel | s20 | | x | | |
| Verdi | Boomtown Casino Hotel | p203 | x | x | | 1 |
| Verdi | Gold Ranch Casino & RV Resort | p105 | | | | 1 |
| Winnemucca | Model T Casino | p50 | x | x | | 1 |

The Nevada Legislature legalized most forms of gambling in the state in 1931, and for nearly 50 years afterward, it was the only state where you could go to casinos. Despite casino expansion in many other states, Nevada still reigns as King Casino, with over 300 casinos – all near or adjacent to interstates and major highways. This section features three popular NV gaming destinations: Las Vegas, Laughlin and Reno, as well as many other casinos throughout the state. Casinos are listed alphabetically by city, and all are RV- friendly.

## Amargosa Valley

### Longstreet Inn & Casino
4400 S Hwy 373
Amargosa Valley, NV 89020

www.longstreetcasino.com
775-372-1777

DESCRIPTION: Located 10 miles from Death Valley Junction. GAMING: 24/7, slots & video poker. FOOD & ENTERTAINMENT: restaurant & bar open 7am-10pm daily. LODGING: Hotel, mini-mart on site. CAMPING: 51-space RV Park, full hookups, heated pool and hot tub. Free dry camping for one overnight only; must park in the truck lot. DIRECTIONS: From junction US-95 & SR-373, southwest for 16 miles on SR-373.

## Carson City

### Carson Nugget
507 N Carson St
Carson City, NV 89701

www.ccnugget.com
775-882-1626

DESCRIPTION: The Nugget is known as the "Happiest Casino In The World." GAMING: 24/7, slots, video poker, keno, gaming tables, bingo. FOOD & ENTERTAINMENT: bistro, deli, bar. Live entertainment weekends. LODGING: Hotel rooms/suites. CAMPING: RV parking lot is at Stuart and Robinson, across the street from the back of the Nugget. Free parking for Prospector's Club Card holders, no hookups; stay limit 72 hours. Check in with Security to get a parking permit. DIRECTIONS: From Hwy-395 south exit 57B (Carson City & Virginia City), continue on Hwy-395 to Carson City. In Carson City, Hwy-395 is the same as Carson Street.

### Gold Dust West Casino
2171 E William St
Carson City, NV 89701

www.gdwcasino.com
775-885-9000 • 877-519-5567

DESCRIPTION: Friendly casino near the action in Carson City. GAMING: 24/7, slots, video poker, pit/table games, sports book, bingo. FOOD & ENTERTAINMENT: grill, cantina, snack bar, sports bar. LODGING: Hotel, outdoor pool/spa, fitness center, business center, 32 bowling lanes. CAMPING: RV Park, 48 paved full-hookup sites, laundry, horseshoes. RV guests invited to use the pool/spa at the hotel. Dry camping is not permitted (prohibited by city ordinance.). RVs planning to stay overnight should check into the RV Park. DIRECTIONS: From Junction US-395 (Carson Street) & US-50E (center of town), east 1 mile on US-50E.

## Elko

### Commercial Casino
345 4th St
Elko, NV 89801

www.northernstarcasinos.com/historic-commercial-casino.com • 800-648-2345

DESCRIPTION: Open since 1869, Commercial is the oldest continually operating casino in Nevada. GAMING: slots, gaming tables, multiplier promotions daily; open 24 hours. Large gunfighter art collection on display. FOOD & ENTERTAINMENT: Lounge is open weekends. Stockman's (across the street) has a full-service restaurant open daily. LODGING: There is no hotel at this location. CAMPING: RVs should use the dirt lot directly in front of the casino; overnight OK. DIRECTIONS: From I-80 exit 301, turn right into downtown.

### Gold Country Inn, Casino & RV Park
2050 Idaho St
Elko, NV 89801

www.goldcountryinnelko.com
775-738-8421 • RV Park: 800-621-1332

DESCRIPTION: Friendly casino, easy on/off access from I-80. GAMING: open 24/7, slots, live-action gaming tables. FOOD & ENTERTAINMENT: restaurant & bar open daily morning till night. LODGING: Hotel, western motif; shopping center nearby. CAMPING: RV Park has 26 back-in, full-hookup sites; must register at the hotel front desk, no dry camping. DIRECTIONS: From I-80 exit 303 (Elko East), Gold Country visible from interstate.

### Red Lion Hotel & Casino

*2065 Idaho St*
*Elko, NV 89801*

www.redlionhotelelko.com
775-738-2111 • 800-545-0044

**DESCRIPTION:** Largest casino in Elko. **GAMING:** 24/7, slots, gaming tables, sports book, live keno, poker room. **FOOD & ENTERTAINMENT:** casual restaurant, bar & grill. **LODGING:** Contemporary hotel. **CAMPING:** RV parking prohibited at this location. RV Park (fee pay) is at Gold Country, directly across the street. **DIRECTIONS:** From I-80 exit 303, Red Lion is visible from interstate.

### Stockmen's Hotel & Casino

*340 Commercial St*
*Elko, NV 89801*

www.northernstarcasinos.com/stockmens-hotel-casino
775-738-5141 • 800-648-2345

**DESCRIPTION:** Old West-themed property recaptures charm of Elko's heritage. Directly across from historic Commercial Casino. **GAMING:** 24/7 slots, video poker, live-action table games, sports book. **FOOD & ENTERTAINMENT:** full-service restaurant, bar. **LODGING:** Ramada hotel. **CAMPING:** RV overnight parking lot in front of Commercial Casino directly across the street. **DIRECTIONS:** From I-80 exit 301, turn right into the downtown area.

## Hawthorne

### El Capitan Lodge & Casino

*540 F Street*
*Hawthorne, NV 89415*

www.northernstarcasinos.com/el-capitan
775-945-3321 • 800-922-2311

**DESCRIPTION:** On US-95, convenient stop between Vegas & Reno; look for glitzy pink & blue neon sign. **GAMING:** slots-only 24-hour casino, video poker. **FOOD & ENTERTAINMENT:** restaurant open daily, morning till night. **LODGING:** Travelodge Hotel. **CAMPING:** Free overnight RV parking behind the hotel, no hookups, walking distance to the casino.

**DIRECTIONS:** On northbound side of US-95, corner of 6th St. in Hawthorne.

## Jackpot

### Cactus Pete's Resort Casino

*1385 Hwy 93*
*Jackpot, NV 89825*

www.ameristar.com/cactus-petes
775-755-2321

**DESCRIPTION:** Popular casino destination resort near the Idaho State line. open 24/7. **GAMING:** slots, video poker, pit/table games, live keno, sports book, poker room. **FOOD & ENTERTAINMENT:** steakhouse, buffet, express food, bar, ticketed events in Showroom, golf course. **LODGING:** Luxury hotel, heated outdoor pool (seasonal), spa, convention, meeting facilities. **CAMPING:** 91-space RV Park, open year-round, full hookup sites, general store, gas station. RV guests invited to use amenities at the hotel. Free overnight RV parking permitted in the south area truck parking lot. Also, parking for RVs available at the sister casino Horseshu across the street. **DIRECTIONS:** To Jackpot from I-84 exit 173 in Idaho, go 42 miles south on US-93, or From I-80 exit 352 in Nevada go 68 miles north on US-93.

## Las Vegas

Even though travelers can now enjoy casinos in many parts of the country, Las Vegas remains the premier gaming destination. But the Vegas area can be overwhelming. The volume of casinos, restaurants and entertainment venues make it difficult to decide how to spend your time during your Vegas visit.

Three major gaming hubs in the Las Vegas area are:

THE STRIP consists of three miles along Las Vegas Blvd. where you'll find some of the most lavish, bigger-than-life themed casino resorts. Explore on foot or take the monorail.

DOWNTOWN VEGAS, Fremont Street is the soul of Las Vegas. Golden Gate, the first casino opened in 1906, is still there, along with many downtown casinos near an outdoor pedestrian mall.

BOULDER STRIP: Many other casinos, located along Boulder Highway, are popular among the locals.

### Some free shows/attractions in Las Vegas include:

- Bellagio: Synchronized laser lights and music shows at the fountains in front of the casino every half hour during the day and every 15 minutes evenings until midnight.
- Bellagio: The Conservatory & Botanical Gardens, open 24 hours daily, features elaborate floral arrangements, crafted by a team of 100 horticulturists, beneath a 55-foot tall glass ceiling in a bright, airy atrium filled with lovely color and rich fragrance.
- Caesar's Palace: Statues come alive during a seven-minute show at the Festival Fountains every hour on the hour in the Forum Shops Mall below the casino.
- Circus Circus: Acts featuring clowns, acrobats, jugglers, tightrope walkers and more, perform continuously daily from 11am.
- Downtown Area: The Fremont Street Experience, a one-of-a-kind light & sound computer-generated show 90 feet in the sky over a pedestrian mall stretching four city blocks in downtown Las Vegas. Shows take place five times per night from 7pm.
- Flamingo: The Wildlife Habitat is home to more than 300 birds (including a flock of Chilean flamingos) as well as turtles and koi. The habitat is filled with lush foliage imported from around the world. Open 8am to dusk.
- Harrah's: The "Big Elvis" tribute (free show) is on stage at Harrah's Piano Bar. Mon, Tue, Thu & Fri - 2, 3 & 5pm.
- M&M's World: Located near the corner of the Strip & Tropicana Ave (next door to MGM Grand), check out the 2nd, 3rd and 4th floors that include a 3D movie theater, interesting displays of the sweet treat and a replica of NASCAR's #38. Open daily.
- Mirage: Outside the Mirage Resort, a peaceful waterfall during daylight hours transforms to a volcano once darkness falls. Beginning at 6pm, the volcano erupts for a stunning show choreographed

for music, fire and water. Shows are every hour on the hour until midnight. Best place to view is from the Strip side.
- Sam's Town: A water and laser show is featured daily at 2, 6, 8 & 10pm in the waterfall area of the indoor park. Sam's Town is located on Boulder Highway.
- Silverton: The Aquarium features 4,000 exotic fish and breathtaking coral in an 117,000-gallon saltwater aquarium. Fish feedings are at 1:30 and 4:30 when a marine biologist is available to answer questions. Live mermaid shows four days a week. There are also two 500-gallon jellyfish aquariums in the lounge. Silverton is located on Blue Diamond Road (south of the Strip).
- Golden Nugget: See the world's largest gold nugget housed inside a wall display in a hallway near the Gold Tower hotel lobby. "The Hand of Faith" weighs in at 61 pounds and is worth $1.5 million.
- Venetian Grand: Life-size puppets, magicians, stilt-walkers and living statues vie for your attention all day in St. Mark's Square. Accompanied by musicians, they perform in five shows daily.

Campers going into Las Vegas should stay in a secure RV Park or campground. Dry camping in a casino parking lot is NOT smart…there are safety and security concerns when motor homes are left unattended in parking areas open to the public. The best strategy is to reserve a site at an RV Park for your Vegas stay. Casino resorts that have campgrounds are Sam's Town, Arizona Charlie's, Main Street Station Hotel & RV Park, and Circus Circus (the only one on the Vegas Strip). Details on these four resorts are listed below.

### Arizona Charlie's Boulder Hotel, RV Park & Casino
*4575 Boulder Hwy*
*Las Vegas, NV 89121*

www.arizonacharliesboulder.com
702-951-9000 • RV Park: 888-236-9066

DESCRIPTION: On "Boulder Strip," with easy on/off access from the highway. GAMING: slots, video poker, live pit/table games & only 24-hour bingo room in

Vegas. Walkway to the casino from RV Park. **FOOD & ENTERTAINMENT:** café, buffet, grille & deli. Several bars & lounges, live music. **LODGING:** Hotel rooms/suites pool & hot tub. **CAMPING:** 200 paved full hookup sites, free Wi-Fi, 24-hour security, dog run, workout facilities, heated pool & spa, shuffleboard & horseshoes. Last year's rates were $32; weekly and monthly rates available. **DIRECTIONS:** From junction I-515/93/95 exit 70, south 1.1 miles on Boulder Hwy.

### Circus Circus Hotel, Casino & RV Park
*2880 Las Vegas Blvd*
*Las Vegas, NV 89109*

www.circuscircus.com
800-444-2472

**DESCRIPTION:** Casino resort at north end of the Strip. **GAMING:** slots, video poker, keno, live action pit/gaming tables, race book/sports book. **FOOD & ENTERTAINMENT:** steakhouse, buffet, cafes, grill, deli, quick food, bars, theme park, circus acts, midway entertainment. **LODGING:** Two hotel towers. **CAMPING:** RV Park, 170 sites, full hookups, free Wi-Fi, dog run. Reservations made through the hotel. **DIRECTIONS:** From I-15 exit 40 go east .4 mile on Sahara Ave, then .3 mile west on South Bridge Lane (follow sign), then .2 mile south on Industrial Road. Turn left.

### Main Street Station Hotel & RV Park
*200 N Main St*
*Las Vegas, NV 89101*

www.mainstreetcasino.com
702-387-1896 • RV Park: 800-465-0711

**DESCRIPTION:** RV Park on Main Street, half block from casino. **GAMING:** 24/7 slots, keno and table games. **FOOD & ENTERTAINMENT:** fine dining, buffet & casual dining, micro-brewery. Close to the Fremont St. entertainment. **LODGING:** Hotel rooms/suites. Shuttle service to and from Sam's Town. **CAMPING:** 99 full hookup sites (30 are pull thrus), 24-hour security & pet run. Advance reservations by phone or pull into a site and then register at the Main Street Station hotel front desk. Last year's rates were $25 (additional fee for dogs - must be under 35 lbs). **DIRECTIONS:** From I-15 exit 42B, go east for .5 mile to I-515 exit 75B,

two blocks west on Stewart, then one block north on Main St.

### Sam's Town Hotel, Gambling Hall & KOA RV Park
*5111 Boulder Hwy*
*Las Vegas, NV 89122*

www.samstownlv.com
702-456-7777 • RV Park: 800-562-7270

**DESCRIPTION:** On Boulder Strip nestled in the shadow of the Sunrise Mountains. **GAMING:** 24/7, slots, pit/table games, poker room, race & sports book, live keno, bingo. **FOOD & ENTERTAINMENT:** steakhouse, buffet, deli, casual dining, express food, cantina & bars. Bowling center, movie complex, live entertainment. **LODGING:** Hotel rooms/suites. **CAMPING:** Two KOA RV Parks, 500 full hookup sites, heated pool/Jacuzzis, cable TV, pet runs, laundry. Last year's daily RV rate: from $29 to $42. Weekly rate: 7th day free. Monthly rates available for qualified RVs. Free shuttle to the Strip and downtown casinos daily. **DIRECTIONS:** From I-515 (93/95S) exit 68, go east on Tropicana Avenue for 1.5 miles, then north on Boulder Highway for .7 mile to Sam's Town RV Park entrance on the right. RV guests must check into the RV Park. There is NO overnight parking allowed in the truck lot.

## Laughlin

Laughlin is in the Colorado River Valley where Nevada, Arizona and California meet. Visitors can enjoy a slower-paced casino-hopping experience in the City by the River. Nine casinos are riverfront along Casino Drive, and the Avi Casino Resort is located 14 miles south, also on the river.

For RV parking:
- Harrah's (at the southern end of Casino Dr) has two lots on property where RVs can park free for up to three days. Please check-in at the Shell gas station and they will assign you a place to park. The casino is walking distance, but a shuttle is also available. There is a dump at the gas station (nominal fee charged).
- Laughlin River Lodge also has parking for oversize vehicles in the truck lot, 4th parking garage level overflow lot.

There are two full-hookup RV Resorts in Laughlin: Riverside on the northern end of Casino Drive & KOA at Avi Resort south of town. Details are below:

### Avi Resort & Casino
*10000 Aha Macav Pkwy*
*Laughlin, NV 89029*

www.avicasino.com
702-535-5555 • 800-284-2946
KOA RV Park: 702-535-5450

**DESCRIPTION:** Resort with white sand beach, largest along the banks of the Colorado River. **GAMING:** slots, live table games, poker room, bingo, keno. **FOOD & ENTERTAINMENT:** fine & casual dining, buffet, food court. Ticketed events weekends. Live entertainment at the lounge. **LODGING:** Luxury hotel, golf courses, movie theaters. **CAMPING:** KOA RV Park, 300 full service sites, pool, laundry, pavilion, lounge, beach, boat launch. Casino shuttle. Free parking for RVs is in the north lot. Casino issues permit to be displayed on your rig, limit 4 days parking for Players Club card holders only. Outside camping activity, like BBQs, slideouts & outside chairs not allowed: $5 fee for use of dump station. **DIRECTIONS:** From I-40, River Road cutoff, which becomes Needles Highway, north for 14 miles to Aha Macav Pkwy. Follow Avi signs.

### Don Laughlin's Riverside Resort Hotel & Casino
*1650 S Casino Dr*
*Laughlin, NV 89029*

www.riversideresort.com
800-227-3849

**DESCRIPTION:** First casino resort in Laughlin, northern end of Casino Dr. **GAMING:** slots, gaming tables, live keno, bingo. **FOOD & ENTERTAINMENT:** steakhouse, cafe, buffet, food court, music in the lounge, bowling center. River access for boating & fishing. **LODGING:** Hotel, outdoor pools, jacuzzi. **CAMPING:** Terraced RV Park, 700 full hookup spaces. RV guests invited to use amenities at the hotel. Enclosed walkway connects RV Park with the hotel/casino. **DIRECTIONS:** Laughlin south of Las Vegas. From junction of US-95 & SR-163, east for 19.9 miles on SR-163 to Casino Drive, then south for .4 mile.

## Mesquite

### CasaBlanca Resort Casino
*950 W Mesquite Blvd*
*Mesquite, NV 89027*

www.casablancaresort.com
702-346-7529 • 877-438-2929

**DESCRIPTION:** Largest resort in Mesquite, open 24/7. **GAMING:** slots, video poker, video keno, pit/gaming tables, race/sports book. **FOOD & ENTERTAINMENT:** steakhouse, cafe, buffet. Live entertainment in lounge. Movies by the pool. Ticketed shows in event center. **LODGING:** Hotel, golf course. **CAMPING:** RV Park has 45 paved sites, full-hookups & patios. Lot for RV dry camping is east of the hotel building. **DIRECTIONS:** From I-15 exit 120, east .1 mile. Resort is visible from the interstate.

### Eureka Casino Resort
*275 Mesa Blvd*
*Mesquite, NV 89027*

www.eurekamesquite.com
702-346-4600 • 800-346-4611

**DESCRIPTION:** Relaxing casino resort, mountain views. **GAMING:** 24/7, live gaming tables, bingo, race & sports book. **FOOD & ENTERTAINMENT:** fine dining, buffet, quick bites. Live lounge entertainment weekends. **LODGING:** Hotel. **CAMPING:** RVs are welcome to park alongside the Eureka Hotel. Overnight is OK. **DIRECTIONS:** From I-15 exit 122, Eureka visible from the north side of interstate.

### Virgin River Hotel Casino
*100 N Pioneer Blvd*
*Mesquite, NV 89027*

www.virginriver.com
702-346-7777 • 877-438-2929

**DESCRIPTION:** Popular local 24-hour casino. **GAMING:** slots, gaming tables, race/sports book, bingo daily, live keno. **FOOD & ENTERTAINMENT:** buffet, cafe, fast food, bowling center. Live country music & dancing in lounge. **LODGING:** Motel. **CAMPING:** Free overnight parking is permitted for self-contained vehicles.

**DIRECTIONS:** From I-15 exit 122, north for .25 mile on the exit road.

## Minden

### Carson Valley Inn Casino
*1627 Hwy 395 N*
*Minden, NV 89423*

www.carsonvalleyinn.com
775-782-9711

**DESCRIPTION:** Charming resort at the foot of mountains surrounding Lake Tahoe. **GAMING:** slots, table games, bingo, sports book. **FOOD & ENTERTAINMENT:** steakhouse, casual dining, coffee shop. Free live entertainment in the lounge. Ticketed shows in outdoor event center. **LODGING:** Hotel rooms/suites. **CAMPING:** RV Park, 60 full hookup sites, maximum 14-day stay, pool/spa, game room, laundry, enclosed dog park. RVs must check into the RV park; NO free overnight parking. **DIRECTIONS:** From junction US-395 & SR-88, south one mile on US-395.

## Pahrump

### Saddle West Hotel Casino & RV Resort
*1220 S Hwy 160*
*Pahrump, NV 89048*

www.saddlewest.com
775-727-1111 • 800-433-3987

**DESCRIPTION:** Cozy casino & RV park in downtown Pahrump. **GAMING:** slots, video poker, electronic gaming tables, bingo. **FOOD & ENTERTAINMENT:** cafe & buffet open daily. **LODGING:** Hotel. **CAMPING:** RV Park, 80 full-hookup sites, free Wi-Fi, laundry, pool/spa. Check in at the desk in the back of the casino. Free RV dry camping in the parking lot is prohibited. **DIRECTIONS:** From junction of SR-160 & SR-372, south on SR-160 for .5 mile.

## Primm

### Primm Valley Casino Resorts
*I-15 at milepost 1*
*Primm, NV 89019*

www.primmvalleyresorts.com
702-386-7867 • 800-386-7867

**DESCRIPTION:** Three casino hotels in Primm Valley, near CA/NV state line are: Primm Valley Resort, Buffalo Bill's & Whiskey Pete's. **GAMING:** All casinos are open 24/7; slots, video poker, keno & pit/table games. **FOOD & ENTERTAINMENT:** fine dining, casual dining, quick food & fast food. Live entertainment in lounges. Ticketed events in the arena. Outdoor family entertainment. **LODGING:** Three luxury hotels, two golf courses, outlet shopping. Casino shuttle service on weekends. **CAMPING:** RVs are welcome to dry camp in the lot behind Buffalo Bill's; overnight parking is permitted for self-contained vehicles. There are no RV hookups in Primm. **DIRECTIONS:** The resorts are accessible from both sides of I-15 at the CA/NV state line.

## Reno

Reno's famed landmark is the glitzy arch over Virginia Street proclaiming, "Reno – The Biggest Little City in the World." Reno is near the California border on I-80. There are 20 casinos in Reno. NOTE: Reno has a local ordinance prohibiting RV parking at any Reno casino resort unless that resort has an RV Park or campground. It is not advisable to park an RV or camper in the city of Reno, even for a brief time. RV accommodations available near Reno are listed below.

### Bordertown Casino RV Resort
*19575 Hwy 395 N*
*Reno, NV 89508*

www.bordertowncasinorv.com
775-972-1309 • 800-218-9339

**DESCRIPTION:** High desert mountain campground near Reno. **GAMING:** 24/7, video poker, slots, sports book. **FOOD & ENTERTAINMENT:** Restaurant open morning till night; deli. **LODGING:** There is no hotel at this location. **CAMPING:** 50 paved & grassy full hookup sites, cable TV, Wi-Fi, laundry. Open all year. Gas station, gift shop. NO free overnight parking; must check into the RV Park. **DIRECTIONS:** From I-80 & US-395, north on US-395 for 17.5 miles to the CA/

NV border, exit 83. Go a quarter mile on Frontage Road. Located 15 miles north of downtown Reno.

### Grand Sierra Resort & Casino
*2500 E Second St*
*Reno, NV 89595*

www.grandsierraresort.com
775-789-2147 • 800-501-2651

**DESCRIPTION:** Destination resort, largest casino in Reno. **GAMING:** slots, pit/gaming tables, poker room, keno, race/sports book. **FOOD & ENTERTAINMENT:** fine dining, buffet, cafe, express food, bars & lounges. Ticketed shows weekends. Live music & DJs in lounges. **LODGING:** Hotel rooms/suites, day spa & health club, fitness center, arcade, bowling, movies, outdoor pool & beach, miniature golf, shopping. **CAMPING:** RV Park has 164 full hookup sites (some river view), Wi-Fi, laundry. RV guests have access to amenities at the hotel. Dry camping in the parking lot is prohibited. **DIRECTIONS:** From junction I-80 (exit 15) & US-395, south on US-395 for one mile to Glendale Avenue (exit 67), then east on Glendale.

## Sparks

### Alamo Casino & Travel Center
*1950 E. Greg St*
*Sparks, NV 89431*

www.thealamo.com/alamo-casino-sparks-petro
775-355-8888

**DESCRIPTION:** Casino at a truck stop. **GAMING:** 24/7, slots, pit/gaming tables, race book, sports book. **FOOD & ENTERTAINMENT:** restaurant and sports bar. **LODGING:** Motel nearby. **CAMPING:** RV overnight parking OK for self-contained vehicles. **DIRECTIONS:** At I-80 exits 20 and 21.

## Tonopah

### Tonopah Station Casino & Hotel
*1137 Erie St*
*Tonopah, NV 89049*

www.tonopahstation.com
775-482-9777

**DESCRIPTION:** An oasis from the hot road, mid-way between Las Vegas & Reno. **GAMING:** 24/7, slots, blackjack tables. **FOOD & ENTERTAINMENT:** restaurant & bar, sports on a giant-screen TV. **LODGING:** Hotel. **CAMPING:** 20 full hookup spaces, 50-amp & 30-amp, many pull-thrus, laundry facilities. Pull in, register & pay at the hotel. Supermarket nearby. **DIRECTIONS:** Located directly on US-95 at the south end of Tonopah.

## Verdi

### Boomtown Casino Hotel & KOA RV Park
*I-80 at Exit 4*
*Verdi, NV 89439*

www.boomtownreno.com
775-345-6000 • RV Park: 775-345-2444

**DESCRIPTION:** Alongside I-80 near Reno. **GAMING:** 24/7, slots, table games, video poker. **FOOD & ENTERTAINMENT:** Lobster buffet weekends, bistro, coffee shop, deli, sports lounge. **LODGING:** Best Western hotel. **CAMPING:** KOA RV Park, 203 full hookup sites. Free overnight RV parking is prohibited -- RVs must stay at KOA. **DIRECTIONS:** From I-80 exit 4 (Boomtown/Garson Road), north for .25 mile.

### Gold Ranch Casino & RV Resort
*350 Gold Ranch Rd*
*Verdi, NV 89439*

www.goldranchrvcasino.com
775-345-6789

**DESCRIPTION:** Modern resort in the scenic Sierra Nevada area. **GAMING:** slots, video poker, sports book & full wall of TVs for watching the games. **FOOD & ENTERTAINMENT:** cafe, quick food, coffee shop. **LODGING:** There is no hotel at this location. **CAMPING:** 105 paved, full hookup RV sites, heated pool/spa, horseshoes, laundry, showers, general store. If staying overnight, RVs must check into the RV Park. No free overnight parking at the casino. **DIRECTIONS:** From I-80 exit 2 (Gold Ranch Road) on the north side of the interstate.

# Winnemucca

### *Model T Casino*
*1130 W Winnemucca Blvd*
*Winnemucca, NV 89446*

www.northernstarcasinos.com/model-t-casino
775-623-2588

**DESCRIPTION:** Friendly casino in an historic northern Nevada town. **GAMING:** open 24/7, slots, live table games. **FOOD & ENTERTAINMENT:** diner is open daily, morning till night. **LODGING:** Quality Inn Hotel. **CAMPING:** 50 level, paved full-hookup pull-thru sites on the west side of the casino, outdoor, game room. Limited dry camping permitted in the truck parking area behind the hotel building. **DIRECTIONS:** From I-80 exit 176, go .5 mile east on Winnemucca Blvd.

# New Mexico

UT

COLORADO

OK

AZ

285

550

25

Ohkay Owingeh

550

Santa Fe

54

Church Rock

40

Algodones

Bernalillo

Albuquerque

Acoma

Casa Blanca

40

25

NEW MEXICO

60

60

54

285

70

180

70

54

380

380

Mescalero

70

25

70

10

285

54

Sunland Park

TEXAS

CHIHUAHUA

1    2    3    4

# New Mexico

| City | Casino | 🚐 | P | 🛏 | 🧍 | 🛡 |
|------|--------|-----|---|-----|-----|-----|
| Acoma | Sky City Casino Hotel | p42 | x | x | | 1 |
| Albuquerque | Isleta Resort & Casino | p50 | x | x | x | 1 |
| Albuquerque | Route 66 Casino Hotel & RV Resort | p100 | x | x | | 1 |
| Albuquerque | Sandia Resort & Casino | | x | x | x | 1 |
| Algodones | Black Mesa Casino | p50 | x | | | 1 |
| Bernalillo | Santa Ana Star Casino | | x | | | 2 |
| Casa Blanca | Dancing Eagle Casino | p35 | x | | | 1 |
| Church Rock | Fire Rock Navajo Casino | | x | | | 3 |
| Mescalero | Casino Apache Travel Center | | x | | | |
| Ohkay Owingeh | Ohkay Hotel Casino | | x | x | | |
| Santa Fe | Buffalo Thunder Resort & Casino | | | x | x | |
| Santa Fe | Cities of Gold Casino | | x | x | | |
| Santa Fe | Tesuque Casino | | x | | | |
| Sunland Park | Sunland Park Racetrack & Casino | s8 | x | x | | 1 |

Various Indian tribes own and operate New Mexico's casinos; most are open 24 hours. The majority of casinos are located in the north central part of the state – Santa Fe and Albuquerque areas. Full-service RV parks can be found at Route 66, Sky City and Dancing Eagle on I-40 west of Albuquerque, at Isleta on I-25 south of Albequerque and Black Mesa Casino on I-25 north of Albuquerque.

## Acoma

### Sky City Casino Hotel
*I-40 exit 102 Acoma Pueblo*
*Acoma, NM 87034*

www.skycity.com
505-552-6123

**DESCRIPTION:** Resort adjacent to the interstate, hosted by the Acoma Pueblo. **GAMING:** slots, live gaming tables, bingo. Open 24/7. **FOOD & ENTERTAINMENT:** restaurant/buffet, coffee shop, snack bar. Live music in the lounge. **LODGING:** Hotel, gift shop. **CAMPING:** RV Park, 42 full hookup sites, free Wi-Fi, laundry, clubhouse. RV guests should pull into a space & call

the hotel at 505-552-1075 to complete registration. Dry camping prohibited in the casino lot. **DIRECTIONS:** From I-40 exit 102, the casino can be seen from the westbound lanes. The adjacent 24-hour Sky City Travel Center, a popular stop for truckers & RVers has fuel, convenience store, laundry & a small non-smoking slots-only area.

## Albuquerque

### Isleta Resort & Casino
*11000 Broadway Blvd SE*
*Albuquerque, NM 87105*

www.isleta.com
505-724-3800

**DESCRIPTION:** Modern American-Indian style resort. **GAMING:** open 24/7, slots, video poker, pit/gaming tables, poker room, live keno, bingo, high limit gaming room, non-smoking slots area. **FOOD & ENTERTAINMENT:** steakhouse, bistro, grill, coffee shop, snack bar, lounge, center bar. Live lounge entertainment. **LODGING:** Luxury hotel tower, bowling, arcade, golf course. **CAMPING:** Isleta Lakes

RV Park, 50 full-hookup sites, free Wi-Fi, Direct TV, laundry, fishing, convenience store, casino shuttle. Free limited dry camping area in the trucker lot, south side of the hotel. **DIRECTIONS:** From I-25 exit 215, south on Hwy-47 for .5 mile.

### Route 66 Casino Hotel & RV Resort
14500 Central Ave SW
Albuquerque, NM 87121

www.rt66casino.com
505-352-7866

**DESCRIPTION:** 50's-themed resort, casual, classy atmosphere. **GAMING:** Open 24 hours, slots, pit/table games, poker room, bingo daily. **FOOD & ENTERTAINMENT:** Varied food venues, fine & casual dining, casino bar, live music weekends at steakhouse/cantina. Ticketed shows in Legends Theater. **LODGING:** Hotel, gift shop with 50's-themed items. **CAMPING:** RV resort, 100 full-hookup sites, many amenities, clubhouse, pool, dog park, rally barn with kitchen, shuttle service. RVs are required to stay at the RV park; dry camping is prohibited in the casino parking lot. **DIRECTIONS:** The casino complex is visible from I-40 eastbound lanes at exit 140. Adjacent travel center caters to truckers & RVers with fuel services, diner, convenience store, gift shop, snack bar and slots-only casino. Trucker parking lot is behind the travel center.

### Sandia Resort & Casino
30 Rainbow Rd
Albuquerque, NM 87113

www.sandiacasino.com
505-796-7500

**DESCRIPTION:** Destination resort in view of majestic Sandia Mountains. **GAMING:** open 24/7, slots, pit/table games, live keno, bingo, largest poker room in NM, separate non-smoking area, high limits area. **FOOD & ENTERTAINMENT:** Ten dining options. bars and lounges. Live lounge entertainment. **LODGING:** Luxury hotel, golf course. **CAMPING:** Overnight RV parking is permitted up to 3 nights. RVs should use Lot D. **DIRECTIONS:** From I-25 exit 234, east on Tramway Road and turn left into the casino's main entrance.

## Algodones

### Black Mesa Casino
25 Hagan Rd
Algodones, NM 87001

www.blackmesacasino.com
505-867-6700

**DESCRIPTION:** Friendly casino & RV Park between Albuquerque and Santa Fe. **GAMING:** slots in all denominations, open 8am–4am/24hrs (Fri–Sat). **FOOD & ENTERTAINMENT:** Homestyle restaurant. **LODGING:** There is no hotel at this location. **CAMPING:** 50 RV sites, water & electric, central dump. Check in & pay at the casino. Free dry camping is permitted in the travel plaza. All parking areas walking distance to casino. **DIRECTIONS:** I-25 at exit 252. The casino can be seen from the northbound side of the interstate.

## Bernalillo

### Santa Ana Star Casino
54 Jemez Canyon Dam Rd
Bernalillo, NM 87004

www.santaanastar.com
505-867-0000

**DESCRIPTION:** Casino-hotel on the Pueblo of Santa Ana near Albuquerque. **GAMING:** slots, pit/gaming tables, high limits room, poker room. Open 24 hours. **FOOD & ENTERTAINMENT:** Five restaurants, lounge, nightclub. Ticketed events in Star Center. **LODGING:** Luxury hotel, pool, spa, fitness center. **CAMPING:** RV parking for day-use only in lot directly across from the casino. NO overnight camping allowed. **DIRECTIONS:** From I-25 exit 242, west on Hwy-550 for two miles.

## Casa Blanca

### Dancing Eagle Casino
167 Casa Blanca Rd
Casa Blanca, NM 87007

www.dancingeaglecasino.com
505-552-7777 • RV Park: 505-552-7730

**DESCRIPTION:** Friendly casino & RV Park hosted by the Pueblo of Laguna tribe. **GAMING:** slots, gaming tables, non-smoking slots room, bingo. Open 8am–4am/24hrs (Thur–Sat). **FOOD & ENTERTAINMENT:** diner, cafe, grille, movies in the event center. **LODGING:** There is no hotel at this location. **CAMPING:** RV Park, 35 level full hookup gravel sites (some pull thrus), pet run, showers, laundry, reasonable rate. RV parking also permitted on any of the gravel areas adjacent to the paved casino parking lot. **DIRECTIONS:** From I-40 take exit 108 toward Casa Blanca/Paraje, visible from the interstate. Travel center in the adjacent village includes a supermarket, bakery, fast food, gas station.

## Church Rock

*Fire Rock Navajo Casino*
*249 Historic Route 66*
*Church Rock, NM 87311*

www.firerocknavajocasino.com
505-905-7100

**DESCRIPTION:** First Navajo casino in NM, located just east of Gallup on Route 66. **GAMING:** slots, gaming tables, bingo daily. Casino hours: Mon-Thur 8am-4am, weekends 24hrs. **FOOD & ENTERTAINMENT:** pub, Navajo food court & restaurant. Live entertainment weekends. **LODGING:** There is no hotel at this location. **CAMPING:** RVs should park at the back of the southwest side of the lot (near the blue building.) Free overnight stays up to 3 days. No hookups. **DIRECTIONS:** From I-40 exit 26 (Old Route 66), go east on SR-118N for 2.2 miles.

## Mescalero

*Casino Apache Travel Center*
*25845 US Hwy 70*
*Mescalero, NM 88340*

www.casinoapachetravelcenter.com
575-464-7910

**DESCRIPTION:** Casino & Travel Center west of Ruidoso, open 24 hours. **GAMING:** slots, video poker, blackjack, roulette, poker. **FOOD & ENTERTAINMENT:** full-service restaurant, discount gas prices, convenience store. **LODGING:** There is no hotel at this location. **CAMPING:** Ample space for RV overnight dry camping in the parking lot. **DIRECTIONS:** From I-25 exit 6, follow US-70 for 105 miles. Travel center is on US-70.

## Ohkay Owingeh

*Ohkay Hotel Casino*
*68 New Mexico-291*
*Ohkay Owingeh, NM 87566*

www.ohkay.com
505-747-1668

**DESCRIPTION:** Rio Grand Valley casino located between Santa Fe & Taos. **GAMING:** slots, video poker, pit/gaming tables, bingo; open 24 hours. **FOOD & ENTERTAINMENT:** buffet, cantina, coffee shop, snack bar. DJs, live music in lounge, weekends. **LODGING:** smoke-free hotel. **CAMPING:** Free overnight parking permitted for RVs on the dirt lot south of the casino. **DIRECTIONS:** From Espanola take Riverside Dr (Hwy-68) north for 4 miles. Casino is 24 miles north of Santa Fe.

## Santa Fe

*Buffalo Thunder Resort & Casino*
*20 Buffalo Thunder Trail*
*Santa Fe, NM 87506*

www.buffalothunderresort.com
505-455-5555

**DESCRIPTION:** Upscale resort on 587 acres at the foot of Sangre de Cristo Mountains. **GAMING:** slots, gaming tables, poker room, racebook; open 24 hours. **FOOD & ENTERTAINMENT:** fine dining, buffet, casual, quick food, bars & lounges. Bar entertainment. Ticketed events/shows. **LODGING:** Hilton hotel, golf course. **CAMPING:** RV parking lot next to the golf course. Overnight permitted. Roadrunner RV Park (505-455-2626), about a mile from the casino, offers shuttle service. **DIRECTIONS:** From I-25 exit 282B go north on Hwy-84/285 for 17.7 miles to exit 177.

### Cities of Gold Casino
*10-B Cities of Gold Rd*
*Santa Fe, NM 87506*

www.citiesofgold.com
800-455-3313 • 877-455-0515

**DESCRIPTION:** Native-American casino & hotel located 15 miles north of Santa Fe. **GAMING:** slots, video poker, bingo. Open 8am-4am/24hrs (Fri-Sat). **FOOD & ENTERTAINMENT:** buffet, snack bar, restaurant in the hotel. DJs, live music in the cantina. **LODGING:** Hotel, golf course, bowling. **CAMPING:** RV dry camping at the back of the casino building; follow signs for RV/truck parking. **DIRECTIONS:** From I-25 exit 282-B (St. Francis Dr. exit), north on Hwy-84/285 for 19 miles to Cities of Gold Road exit at SR-502. The casino is visible from the northbound side of the highway.

### Tesuque Casino
*7 Tesuque Rd*
*Santa Fe, NM 87506*

www.tesuquecasino.com
800-462-2635

**DESCRIPTION:** New casino near downtown Santa Fe, opened in November 2018. **GAMING:** 24 hour slots, pit/table games, keno. **FOOD & ENTERTAINMENT:** full service dining, casual, grab & go. Lounge and bar areas overlook casino. Open 11am-10pm. **LODGING:** No hotel at this location. **CAMPING:** RV parking in the lot at the south side of the casino. Free overnight parking is permitted. **DIRECTIONS:** On west side of US 84/285 approximately 7 miles north of Santa Fe.

## Sunland Park

### Sunland Park Racetrack & Casino
*1200 Futurity Dr*
*Sunland Park, NM 88063*

www.sunland-park.com
575-874-5200

**DESCRIPTION:** Racino combines racing with casino gaming, in southern NM. **GAMING:** slots, plus electronic blackjack, 3-card poker machines with five individual player stations. Open: 10am-1am/4am(weekends). Thoroughbred, Quarter Horse racing Dec-Apr. Admission to the races is free. Simulcast wagering daily year-round. **FOOD & ENTERTAINMENT:** restaurant, buffet, grill, lounge, cantina. Live music weekends in lounge. **LODGING:** Boutique hotel. **CAMPING:** 8 RV spaces with electric & water, $13 per night, maximum stay 30 days. RV's must pull into hookups; dry camping is prohibited. **DIRECTIONS:** Sunland is just off I-10 at exit 13 (5 miles west of El Paso, TX). Follow signs.

# New York

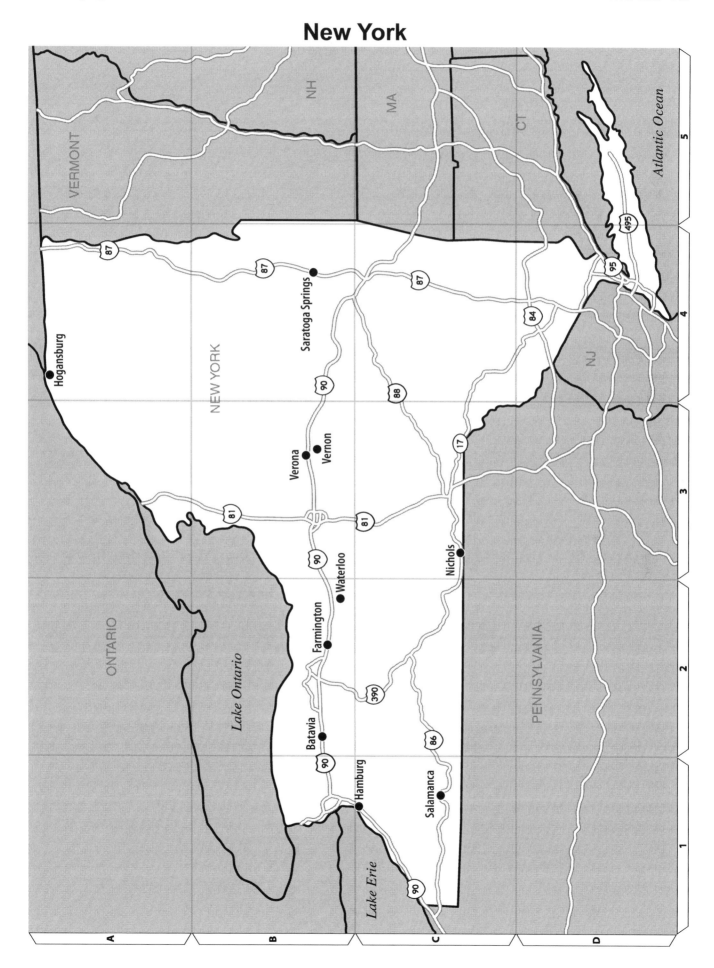

# New York

| City | Casino | 🚐 | P | 🛏 | 🏌 | 🛡 |
|------|--------|-----|-----|-----|-----|-----|
| Batavia | Batavia Downs Casino | | x | x | | 1 |
| Farmington | Finger Lakes Casino & Racetrack | | x | | | 2 |
| Hamburg | Hamburg Gaming | | x | | | 4 |
| Hogansburg | Akwesasne Mohawk Casino | | x | x | | |
| Nichols | Tioga Downs | | x | | | |
| Salamanca | Seneca Allegany Casino & Hotel | | x | x | | 1 |
| Saratoga Springs | Saratoga Casino & Raceway | | x | x | | 3 |
| Vernon | Vernon Downs Casino Hotel | | x | x | | 3 |
| Verona | Turning Stone Resort Casino | p175 | | x | x | 2 |
| Waterloo | del Lago Resort & Casino | | x | x | | 1 |

New York State's gaming consists of Indian casinos and racinos (casinos at horse and harness race tracks.) Some casinos in crowded areas do not allow RV parking due to space limitations.

## Batavia

### Batavia Downs Casino
8315 Park Rd
Batavia, NY 14020

www.bataviadownscasino.com
585-343-3750

**DESCRIPTION:** The oldest lighted harness track in the country is also a casino destination. **GAMING:** slots in all denominations; casino hours 8am-4am. Live harness racing July-Dec. Simulcasting of Thoroughbred & harness racing. **FOOD & ENTERTAINMENT:** sports bar, fine dining, casual dining with view of the track, grill. **LODGING:** contemporary hotel. **CAMPING:** RVs should park on the perimeter of the back of the lot. If staying overnight please register with Security in the casino. **DIRECTIONS:** From I-90 exit 48, go through the toll booth and proceed straight through on to Veterans Memorial Dr for .2 mile to Park Rd for .3 mile to Batavia Downs.

## Farmington

### Finger Lakes Casino & Racetrack
5857 Rt 96
Farmington, NY 14425

www.fingerlakesracetrack.com
585-924-3232 • 585-935-5252

**DESCRIPTION:** Western NY racino, Thoroughbreds plus lots of slots. **GAMING:** smoke-free casino open 8am-4am daily, slots, many progressives, video poker. Live Thoroughbred racing mid-Apr to late-Nov. Simulcasting daily. **FOOD & ENTERTAINMENT:** steakhouse, buffet, grill, casual dining, express food, sports bar. **LODGING:** There is no hotel at this location. **CAMPING:** Before parking, check in with Security in the casino to register for free overnight RV parking. **DIRECTIONS:** From NY State Thruway I-90 exit 44, take Rt-332 south for one mile to Rt-96, then left on Rt-96 for one-half mile.

## Hamburg

### Hamburg Gaming
5820 S Park Ave
Hamburg, NY 14075

www.the-fairgrounds.com
716-646-6109

**DESCRIPTION:** Gaming & harness racing at Erie County Fairgrounds. **GAMING:** Non-smoking casino open 8am-4am daily, many gaming machines, live harness racing Jan-Jul. Simulcast wagering year-round. **FOOD & ENTERTAINMENT:** buffet, cafe, grill, fast food, sports bar. **LODGING:** There is no hotel at this location. **CAMPING:** Free overnight parking permitted (except during county fair, 3rd week of Aug). **DIRECTIONS:** I-90E take exit 57 to Rt-75 north. Turn right on Southwestern Blvd (Rt-20). Turn right on South Park (US-62) for 4 miles. From I-90W take exit 56 (Blasdell/Milestrip). Turn right on Milestrip Rd (Rt-179). Turn left on South Park for 4 miles.

## Hogansburg

### Akwesasne Mohawk Casino
*873 State Rt 37*
*Hogansburg, NY 13655*

www.mohawkcasino.com
518-358-2222 • 877-992-2746

**DESCRIPTION:** Native-American casino near US/Canada border in Hogansburg. **GAMING:** 24-hour casino, slots, video poker, gaming tables, poker room, bingo. **FOOD & ENTERTAINMENT:** steakhouse, buffet, bar & grill, food court, sports bar. Entertainment at lounge weekends. **LODGING:** Luxury hotel, gift shop. **CAMPING:** There are 20 electric hookup parking spots in a designated section of the parking lot. Check in & pay at the hotel front desk. Free dry camping is also available in the large vehicle area. 24-hour security. **DIRECTIONS:** From I-81 exit 49, north on Rt-411 for 3 miles, then follow Rt-37 north for 80 miles.

## Nichols

### Tioga Downs
*2384 W River Rd*
*Nichols, NY 13812*

www.tiogadowns.com
888-946-8464

**DESCRIPTION:** Popular harness race track combined with casino. **GAMING:** slots, electronic table games, live-action pit/table games, poker room. Open 9am-3am, 24hrs weekends. Live harness racing May to mid-Sep. Simulcasting. **FOOD & ENTERTAINMENT:** buffet, casual dining, sports bar & quick food. Music in the lounge, weekends. Ticketed concerts & shows. **LODGING:** Smoke-free hotel. **CAMPING:** RVs should use the back of the parking lot, shuttle available. Limited free overnight parking permitted. **DIRECTIONS:** From NY-17W take exit 61 toward Nichols/Tioga Downs. Turn left on NY-282S, then right onto W River Rd for 1.6 miles.

## Salamanca

### Seneca Allegany Casino & Hotel
*777 Seneca Allegany Blvd*
*Salamanca, NY 14779*

www.senecaalleganycasino.com
888-913-3377

**DESCRIPTION:** Destination resort in southwestern NY State. **GAMING:** 24/7, slots, high limit area, video poker, live-action gaming tables, separate non-smoking casino. **FOOD & ENTERTAINMENT:** Seven restaurants: casual to gourmet dining, quick food. Live music in the bar. Ticketed shows in event center weekends. **LODGING:** Hotel. **CAMPING:** RVs should park at the back of the lot. Free overnight parking permitted. Inform Security if you plan to stay overnight. **DIRECTIONS:** From I-86 take exit 20. The casino can be seen on the south side of the interstate.

## Saratoga Springs

### Saratoga Casino & Raceway
*342 Jefferson St*
*Saratoga Springs, NY 12866*

www.saratogacasino.com
518-584-2110 • 800-727-2990

**DESCRIPTION:** Racino in historic Saratoga Springs, open daily 9am-5am. **GAMING:** slots, video poker, progressives, electronic table games. Live harness racing Mar to mid-Dec. Simulcasting daily. **FOOD & ENTERTAINMENT:** steakhouse, buffet, cafe, bar. Restaurant overlooking the track. Live entertainment weekends. **LODGING:** Modern hotel. **CAMPING:** RVs should use south entrance, park in the cobblestone area of the lot. Free overnight parking permitted.

**DIRECTIONS:** Take I-87 to exit 13N towards Saratoga Springs. Follow US-9 north for about 2 miles and turn right on Crescent Ave for about one mile.

## Vernon

### Vernon Downs Casino Hotel

*4229 Stuhlman Rd*
*Vernon, NY 13476*

www.vernondowns.com
877-888-3766

**DESCRIPTION:** Gaming getaway in the heart of Central NY's rolling hills. **GAMING:** Casino hours: 9am-2am/3am (Fri-Sat). Slots, many progressives, video poker, daily simulcasting year-round. Live harness racing Apr-Nov. **FOOD & ENTERTAINMENT:** buffet, cafe, quick food, bar. Full-service restaurant with simulcast wagering at tables. Ticketed shows weekends. Smoke-free hotel. **CAMPING:** RVs should use the back of the parking lot. Free overnight parking permitted for self-contained vehicles. **DIRECTIONS:** From I-90 exit 33 take Rt-365E for 1 mile then south on Rt-31 for 1.3 miles.

## Verona

### Turning Stone Resort Casino

*5218 Patrick Rd*
*Verona, NY 13478*

www.turning-stone.com
800-771-7711 • RV Park: 315-361-7275

**DESCRIPTION:** Four season destination resort in Upstate New York. **GAMING:** open 24/7, slots, live action table games, keno lounge, poker room, bingo. **FOOD & ENTERTAINMENT:** Nine dining venues, fine dining to quick food, lounge, tavern and bars. Ticketed shows in event center, Music in the cabaret. **LODGING:** All-suites hotel, Inn, Lodge, golf course. **CAMPING:** RV Park, 175 full-hookup paved sites, 50 pull thrus, heated pool, jacuzzi, nature trails, other recreation activities. Open Apr-Oct. Shuttle service to the casino. RVers who plan to stay overnight must check into the RV Park. Overnight parking in the casino lot is NOT permitted. **DIRECTIONS:** From I-90 exit 33 follow Rt-365W for 1.6 miles.

## Waterloo

### del Lago Resort & Casino

*1133 NY-414*
*Waterloo, NY 13165*

www.dellagoresort.com
315-946-1777

**DESCRIPTION:** Friendly casino resort in Finger Lakes region. **GAMING:** slots, pit/table games, open 24 hours. **FOOD & ENTERTAINMENT:** Eight dining venues, music in bars, ticketed events weekends. **LODGING:** Modern hotel. **CAMPING:** RV free parking is available in the back section of the lot. Overnight OK. **DIRECTIONS:** At I-90 exit 41, the resort is just north of the thruway.

# North Dakota

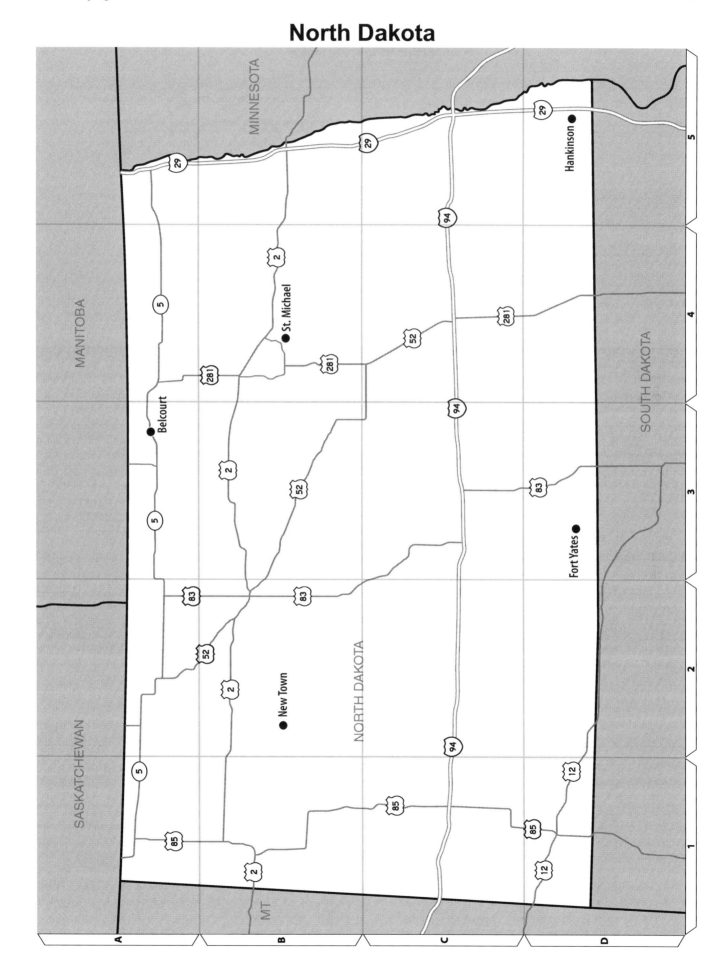

# North Dakota

| City | Casino | 🚐 | 🅿 | 🛏 | 🏌 | 🛡 |
|------|--------|-----|-----|-----|-----|-----|
| Belcourt | Sky Dancer Casino & Resort | s | x | x | | |
| Fort Yates | Prairie Knights Casino & Resort | s12 | | x | | |
| Hankinson | Dakota Magic Casino & Resort | s25 | | x | x | 1 |
| New Town | 4 Bears Casino & Lodge | p85 | | x | | |
| St. Michael | Spirit Lake Casino & Resort | s53 | x | x | | |

North Dakota's casino resorts have hotels and most have campgrounds or hookups available for RV travelers. Although the casinos and hotels are open all year, some campgrounds close during winter months.

## Belcourt

### Sky Dancer Casino & Resort
*Hwy 5 W, 3965 Sky Dancer Way*
*Belcourt, ND 58316*

www.skydancercasino.com
701-244-2400 • 866-244-9467

**DESCRIPTION:** Cozy casino ten miles south of the Canada border. **GAMING:** open 24 hours, slots, video poker, video keno, video blackjack, live action gaming tables, poker room, simulcast racing, bingo. **FOOD & ENTERTAINMENT:** steakhouse, buffet & grill, snack bar. **LODGING:** smoke free hotel, gift shop. **CAMPING:** RV parking with free electric hookups in the casino lot, overnight is OK. **DIRECTIONS:** From I-29 exit 203 go west on SR-5 for 125 miles.

## Fort Yates

### Prairie Knights Casino & Resort
*7932 Hwy 24*
*Fort Yates, ND 58538*

www.prairieknights.com
701-854-7777

**DESCRIPTION:** Casino resort hosted by the Standing Rock Sioux Indian Community. **GAMING:** open 24/7, slots, gaming tables, video poker, video keno, high limits area. **FOOD & ENTERTAINMENT:** buffet every day, fine dining at Hunters Club. **LODGING:** Rooms/suites at the Lodge. Marina, boat ramp access, fishing. **CAMPING:** 16 RV (electric-only) spaces, walking distance to casino; pull in, register & pay at hotel front desk, online booking also available. 24-hour gas station, quick mart, 24-hour security. **DIRECTIONS:** From I-94 exit 152 follow SR-6 south for 62.8 miles, then east on SR-24 for 1.3 miles.

## Hankinson

### Dakota Magic Casino & Resort
*16849 100th St*
*Hankinson, ND 58041*

www.dakotamagic.com
701-634-3000

**DESCRIPTION:** Premier destination resort along the ND/SD border. **GAMING:** open 24/7, slots, many progressives, pit/gaming tables, high limits area, poker room, live keno, pari-mutuel betting parlor, non-smoking area. **FOOD & ENTERTAINMENT:** buffet, grill, deli at casino; bar & grill at golf clubhouse. Live music in lounge. **LODGING:** Luxury hotel, golf course. **CAMPING:** 25 RV spaces with full hookups on the north side of the casino (electric-only in winter months). Register at the hotel front desk. **DIRECTIONS:** Resort is just off I-29 at exit 1 in North Dakota.

## New Town

### 4 Bears Casino & Lodge
*202 Frontage Rd*
*New Town, ND 58763*

www.4bearscasino.com
701-627-4018

**DESCRIPTION:** Casino resort on the shores of Lake Sakakawea. **GAMING:** open 24/7, slots, pit/gaming tables, poker room. **FOOD & ENTERTAINMENT:** steakhouse, buffet, cafe, lounge. Ticketed shows in event center; music in the lounge. **LODGING:** Hotel overlooking lake. **CAMPING:** RV Park, 115 full-hookup sites, open May to mid-Oct, advance reservations required, monthly rates available. For limited overnight RV parking, check in with Security Control at event center and they will assign space. **DIRECTIONS:** From I-94 exit 159 follow US-83 north for 90.3 miles, then 55 miles west on SR-23. Located 4 miles west of New Town.

## St. Michael

### Spirit Lake Casino & Resort
*7889 Hwy 57*
*St. Michael, ND 58370*

www.spiritlakecasino.com
701-766-4747 • 800-946-8238

**DESCRIPTION:** Destination resort on scenic shores of Devil's Lake. **GAMING:** open 24/7, slots, pit/table games, poker room, bingo. **FOOD & ENTERTAINMENT:** buffet and quick food, ticketed events in the showroom. **LODGING:** Hotel, indoor pool, exercise room. Marina, fishing. **CAMPING:** RV Park (seasonal), 73 full-hookup sites. 24-hour security. Grocery store. RV guests are invited to use amenities at the hotel. Some electric-only spaces in the casino parking lot. Advance reservations suggested. No free overnight parking. **DIRECTIONS:** From I-29 exit 141, west on US-2 for 86 miles to Devil's Lake, then south on SR-20 for five miles and continue on SR-57 for another 1.5 miles.

# Ohio

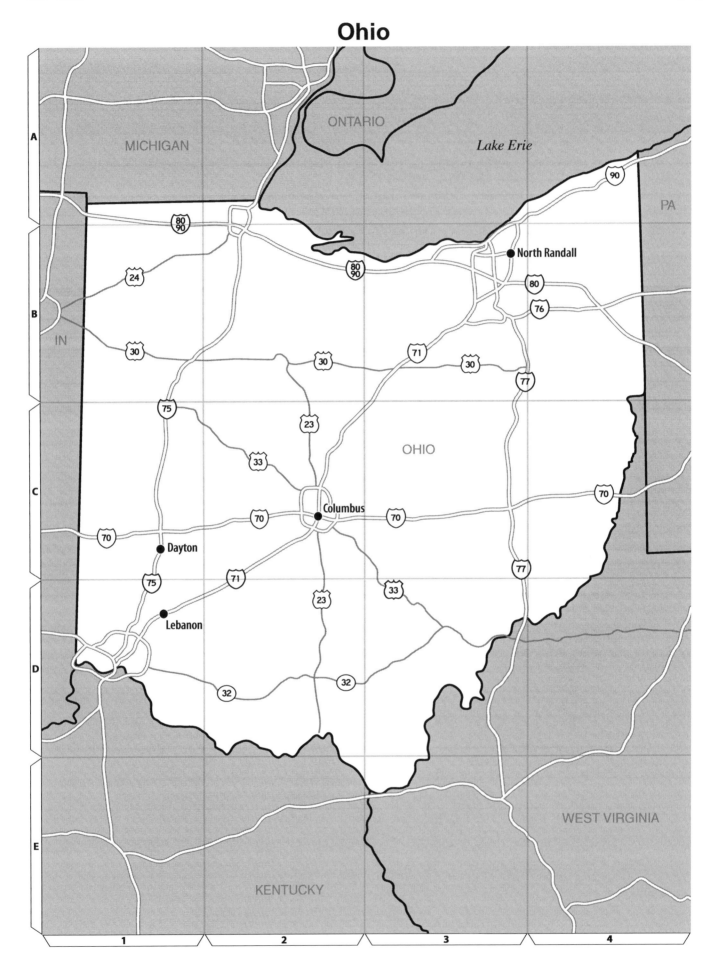

# Ohio

| City | Casino | 🚐 | **P** | 🛏 | 🏌 | 🛡 |
|------|--------|---|---|---|---|---|
| Columbus | Hollywood Casino | | x | | | 1 |
| Columbus | Elderado Scioto Downs | | x | | | 3 |
| Dayton | Hollywood Gaming at Dayton Raceway | | | | | |
| Lebanon | Miami Valley Gaming | | x | | | 1 |
| North Randall | JACK Thistledown Racino | | x | | | 1 |

Ohio voters passed a ballot referendum in 2009 that allows casinos to operate in four major cities and at race tracks. Casinos listed here are those that permit RV parking at their property.

## Columbus

### Hollywood Casino
*200 Georgesville Rd*
*Columbus, OH 43228*

www.hollywoodcolumbus.com
614-308-3333

**DESCRIPTION:** Hollywood-themed traditional casino, quality gaming. **GAMING:** open 24/7, slots, video poker, live gaming tables, poker room. **FOOD & ENTERTAINMENT:** steakhouse, buffet, sports bar, grill, noodle bar, express food. Live lounge entertainment, concerts on weekends. **LODGING:** There is no hotel at this location. **CAMPING:** Follow signs for the truck & RV parking area. Free overnight parking is permitted. **DIRECTIONS:** From I-270 take exit 74, merge onto US-40 E/W Broad St for .8 mile, then right onto Georgesville Rd.

### Elderado Scioto Downs
*6000 S High St*
*Columbus, OH 43207*

www.sciotodowns.com
614-295-4700

**DESCRIPTION:** First racino to open in Ohio combines live harness racing with casino slots. **GAMING:** open 24/7, slots, keno machines. Live harness racing May-

Sep, simulcasting. **FOOD & ENTERTAINMENT:** buffet, clubhouse restaurant, quick food, center bar. Live entertainment weekends. **LODGING:** Hampton Inn. **CAMPING:** RVs should park in the gravel area next to the hotel. Free overnight RV parking permitted. **DIRECTIONS:** From I-270 exit 52, go south 2.5 miles on US-23.

## Dayton

### Hollywood Gaming at Dayton Raceway
*777 Hollywood Blvd*
*Dayton, OH 45414*

www.hollywooddaytonraceway.com
844-225-7057

**DESCRIPTION:** Slots casino combined with harness racing. **GAMING:** slots, simulcasting year-round, live harness racing Sep-Dec. **FOOD & ENTERTAINMENT:** sportsbar & grill, food court, live entertainment weekends. **LODGING:** There is no hotel at this location. **CAMPING:** RVs may park in the truck lot at the front of the casino. Overnight is OK. **DIRECTIONS:** I-75 north to exit 58 for direct access to the raceway.

## Lebanon

### Miami Valley Gaming
*6000 State Rd 63*
*Lebanon, OH 45036*

www.miamivalleygaming.com
513-934-7070

**DESCRIPTION:** Popular harness racing track and slots casino. **GAMING:** open 24/7, slots, high limits area, live harness racing Jan-May, simulcasting noon-midnight daily. Ticketed shows & special events. **FOOD & ENTERTAINMENT:** steakhouse, buffet, quick bites, bars. **LODGING:** There is no hotel at this location. **CAMPING:** Follow signs for designated area for oversized vehicles, west side of the building. Overnight parking permitted for self-contained RVs. **DIRECTIONS:** Located just off I-75 at exit 29, east of the interstate.

## North Randall

### JACK Thistledown Racino
*21501 Emery Rd*
*North Randall, OH 44128*

www.jackentertainment.com/thistledown/
216-662-8600

**DESCRIPTION:** Horse racing & slots casino near Cleveland. **GAMING:** 24/7 slots, live Thoroughbred racing Apr-Nov, simulcasting daily. **FOOD & ENTERTAINMENT:** grill, diner, quick food, bars. **LODGING:** No hotel at this location. **CAMPING:** Parking for RVs available in the back section of the lot. Overnight is permitted for casino players. **DIRECTIONS:** Located one mile west of I-271, two blocks north of I-480 (exit 25C) at the intersection of Warrensville and Emery Roads.

# Oklahoma

MO

Quapaw

Wyandotte

Miami

412

169

Claremore

Catoosa

44

Newkirk

35

412

Concho

270

Hinton

Newcastle

412

183

Clinton

281

412

412

83

54

412

NM

KANSAS

COLORADO

Salisaw

Roland

Pocola

AR

40

Okemah

Shawnee

Norman

OKLAHOMA

7

44

Lawton

62

Devol

40

183

62

Grant

69

Durant

Davis

35

Thackerville

TEXAS

A

B

C

D

1

2

3

4

5

# Oklahoma

| City | Casino | 🚐 | **P** | 🛏 | 🏌 | 🛡 |
|------|--------|-----|-------|------|------|------|
| Catoosa | Hard Rock Hotel & Casino — Tulsa | | x | x | x | 1 |
| Claremore | Cherokee Casino Will Rogers Downs | p400 | | | | 4 |
| Clinton | Lucky Star Casino | s2 | x | | | 2 |
| Concho | Lucky Star Casino | s10 | x | | | 8 |
| Davis | Treasure Valley Casino | | x | x | | 1 |
| Devol | Comanche Red River Casino | s10 | x | | | 7 |
| Devol | Kiowa Casino | | x | | | 2 |
| Durant | Choctaw Casino Resort | p77 | | x | | |
| Grant | Choctaw Casino | | x | x | | |
| Hinton | Sugar Creek Casino | | x | | | 1 |
| Lawton | Comanche Nation Casino | s4 | x | | | 1 |
| Miami | Buffalo Run Casino & Hotel | s7 | x | x | | 2 |
| Miami | Quapaw Casino | s8 | x | | | 4 |
| Newcastle | Newcastle Casino | | x | | | 1 |
| Newkirk | Native Lights Casino | s15 | x | | | |
| Norman | Riverwind Casino | | x | x | | 1 |
| Norman | Thunderbird Casino | | x | | | |
| Okemah | Golden Pony Casino | | x | | | 1 |
| Pocola | Choctaw Casino | | x | x | | 10 |
| Quapaw | Downstream Casino Resort | s70 | | x | x | 1 |
| Roland | Cherokee Casino | | x | x | | 1 |
| Sallisaw | Cherokee Casino | | x | | | 1 |
| Shawnee | Grand Casino Hotel Resort | s20 | x | x | x | 1 |
| Thackerville | WinStar World Casino & Resort | p150 | | x | x | 1 |
| Wyandotte | Indigo Sky Casino Resort | p44 | | x | | |

Oklahoma has more Native American tribes and more Indian gaming than any other state, with over 100 gaming locations throughout Oklahoma. This guide includes facilities that are accessible for secure RV parking and convenient to major highways for road travelers.

## Catoosa

### Hard Rock Hotel & Casino — Tulsa
777 W Cherokee St
Catoosa, OK 74015

www.hardrockcasinotulsa.com
918-266-4352

**DESCRIPTION:** Hard Rock-themed resort in suburban Tulsa. **GAMING:** open 24/7, slots, gaming tables, poker room. **FOOD & ENTERTAINMENT:** Eight dining venues, bars, lounge. Live nightclub entertainment. Ticketed shows in amphitheater. **LODGING:** Hotel, golf course. **CAMPING:** Parking for RVs and motor coaches in Lot I, north of the casino building. Dump station on site. Follow signs, check in with Security if you plan to stay overnight. Call casino for shuttle service, let them know you are in Lot I. **DIRECTIONS:** From I-44 exit 240A (193rd East Ave) turn right, stay in the left lane and turn left at the light.

## Claremore

### Cherokee Casino Will Rogers Downs
*20900 S 4200 Rd*
*Claremore, OK 74017*

www.cherokeecasino.com/will-rogers-downs
918-283-8800

**DESCRIPTION:** Horse racing track & gaming facility. **GAMING:** slots, video poker, open 11am-1am/4am (Fri-Sat). Live racing Mar-May, simulcasting. **FOOD & ENTERTAINMENT:** restaurant open morning till night, lounge. **LODGING:** There is no hotel at this location. **CAMPING:** KOA RV Park, 400 full hookup sites, open year round, clubhouse, event center. Overnight RV parking is NOT permitted in the casino lot. If staying overnight, check into the RV Park. Dry camping rates are available. **DIRECTIONS:** On Hwy-20 east of Claremore. From I-44 (Will Rogers Tpk) take exit 255, then east on Hwy-20 four miles.

## Clinton

### Lucky Star Casino
*10347 N 2274 Rd*
*Clinton, OK 73601*

www.luckystarcasino.org
580-323-6599

**DESCRIPTION:** Friendly casino just north of I-40 in Clinton. **GAMING:** slots open 24/7, live-action blackjack tables, poker room. **FOOD & ENTERTAINMENT:** cafe open morning till night. **LODGING:** No hotel at this location. **CAMPING:** RVs welcome. Two spaces with free electric hookup in the parking lot. first come-first serve. Overnight is OK. **DIRECTIONS:** From I-40 exit 66 take S. 4th St/US-183 exit toward Cordell. Keep left to take the S. 4th St. ramp, turn left onto US-183N/S. 4th St. Go 1.1 miles, then turn right on W. Gary Blvd/I-40 Bus. E. for 1.8 miles to N. 2274 Rd., turn left to the casino.

## Concho/El Reno

### Lucky Star Casino
*7777 N Hwy 81*
*El Reno, OK 73036*

www.luckystarcasino.org
405-262-7612

**DESCRIPTION:** Casino hosted by the Cheyenne & Arapaho Tribes. **GAMING:** open 24/7, slots, blackjack & poker tables. **FOOD & ENTERTAINMENT:** restaurant serves traditional American food daily, sports bar. **LODGING:** There is no hotel at this location. **CAMPING:** 10 free RV spaces with hookups, east side of the casino building, first-come, first-served. Sign in and register at the security desk in the casino before hooking up. **DIRECTIONS:** From I-40 exit 125, take US-81 north for eight miles to the casino, on the southbound side of US-81.

## Davis

### Treasure Valley Casino
*12252 Ruppe Rd*
*Davis, OK 73030*

www.treasurevalleycasino.com
580-369-2895 • 580-369-3223

**DESCRIPTION:** Gaming Center and Inn hosted by the Chickasaw Nation. **GAMING:** open 24/7, slots, blackjack & poker tables, off track betting. **FOOD & ENTERTAINMENT:** Sports bar & quick food. **LODGING:** Inn. **CAMPING:** Free RV parking east side of the casino building. Notify Security if you plan to stay overnight. **DIRECTIONS:** From I-35 exit 55, follow signs to the casino.

## Devol

### Comanche Red River Casino
*Hwy 36 & Hwy 70*
*Devol, OK 73531*

www.comancheredrivercasino.com
580-250-3060

**DESCRIPTION:** Near the Texas border, casino is hosted by the Comanche Nation. **GAMING:** open 24/7, slots, blackjack tables, poker room. **FOOD & ENTERTAINMENT:** cafe, bar & grill. **LODGING:** Modern hotel. **CAMPING:** 10 spaces with free RV electric hookups, south side of the parking lot, available for RVers playing in the casino. First come-first served. Must register at the security office. **DIRECTIONS:** From I-44 exit 5, take US-70 west for about seven miles to the casino.

### Kiowa Casino
*198131 Hwy 36*
*Devol, OK 73531*

www.kiowacasino.com
580-299-3333

**DESCRIPTION:** Casino hosted by Kiowa Tribe. **GAMING:** open 24/7, slots, gaming tables, poker room. **FOOD & ENTERTAINMENT:** steakhouse, buffet, bar & grill. **LODGING:** Modern hotel. **CAMPING:** RV dry camping permitted in parking lot in front of the hotel. **DIRECTIONS:** From I-44 exit 1, OK-36 north for 1.1 mile.

## Durant

### Choctaw Casino Resort
*4216 S Hwy 69/75*
*Durant, OK 74701*

www.choctawcasinos.com/choctaw-durant
580-920-0160 • RV Park: 800-562-6073

**DESCRIPTION:** Luxury destination resort hosted by the Choctaw Nation. **GAMING:** open 24/7, slots, gaming tables, poker room, OTB/race book, bingo. **FOOD & ENTERTAINMENT:** Nine restaurants, four lounges, one with live entertainment. Ticketed events weekends. **LODGING:** Grand Tower & Inn. **CAMPING:** KOA RV Park, 77 pull-thru, full hookup sites, clubhouse, game room, shuffleboard, dog park, 24-hour shuttle. Limited (one-night) free dry camping permitted in the event center lot. For longer stays, please register at the KOA. **DIRECTIONS:** Located just north of the Texas state line on the northbound side of Hwy-69/75. Travel Plaza has fuel, food, 24-hour slots.

## Grant

### Choctaw Casino
*1516 US Hwy 271 S*
*Grant, OK 74738*

www.choctawcasinos.com/choctaw-grant
580-326-8397

**DESCRIPTION:** Casino resort just north of Paris, TX. **GAMING:** open 24/7, slots, blackjack tables, poker room. **FOOD & ENTERTAINMENT:** buffet, grill, bar. Ticketed shows weekends at the event center. **LODGING:** Hotel. **CAMPING:** RV dry camping permitted on the perimeter of the parking lot; overnight OK. **DIRECTIONS:** The resort is north of the Texas/Oklahoma state line, directly on US-271 in Grant.

## Hinton

### Sugar Creek Casino
*5304 N Broadway Ave*
*Hinton, OK 73047*

www.sugarcreekcasino.net
405-542-2946

**DESCRIPTION:** Friendly casino in western OK. **GAMING:** open 24/7, slots, live gaming tables. **FOOD & ENTERTAINMENT:** cafe, sports bar, quick food. Ticketed shows weekends at event center. **LODGING:** smoke-free Inn. **CAMPING:** RVs welcome, see Security for parking directions; overnight permitted. **DIRECTIONS:** From I-40 exit 101 toward Anadark/Watongam go .2 mile then right onto N. Broadway.

## Lawton

### Comanche Nation Casino
*402 S Interstate Dr*
*Lawton, OK 73501*

www.comanchenationcasinos.com
580-250-3030

DESCRIPTION: Non-stop gaming, friendly casino, easy on/off access from interstate. GAMING: open 24/7 slots, live gaming tables. FOOD & ENTERTAINMENT: sports bar & grill. LODGING: No hotel at this location. CAMPING: Four RV spaces with free electric hookups in the parking lot. First come-first serve. Check in with Security. DIRECTIONS: From I-44 exit 37 (Gore Blvd), casino visible from the eastbound lanes.

## Miami

### Buffalo Run Casino & Hotel
1000 Buffalo Run Blvd
Miami, OK 74354

www.buffalorun.com
918-542-7140

DESCRIPTION: Charming casino just off the interstate near Joplin, MO. GAMING: open 24/7, slots, live table games. FOOD & ENTERTAINMENT: restaurant, grill, bistro, diner, lounge. Ticketed shows weekends. LODGING: Suite hotel, golf course. CAMPING: 7 spaces with electric hookups at the casino. Register at hotel. DIRECTIONS: From I-44 exit 313 (Miami), after the toll booth, go straight on US-69A for 1.5 miles.

### Quapaw Casino
58100 E 64th Rd
Miami, OK 74355

www.quapawcasino.com
918-540-9100

DESCRIPTION: Cozy casino hosted by the Quapaw Tribe of OK. GAMING: open 24/7, slots, video poker, live gaming tables. FOOD & ENTERTAINMENT: grill and bar. LODGING: There is no hotel at this location. CAMPING: Eight pull-thru RV spaces, water & electric, central dump. Register at the Dispatch (security) office. No charge for the first three days. DIRECTIONS: From I-44 exit 313, after going through the toll booth, continue straight on US-69A north for 3.5 miles, turn right into the casino.

## Newcastle

### Newcastle Casino
2457 Hwy 62 Service Rd
Newcastle, OK 73065

www.mynewcastlecasino.com
405-387-6013

DESCRIPTION: Popular local casino destination for entertainment & gaming. GAMING: open 24/7 slots, progressives, keno, live gaming tables, OTB, high limits area. FOOD & ENTERTAINMENT: casual dining, sports bar, free live music on weekends. Summer concert series. LODGING: There is no hotel at this location. CAMPING: RVs should park in the far northeast corner of the lot. Please inform security if you wish to stay overnight. DIRECTIONS: From I-44 exit 107 merge on US-277S/US-62W/N Main St toward Newcastle .8 mile, then left on NW 24th St.

## Newkirk

### Native Lights Casino
12375 N Hwy 77
Newkirk, OK 74647

www.nativelightscasino.com
580-448-3100

DESCRIPTION: Casino hosted by the Tonkawa Tribe of OK. GAMING: Vegas-style slots, electronic table games, open 10am-midnight/3am (weekends). FOOD & ENTERTAINMENT: cafe, grill, lounge. LODGING: There is no hotel at this location. CAMPING: 15 RV spaces with full hookup south of the casino, first day free to Players Club members. Check in at the casino cage. DIRECTIONS: Located on US-77, just south of Arkansas City, Kansas.

## Norman

### Riverwind Casino
1544 W State Hwy 9
Norman, OK 73072

www.riverwind.com
405-322-6000

DESCRIPTION: Gaming & premiere entertainment near I-35, just south of OK City. GAMING: open 24/7, slots, video poker, gaming tables, poker room, off-track betting, high limits room. FOOD & ENTERTAINMENT: buffet, restaurant, food court. Ticketed shows weekends. Free lounge entertainment. LODGING:

Contemporary hotel, gift shop. **CAMPING:** Free parking for self-contained RVs at the south end of the lot. Overnight is OK. **DIRECTIONS:** From I-35 exit 106, the casino is on the west side of the interstate.

### Thunderbird Casino
*15700 E Hwy 9*
*Norman, OK 73026*

playthunderbird.com
405-360-9270

**DESCRIPTION:** Western-themed Vegas-style casino. **GAMING:** slots, gaming machines, live blackjack & poker tables. Hours: 9am-2am daily and 24 hrs (weekends.) **FOOD & ENTERTAINMENT:** restaurant, bar, karaoke, live music weekends. **LODGING:** There is no hotel at this location. **CAMPING:** RV parking spaces behind the casino building; overnight is permitted. Must check in with Security on arrival. **DIRECTIONS:** From I-35 exit 108A, take Hwy-9 east toward Tecumseh for 17.3 miles.

## Okemah

### Golden Pony Casino
*109095 Okemah St*
*Okemah, OK 74859*

www.goldenponycasino.com
918-582-4653

**DESCRIPTION:** Friendly slots-only casino adjacent to the interstate. **GAMING:** over 400 machines in all denominations. Open 24 hours. **FOOD & ENTERTAINMENT:** Cafe open daily morning till night, smoke shop & gift shop. **LODGING:** No hotel at this location. **CAMPING:** Free RV parking on the north side of the parking lot; overnight is OK. **DIRECTIONS:** Just south of I-40 exit 227.

## Pocola

### Choctaw Casino
*3400 Choctaw Rd*
*Pocola, OK 74902*

www.choctawcasinos.com/choctaw-pocola
918-436-7761 • 800-590-5825

**DESCRIPTION:** Choctaw casino near Ft. Smith, Arkansas. **GAMING:** 24/7, slots, live action gaming tables, race book, high limits area. **FOOD & ENTERTAINMENT:** buffet, bar & grill, lounge, nightclub. Ticketed entertainment at Center Stage, weekends. **LODGING:** Stylish hotel. **CAMPING:** RV parking is permitted; inform Security if planning to stay overnight. **DIRECTIONS:** Just off US-271 at the Oklahoma/Arkansas state line.

## Quapaw

### Downstream Casino Resort
*69300 E Nee Rd*
*Quapaw, OK 74363*

www.downstreamcasino.com
918-919-6000

**DESCRIPTION:** Luxury resort in northeastern corner of OK near Kansas & Missouri. **GAMING:** open 24/7, slots, live table games, poker room, non-smoking section. **FOOD & ENTERTAINMENT:** Six dining options, sports bar, coffee shop, quick bites. Live entertainment in casino. Ticketed touring national shows. **LODGING:** Hotel, golf course, gift shop. **CAMPING:** 70 RV spaces in the parking area, water & electric hookups, central dump. Check in & pay at the gift shop. Shuttle service available. Limited dry camping is permitted. **DIRECTIONS:** From I-44 exit 1 (in Missouri) take US-166 north to the roundabout and follow signs.

## Roland

### Cherokee Casino
*205 Cherokee Blvd*
*Roland, OK 74954*

www.cherokeecasino.com/roland
918-427-7491

**DESCRIPTION:** Casino, hotel & travel plaza. **GAMING:** open 24/7, slots, live blackjack & poker tables, daily casino promotions. **FOOD & ENTERTAINMENT:** buffet, quick food, tavern. **LODGING:** Hotel connected to casino. Travel Plaza has fuel, fast food and snacks. **CAMPING:** RV area is next to the parking garage. Free overnight parking only for players in the casino.

Obtain a Players Card & inform Security if you plan to stay overnight. **DIRECTIONS:** From I-40 exit 325 take US-64W for .4 mile, then right at Paw Paw Rd & immediate right on Cherokee Blvd for .3 mile.

## Sallisaw

### Cherokee Casino
*1621 W Ruth Ave*
*Sallisaw, OK 74955*

www.cherokeecasino.com/sallisaw
800-256-2338

**DESCRIPTION:** Local casino has slots plus daily simulcasting. **GAMING:** slots, open 24 hours. Off track betting in simulcast room, big-screen TVs & 20 individual carrel stations to view live horse racing around the world. Simulcasting opens daily at 11am. **FOOD & ENTERTAINMENT:** bar & grill, live music and dancing. **LODGING:** There is no hotel at this location. **CAMPING:** RV parking lot on the east side of the property, on the other side of the parking garage; free overnight up to 3 days. **DIRECTIONS:** From I-40 exit 308 for US-59 toward Sallisaw, turn left on US-59N/ S Kerr Blvd, then first left onto Ruth Ave.

## Shawnee

### Grand Casino Hotel Resort
*777 Grand Casino Blvd*
*Shawnee, OK 74804*

www.grandresortok.com
405-964-7263 (Casino)

**DESCRIPTION:** Casino resort, easy on/off access from I-40 in Shawnee. **GAMING:** open 24/7, slots, pit/ gaming tables, poker room. **FOOD & ENTERTAINMENT:** steakhouse, buffet, sushi bar, cafe, sports grill & 3 bars. Ticketed shows in event center. **LODGING:** Hotel, golf course. **CAMPING:** 20 back-in RV spaces, electric & water hookup, central dump; register/pay at hotel front desk. **DIRECTIONS:** Just off I-40 at exit 178 on north side of the interstate. Travel center has fuel, snacks & store.

## Thackerville

### WinStar World Casino & Resort
*777 Casino Dr*
*Thackerville, OK 73459*

www.winstarworldcasino.com
580-276-4229 • 800-622-6317

**DESCRIPTION:** Oklahoma's largest casino resort with eight city-themed gaming plazas. **GAMING:** slots, electronic &table games, poker room, bingo, off-track-betting. **FOOD & ENTERTAINMENT:** Many dining options. Live entertainment at lounges & bars. Ticketed shows weekends. **LODGING:** Hotel, pools open seasonally, day spa, shopping boutiques, golf course. **CAMPING:** RV Park, 152 full hookup sites, pavilion, 24/7 shuttle. **DIRECTIONS:** At I-35 exit 1, one mile north of the Red River Texas/Oklahoma border.

## Wyandotte

### Indigo Sky Casino Resort
*70220 East Hwy 60*
*Wyandotte, OK 74370*

www.indigoskycasino.com
888-992-7591

**DESCRIPTION:** Casino resort getaway near Missouri border. **GAMING:** slots, gaming tables, poker room, bingo, off track betting. **FOOD & ENTERTAINMENT:** restaurant, grill, cafe & bar. **LODGING:** Hotel, free Wi-Fi, pool & hot tub, gift shop. **CAMPING:** RV Park, 44 sites, water & electric hookups, clubhouse, pool access. If staying overnight, must register into the RV park. Dry camping prohibited. **DIRECTIONS:** From I-44 exit 302, follow US-60 east for 19 miles.

# Oregon

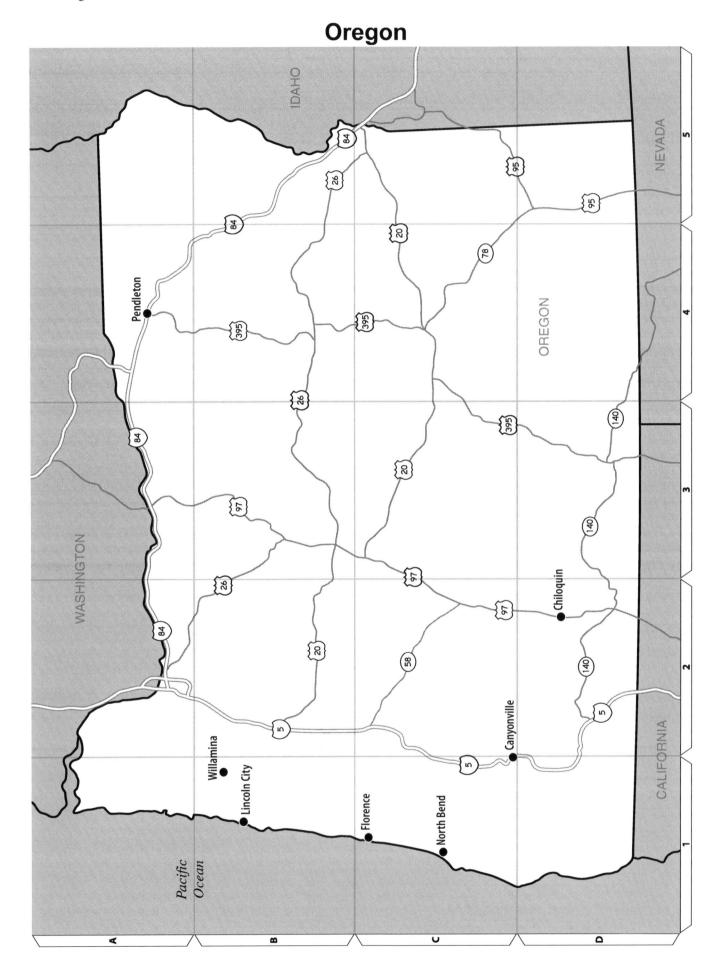

# Oregon

| City | Casino | 🚐 | P | 🛏 | 🏌 | 🛡 |
|------|--------|------|------|------|------|------|
| Canyonville | Seven Feathers Casino Resort | p191/s51 | x | x | x | 1 |
| Chiloquin | Kla-Mo-Ya Casino | | x | | | |
| Florence | Three Rivers Casino & Hotel | | x | x | x | |
| Lincoln City | Chinook Winds Casino Resort | p51 | x | x | x | |
| North Bend | The Mill Casino Hotel & RV Park | p102 | x | x | | |
| Pendleton | Wildhorse Resort & Casino | p100 | x | x | x | 1 |
| Willamina | Spirit Mountain Casino | | x | x | | |

The seven Indian casinos in Oregon, listed here, are located within an easy drive of an interstate or major highway. Some of the casino resorts rank among the top Oregon attractions.

## Canyonville

### Seven Feathers Casino Resort
*146 Chief Miwaleta Ln*
*Canyonville, OR 97417*

www.sevenfeathers.com
541-839-1111 • RV Resort: 877-839-3599

**DESCRIPTION:** Destination resort just off Interstate 5. **GAMING:** open 24/7 slots, pit/table games, live keno, poker room, non-smoking gaming area, bingo. **FOOD & ENTERTAINMENT:** steakhouse, buffet, cafe, bar, coffee house. Live music in lounge. Ticketed touring shows. **LODGING:** Luxury hotel, golf course. **CAMPING:** RV Park, 191 full hookup sites, many pull thrus, pool/spa, fitness center. For short stay, free dry camping (up to 5 days) in the lot across from Burger King (below the casino). Shuttle throughout resort. **DIRECTIONS:** From junction I-5 and Canyonville/ Crater Lake (exit 99), resort is visible.

## Chiloquin

### Kla-Mo-Ya Casino
*3433 US-97 N*
*Chiloquin, OR 97624*

www.klamoyacasino.com
541-783-7529

**DESCRIPTION:** Casino gaming in the scenic Klamath Basin. **GAMING:** 24/7 slots, gaming tables, keno. **FOOD & ENTERTAINMENT:** restaurant, deli, lounge. **LODGING:** Sleep Inn Suites. **CAMPING:** Free dry camping in the parking lot, some shady areas. Players Club welcomes campers; sign up for a card & free slot play. **DIRECTIONS:** Located on US-97, 22 miles north of Klamath Falls.

## Florence

### Three Rivers Casino & Hotel
*5647 Oregon126*
*Florence, OR 97439*

www.threeriverscasino.com
877-374-8377

**DESCRIPTION:** Resort on 100 acres of rolling sand dunes on Oregon coast. **GAMING:** slots, many progressives, non-smoking area, live action pit/table games, bingo, keno parlor. **FOOD & ENTERTAINMENT:** Five restaurants: quick food, sports bar. Ticketed touring shows. **LODGING:** Hotel, golf. **CAMPING:** Free RV dry camping; 1st night free, earn 50 players club points per day to stay up to three additional days. First come-first serve, check in at Security podium, 24-hr security, free coffee, soda in the casino. **DIRECTIONS:** From I-5 exit 195 go west on Beltline Hwy 9.7 miles, then SR-126 west for 54.6 miles. The casino is on SR-126 just east of Florence.

## Lincoln City

### Chinook Winds Casino Resort
*1777 NW 44th St*
*Lincoln City, OR 97367*

www.chinookwindscasino.com
888-244-6665

**DESCRIPTION:** Destination resort on the beach. **GAMING:** 24/7, slots, progressives, high limit slot area, pit/gaming tables, poker room, live keno, bingo, smoke-free areas. **FOOD & ENTERTAINMENT:** steakhouse, buffet, grills, deli, lounges, coffee shop. Ticketed headline shows. **LODGING:** Hotel, golf course. **CAMPING:** Dry camping available, parking permit is required. 30 designated spaces in the casino lot, first-come, first-serve, generators may not be used. Logan Road RV Park (877-564-2678) a few blocks from the casino, has 51 full hookup sites, amenities, shuttle service. **DIRECTIONS:** From I-5 exit 253 follow OR-22 west for 30 miles then OR-18 west for 27 miles to US-101 south for 2.3 miles, then north on Logan Rd for .3 mile and west on 44th St.

## North Bend

### The Mill Casino Hotel & RV Park
*3201 Tremont Ave*
*North Bend, OR 97459*

www.themillcasino.com
541-756-8800 • 800-953-4800

**DESCRIPTION:** A place to play in Coos Bay on Oregon coast. **GAMING:** slots, pit/gaming tables, smoke-free area. **FOOD & ENTERTAINMENT:** steakhouse, buffet, cafe, bakery, sports bar/nightclub. Live entertainment. **LODGING:** Hotel. **CAMPING:** 102-space full hookup RV Park, many pull thrus, pet area. Casino shuttle. Fee-pay dry camping available; register/pay at the RV Park or hotel front desk (evenings.) **DIRECTIONS:** From I-5 exit 162 follow OR-38 west for 56.8 miles & south on US-101 for 24.7 miles.

## Pendleton

### Wildhorse Resort & Casino
*46510 Wildhorse Blvd*
*Pendleton, OR 97801*

www.wildhorseresort.com
541-278-2274 • 800-654-9453

**DESCRIPTION:** Resort in the foothills of Oregon's Blue Mountains just off I-84. **GAMING:** slots, pit/gaming tables, poker room, live keno, bingo, non-smoking slots area. **FOOD & ENTERTAINMENT:** buffet, fine dining, cafe, sports bar. Live music, comedy shows, movie theater. **LODGING:** Luxury hotel, indoor pool, fitness center, golf course. **CAMPING:** RV Park, 100 full-hookup sites, walking distance to casino, heated pool & spa, free breakfast. Free dry camping also available (limited to 24 hours). Must park in the oversize lot (closest to the highway), do not use regular parking area. Call the casino for shuttle & let them know you're in oversize parking. **DIRECTIONS:** From I-84 exit 216, the resort entrance is .8 mile north of the interstate.

## Willamina

### Spirit Mountain Casino
*27100 SW Salmon River Hwy*
*Willamina, OR 97396*

www.spiritmountain.com
503-879-2350 • 800-760-7977

**DESCRIPTION:** Oregon's #1 tourist attraction, getaway resort southwest of Portland. **GAMING:** 24/7, slots, pit/gaming tables, poker room, non-smoking area, bingo, keno. **FOOD & ENTERTAINMENT:** buffet, restaurant, food court, express food, coffee bar, sports bar. Free entertainment at three venues. Ticketed touring concerts in larger venue. **LODGING:** Tribal-decor lodge. **CAMPING:** Designated lot for RV dry camping, for casino players only. No hookups, dump station on site. **DIRECTIONS:** From I-5 exit 253 follow OR-22 west for about 30 miles then OR-18 west for 4.5 miles. (Highway underpass clearance 15 feet 3 inches.)

# Pennsylvania

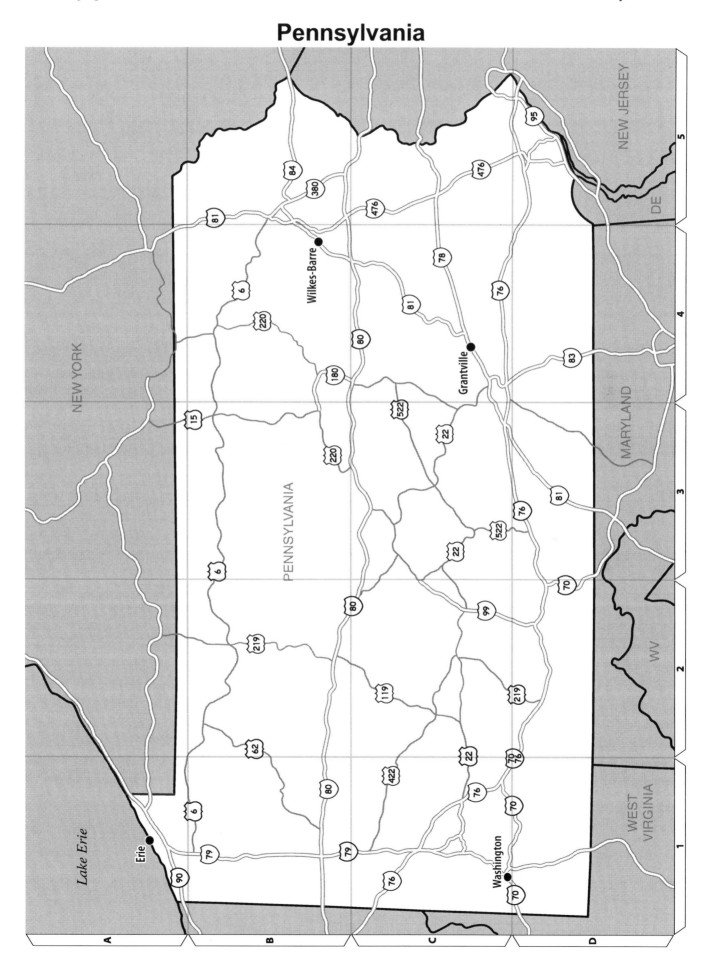

# Pennsylvania

| City | Casino | 🚐 | 🅿 | 🛏 | 🏌 | 🛡 |
|------|--------|----|----|----|----|----|
| Erie | Elderado Presque Isle Downs & Casino | | x | | | 1 |
| Grantville | Hollywood Casino at PNRC | | x | | | 1 |
| Washington | The Meadows | | x | | | 1 |
| Wilkes-Barre | Mohegan Sun at Pocono Downs | | x | | | 4 |

Pennsylvania legalized gambling in 2004 and the state's racetracks are also authorized to offer casino gaming. The casinos listed below are RV-friendly.

## Erie

### Elderado Presque Isle Downs & Casino
8199 Perry Hwy
Erie, PA 16509

www.presqueisledowns.com
814-860-8999

**DESCRIPTION:** Casino/racing complex located in northwest corner of the state. **GAMING:** open 24/7, slots, live pit/gaming tables, electronic table games, poker room, high limit room. Live Thoroughbred racing, May-Sep, 4-5 days a week. Simulcasting daily. **FOOD & ENTERTAINMENT:** Trackside buffet, cafe, steakhouse, bars & lounges. Live entertainment. **LODGING:** There is no hotel at this location. **CAMPING:** RV dry camping in the lower lot. Overnight is permitted; shuttle in parking areas. Note: RVs, do not cross the bridge to the casino area; oversize vehicles must park in the lower lot. **DIRECTIONS:** From I-90 exit 27 take SR-97 south for .2 mile then left into the complex.

## Grantville

### Hollywood Casino at Penn National Race Course
777 Hollywood Blvd
Grantville, PA 17028

www.hollywoodpnrc.com
717-469-2211

**DESCRIPTION:** Hollywood-themed casino & exciting racing on world-class track. **GAMING:** open 24/7, slots, video poker, table games, poker tables. Live Thoroughbred racing all year Wed-Sat, full-card simulcasting daily. **FOOD & ENTERTAINMENT:** steakhouse, trackside restaurant, buffet, casual dining, concessions. Live entertainment weekends. **LODGING:** There is no hotel at this location. **CAMPING:** RV parking in the lot north of the casino building near the red barn (walking distance). Overnight is OK. **DESCRIPTION:** From I-81 exit 80, the track is just north of the exit ramp.

## Washington

### The Meadows
210 Racetrack Rd
Washington, PA 15301

www.meadowsgaming.com
724-503-1200

**DESCRIPTION:** Popular harness racing combined with lively casino gaming. **GAMING:** open 24 hrs, slots, video poker, gaming tables, non-smoking poker room, race book. Harness racing four days a week, all year. **FOOD & ENTERTAINMENT:** steakhouse, trackside dining, food court, bowling. Entertainment weekends. **LODGING:** A Hyatt Hotel. **CAMPING:** RVs should park in far back section of the lot; overnight parking permitted. **DIRECTIONS:** From I-79 exit 41 go east on Racetrack Rd for .3 mile then left into the complex.

# Wilkes-Barre

### *Mohegan Sun at Pocono Downs*
*1280 PA-315*
*Wilkes-Barre, PA 18702*

www.mohegansunpocono.com
570-831-2100

**DESCRIPTION:** Live harness racing and 24 hour casino. **GAMING:** slots, non-smoking area, live-action gaming tables, high limits area. Live harness racing Apr-Nov. Simulcasting daily. **FOOD & ENTERTAINMENT:** 15 dining venues, fine dining to express food, several lounges. Live entertainment at bars & lounges. Ticketed headliner shows. **LODGING:** Luxury hotel. **CAMPING:** Parking for RVs is toward the back of the surface lot. Overnight is OK. Shuttle available. **DIRECTIONS:** From I-81 southbound take exit 175A then follow SR-315 south for 4 miles. From I-81 northbound use exit 170B, the Cross Valley Expressway to exit 1, then left on SR-315 north 1 mile.

# Rhode Island

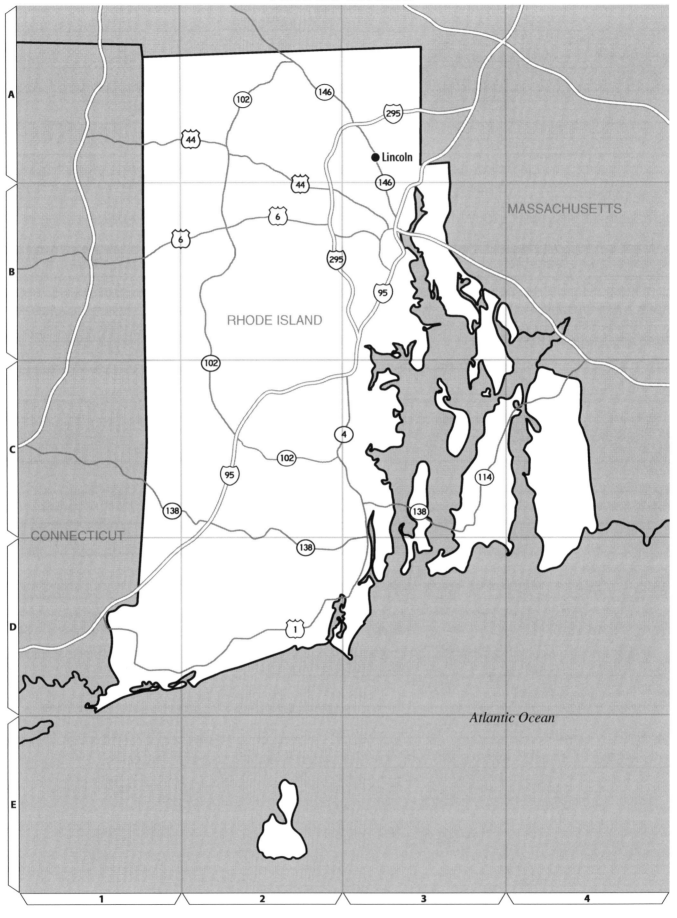

# Rhode Island

| City | Casino | 🚐 | **P** | 🛏 | 🏌 | 🛡 |
|------|--------|----|----|----|----|----|
| Lincoln | Twin River Casino | | x | x | | 5 |

In 2010, voters approved a ballot measure to allow casinos in Rhode Island. The Ocean State's largest casino, Twin River, is RV-Friendly.

## Lincoln

### Twin River Casino
*100 Twin River Rd*
*Lincoln, RI 02865*

www.twinriver.com
401-723-3200

DESCRIPTION: Largest gaming and entertainment venue in RI. GAMING: open 24/7, slots, video poker, virtual gaming tables, live-action pit/table games, separate smoke-free area. Simulcasting, Thoroughbred and greyhound racing daily. FOOD & ENTERTAINMENT: 18 dining options, fine dining to quick food. Bar & lounge feature free entertainment. Ticketed headline concerts and shows in event center. LODGING: Modern hotel. CAMPING: RV parking is available in the south lot. Overnight is OK for self-contained vehicles. DIRECTIONS: From I-95N take exit 23 toward Woonsocket/Lincoln for 4.8 miles, then turn right onto Twin River Road.

# South Dakota

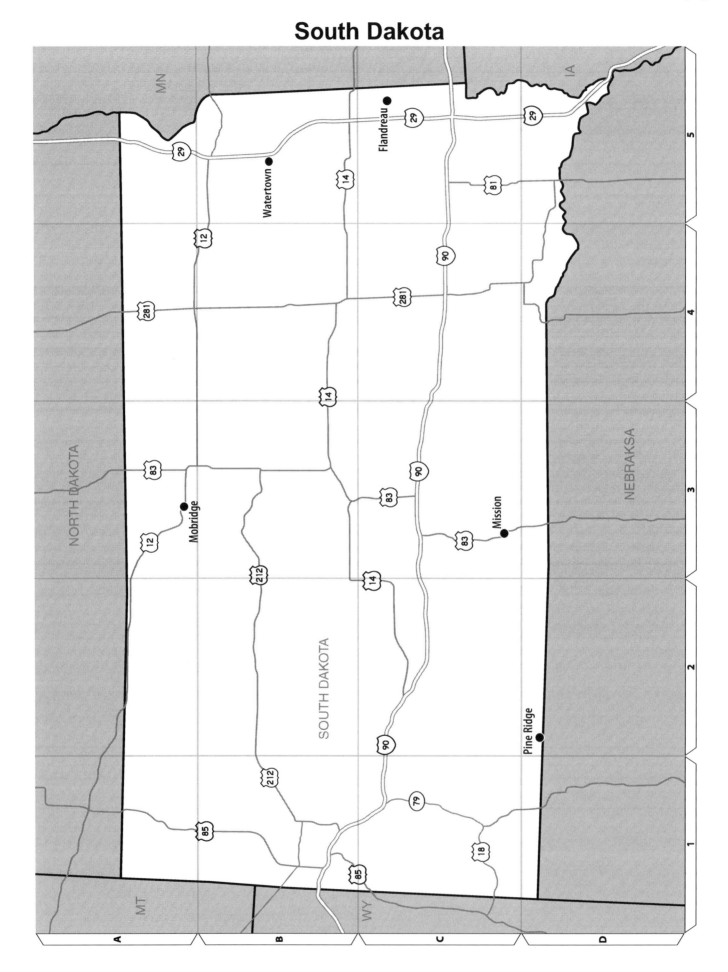

# South Dakota

| City | Casino | 🚐 | 🅿 | 🛏 | 🎣 | 🛡 |
|---|---|---|---|---|---|---|
| Flandreau | Royal River Casino Hotel | s20 | x | x | | 8 |
| Mission | Rosebud Casino | | x | x | | |
| Mobridge | Grand River Casino & Resort | s8 | | x | | |
| Pine Ridge | Prairie Wind Casino | | x | x | | |
| Watertown | Dakota Sioux Casino & Hotel | s12 | x | x | | 5 |

South Dakota's casinos can be found at Indian-operated facilities, many convenient to interstates. Most are RV-Friendly. Note: Dakota Magic Casino, located just off I-29 at the South Dakota/North Dakota state line, is listed in the North Dakota section of this guide.

## Flandreau

### Royal River Casino Hotel
607 S Veterans St
Flandreau, SD 57028

www.royalrivercasino.com
605-997-3746

DESCRIPTION: Friendly hometown casino, gaming 24 hours. GAMING: slots, blackjack & poker tables, roulette. FOOD & ENTERTAINMENT: restaurant open daily morning till night, snack bar. Ticketed shows & concerts. LODGING: Hotel rooms/suites. CAMPING: 20 RV sites with electric & cable TV, central dump & fresh water supply. Check in & pay at the hotel. DIRECTIONS: From I-29 exit 114, go east into Flandreau for 7.6 miles, then right on Veterans Street for .4 mile.

## Mission

### Rosebud Casino
30421 US Hwy 83
Mission, SD 69201

www.rosebudcasino.com
605-378-3800

DESCRIPTION: Cozy casino situated at the Nebraska/South Dakota state line. GAMING: Open 24 hours, slots, gaming tables, poker room, bingo. FOOD & ENTERTAINMENT: Cafe open morning till night. LODGING: Quality Inn. CAMPING: Parking area for large vehicles east side of the lot; overnight RV parking is OK. DIRECTIONS: From I-90 exit 192, follow US-83 south for 95 miles to the Nebraska state line. The casino is 22 miles south of the city of Mission and is on the southbound side of US-83.

## Mobridge

### Grand River Casino & Resort
27903 US Hwy 12
Mobridge, SD 57601

www.grandrivercasino.com
605-845-7104 • 800-475-3321

DESCRIPTION: Casino hosted by the Standing Rock Sioux Tribe since 1994. GAMING: slots, blackjack and poker tables, hours: 7am-2:30am, 24hrs (weekends.) FOOD & ENTERTAINMENT: restaurant open daily morning till night. LODGING: Lodge & cabins. CAMPING: Eight RV sites with electric hookups; register/pay at the lodge. DIRECTIONS: I-29 exit 207 go west on US-12 for 172 miles. Grand River is directly on US-12, two miles west of Mobridge.

## Pine Ridge

### Prairie Wind Casino
US Highway 18
Pine Ridge, SD 57770

www.prairiewindcasino.com
605-867-6300

**DESCRIPTION:** Casino destination in southwestern SD. **GAMING:** slots, pit/gaming tables, non smoking section, open 24/7. **FOOD & ENTERTAINMENT:** restaurant, snack bar. **LODGING:** Hotel. **CAMPING:** RV parking is available in the lot next to the bingo hall; inform security if you plan to stay overnight. **DIRECTIONS:** I-90 from the east take Hwy-73 south from Kadoka (exit 150) to Hwy-18 then travel west through Martin, Pine Ridge & Oglala. From I-90 Rapid City area take exit 61 south and follow Hwy-79 then Hwy-18 east.

## Watertown

### *Dakota Sioux Casino & Hotel*
*16415 Sioux Conifer Rd*
*Watertown, SD 57201*

www.dakotasioux.com
605-884-1700

**DESCRIPTION:** Casino located in popular fishing & hunting area. **GAMING:** open 24 hrs, slots, gaming tables, poker room. **FOOD & ENTERTAINMENT:** steakhouse and buffet, deli, lounge entertainment weekends. **LODGING:** Hotel, gift shop. **CAMPING:** 12 RV spaces on paved parking lot, electric hookups, central dump & fresh water supply. Register/pay at the hotel. **DIRECTIONS:** I-29 exit 185 take CR-6/164th St west 4.5 miles, then south on Sioux Conifer Rd.

# Washington

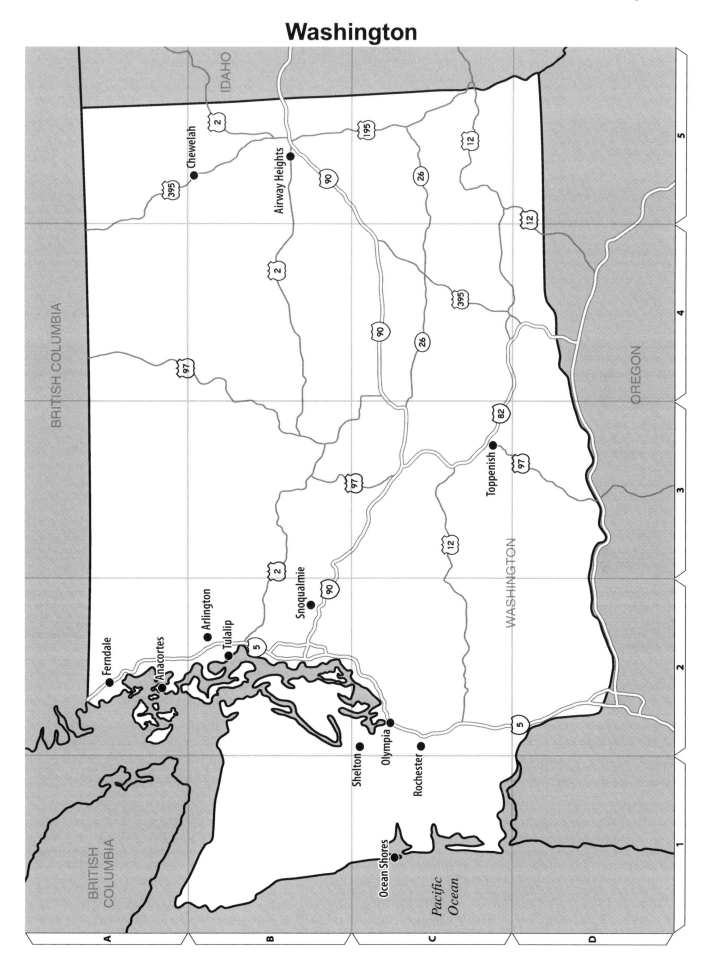

# Washington

| City | Casino | 🚐 | 🅿 | 🛏 | 🏌 | 🛡 |
|------|--------|-----|-----|-----|-----|-----|
| Airway Heights | Northern Quest Resort & Casino | | x | x | | 5 |
| Anacortes | Swinomish Casino & Lodge | p35 | | x | | 9 |
| Arlington | Angel of the Winds Casino | p28 | | | | 2 |
| Chewelah | Chewelah Casino | p10 | x | | | |
| Ferndale | Silver Reef Hotel Casino | | x | x | | 4 |
| Ocean Shores | Quinault Beach Resort & Casino | | x | x | | |
| Olympia | Red Wind Casino | | x | | | 8 |
| Rochester | Lucky Eagle Casino & Hotel | s9 | | x | | 9 |
| Shelton | Little Creek Casino Resort | p44 | | x | x | |
| Snoqualmie | Snoqualmie Casino | | x | | | 4 |
| Toppenish | Yakama Legends Casino | | x | | | 5 |
| Tulalip | Tulalip Resort Casino | | x | x | | 1 |

# Washington

The State of Washington is home to many RV-friendly gaming facilities. The Western Washington casinos are accessible from I-5 and US-101. A casino in South-Central Washington is close to I-82 and, in Eastern Washington, some are convenient to I-90.

## Airway Heights

### Northern Quest Resort & Casino
*100 N Hayford Rd*
*Airway Heights, WA 99001*

www.northernquest.com
877-871-6772 • RV Park: 833-702-2082

DESCRIPTION: Spokane's largest 24/7 casino. GAMING: slots, pit/table games, keno, race book, non-smoking poker room & separate non-smoking gaming area with slots & tables. FOOD & ENTERTAINMENT: 14 dining options, fine dining to quick food, cigar lounge & bars, movie theater, ticketed shows & events, indoor & outdoor venues. LODGING: Luxury hotel. CAMPING: RVs should park in the lot nearest the parking garage; overnight parking permitted. New RV Park to open in 2019. DIRECTIONS: From I-90 exit 277, west on Hwy-2 four miles, right on Hayford Road one mile.

## Anacortes

### Swinomish Casino & Lodge
*12885 Casino Dr*
*Anacortes, WA 98221*

www.swinomishcasinoandlodge.com
360-588-3800 • RV Park: 855-794-6663

DESCRIPTION: On Fidalgo Island in view of Padilla Bay. GAMING: Open 24 hours, slots, pit/gaming tables, poker, keno. FOOD & ENTERTAINMENT: steakhouse, café, deli, bar & grille, quick food. Live music weekends. LODGING: Luxury lodge. CAMPING: RV Park, 35 full hookup sites; register/pay in the casino gift shop. If staying overnight, please check into the RV Park. NO free overnight parking. DIRECTIONS: I-5 exit 230, take Hwy-20 west for 8.5 miles. Resort can be seen on the north side of the highway as you cross the bridge from the mainland to Fidalgo Island at the Swinomish Channel.

## Arlington

### Angel of the Winds Casino

*3438 Stoluckquamish Ln*
*Arlington, WA 98223*

www.angelofthewinds.com
360-474-9740

**DESCRIPTION:** 24-hour casino north of Seattle, near I-5. **GAMING:** pit/table games, poker room, keno, non-smoking gaming area. **FOOD & ENTERTAINMENT:** steakhouse, buffet, cafe, bar, lounge, live music & entertainment; bowling. **LODGING:** Modern hotel, gift shop. **CAMPING:** RV Park, 28 sites, dump station, free Wi-Fi, shuttle to casino, fuel. **DIRECTIONS:** From I-5 exit 210 follow 236th St/Kackman Rd east for 1.5 miles, then north on 35th Ave for .3 mile & west on Stoluckquamish Lane to the casino.

## Chewelah

### Chewelah Casino

*2555 Smith Rd - Hwy 395 S*
*Chewelah, WA 99109*

www.chewelahcasino.com
509-935-6167

**DESCRIPTION:** Friendly hometown casino hosted by the Spokane Tribe. **GAMING:** slots, live-action table games; Casino open 8am–2am daily. **FOOD & ENTERTAINMENT:** Café/buffet, lounge. Smaller Double Eagle Casino, next to the main casino, has slots & deli. **LODGING:** There is no hotel at this location. **CAMPING:** RV parking area, 10 sites, water/electric, Wi-Fi; register & pay at the casino cage. Free overnight dry camping is also permitted in the dirt lot at the front of the casino. **DIRECTIONS:** From I-90 exit 281, go north on US-395 for about 46.3 miles. The casino can be seen on the east side of the highway.

## Ferndale

### Silver Reef Hotel Casino

*4876 Haxton Way*
*Ferndale, WA 98248*

www.silverreefcasino.com
866-383-0777

**DESCRIPTION:** Luxury resort near the Canadian border. **GAMING:** open 24-hrs, slots, pit/gaming tables, race book, smoke-free slots area. **FOOD & ENTERTAINMENT:** 10 restaurants, 2 bars. Ticketed concerts in the event center. **LODGING:** Hotel, day spa, free Wi-Fi, breakfast. **CAMPING:** RVs may park in the back parking lot; overnight dry camping permitted, dump station available. **DIRECTIONS:** From I-5 exit 260, go west on Slater Road for 3.7 miles, turn left on Haxton Way.

## Ocean Shores

### Quinault Beach Resort & Casino

*78 State Rd 115*
*Ocean Shores, WA 98569*

www.quinaultbeachresort.com
888-461-2214

**DESCRIPTION:** Casino resort on the beach, premier coastal destination. **GAMING:** Open 24 hours, slots, pit/gaming tables, poker room, smoke-free gaming area. **FOOD & ENTERTAINMENT:** Sidewalk bistro, fine dining oceanside, buffets, coffee bar, lounge. **LODGING:** Hotel. **CAMPING:** RV dry camping by the sea is available for self-contained vehicles (no hookups), RV lot on the west side of the parking area. Daily fees: $5 mid-week; $10 weekends/holidays. Check in at the front desk, first come-first serve. Free casino shuttle. **DIRECTIONS:** From I-5 exit 88B go west on US-12 for 46.3 miles, then US-101N for 3.7 miles, turn right at Levee St then left on Emerson St for 1.5 miles. Continue on WA-109 for 14.6 miles, then left at WA-115.

## Olympia

### Red Wind Casino

*12819 Yelm Hwy SE*
*Olympia, WA 98513*

www.redwindcasino.com
866-946-2444

**DESCRIPTION:** Casino on the Nisqually Reservation. **GAMING:** open 8am–5am/24hrs (weekends), slots, pit/gaming tables, keno. **FOOD & ENTERTAINMENT:** buffet, grille, deli, sports pub, lounge. Smoke-free bar. Live entertainment. **LODGING:** There is no hotel at this location. **CAMPING:** RV parking across from the casino building. 24-hour limit for dry camping; check in and register with Security when you arrive. **DIRECTIONS:** From I-5 exit 111, go east on Hwy-510 (Marvin Road) for 1.7 miles. At the roundabout, take the third exit to continue on Hwy-510 east for six miles.

## Rochester

### Lucky Eagle Casino & Hotel
*12888 188th Ave SW*
*Rochester, WA 98579*

www.luckyeagle.com
360-273-2000

**DESCRIPTION:** Popular south sound casino, where the locals play. **GAMING:** open 8am–4am/6am (weekends), slots, pit/table games, keno area, bingo, non-smoking slots area. **FOOD & ENTERTAINMENT:** steakhouse, buffet, sidewalk deli, 2 bars. Live bands weekends. Ticketed shows in event center. **LODGING:** Stylish hotel. **CAMPING:** 9 RV back-in sites with electric hookup in the lot (no slideouts allowed), walking distance to the casino; RV Park, with full hookup sites, is a short distance away; on-call shuttle service available. Register and pay for all RV accommodations at the hotel front desk. **DIRECTIONS:** From I-5 exit 88, go west on Hwy-12 for 7.7 miles, then left on Anderson Road for .8 mile, then left on 188th Avenue for .2 mile.

## Shelton

### Little Creek Casino Resort
*W91 WA-108*
*Shelton, WA 98584*

www.little-creek.com
360-427-7711 • 800-667-7711

**DESCRIPTION:** Casino destination resort near US-101 north of Olympia. **GAMING:** Open 8am-5am daily, slots, gaming tables, bingo, keno, non-smoking area. **FOOD & ENTERTAINMENT:** buffet, cafe, grill, seafood bar, lounges. Ticketed shows in event center. Live music, karaoke in the lounge. **LODGING:** Luxury hotel,

indoor pool, hot tub, day spa, golf course. **CAMPING:** RV Park, 44 full hookup sites & full access to hotel amenities, free Wi-Fi, TV, laundry. Free dry camping limited to 24-hour stay, must obtain dry camping permit at the hotel front desk. Fuel, convenience store across the street. **DIRECTIONS:** From I-5 in Olympia, exit 104, north on US-101 for five miles (follow signs to Port Angeles/Shelton), continue north on US-101 for another 7.5 miles. Exit US-101 between mileposts 353 & 354 (at Hwy-108). The casino is next to the southbound lanes.

## Snoqualmie

### Snoqualmie Casino
*37500 SE North Bend Way*
*Snoqualmie, WA 98065*

www.snocasino.com
425-888-1234

**DESCRIPTION:** Non-stop 24/7 gaming at Seattle's closest casino. **GAMING:** slots, live pit/gaming tables, poker room. **FOOD & ENTERTAINMENT:** fine dining, buffet, cafe, deli, 3 bars & lounge. Ticketed headliner shows in ballroom. Live lounge entertainment. **LODGING:** No hotel at this location. **CAMPING:** RV parking area is identified, follow signs. Free dry camping (no hookups). **DIRECTIONS:** From I-90 east, exit 27, turn left (north), follow North Bend Way around the curve, casino on left. From I-90 west, exit 31 turn right (north), follow Bendigo Blvd to North Bend Way, turn left (west) onto North Bend Way and head west about 4 miles.

## Toppenish

### Yakama Legends Casino
*580 Fort Rd*
*Toppenish, WA 98948*

www.legendscasino.com
509-865-8800

**DESCRIPTION:** Casino destination resort in South-Central Washington. **GAMING:** open 9am-4am/5am (Fri–Sat,) slots, pit/gaming tables, poker, keno, bingo. **FOOD & ENTERTAINMENT:** buffet, deli, food court, cafe. **LODGING:** Hotel. **CAMPING:** Free overnight parking is permitted in the far end of casino lot, shuttle service. **DIRECTIONS:** From I-82 exit 50, take WA-22E (through the town of Toppenish) for 2.8 miles, continue straight on to Washington St and Elm St for .4 mile, turn right at W 1st Ave for .5 mile and continue on Fort Rd/WA-220 for .7 mile.

## Tulalip

### *Tulalip Resort Casino*
*10200 Quil Ceda Blvd*
*Tulalip, WA 98271*

www.tulalipcasino.com
360-716-6000

**DESCRIPTION:** Premier destination resort for non-stop gaming, most cash-back in WA. **GAMING:** slots, pit/ gaming tables, non-smoking poker room, high roller room, keno, bingo, separate non-smoking area. **FOOD & ENTERTAINMENT:** fine dining, buffet, 24-hour cafe, coffee shop. Live music in cabaret. Ticketed touring shows in ballroom; outdoor amphitheater concerts. **LODGING:** Luxury hotel. **CAMPING:** Free RV parking on the west side of the casino; overnight parking permitted. Please check in with Security to get a parking permit for up to 3 days. **DIRECTIONS:** From I-5 exit 200, follow casino signs. The resort complex is visible from southbound lanes of the interstate.

# West Virginia

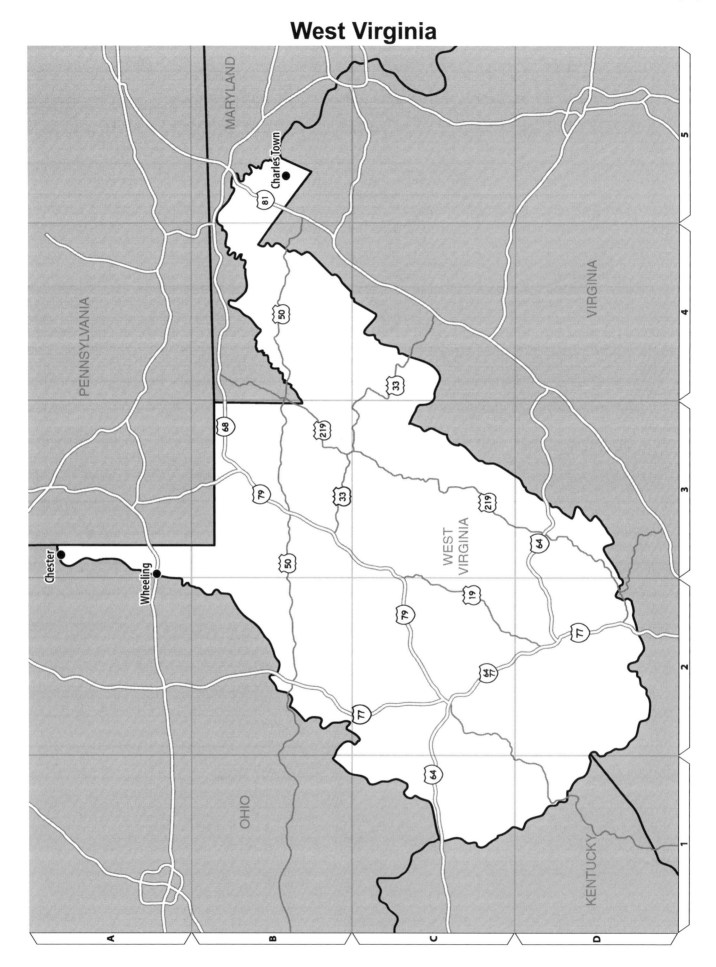

# West Virginia

| City | Casino | 🚐 | 🅿 | 🛏 | 🏌 | 🛡 |
|------|--------|-----|-----|-----|-----|-----|
| Charles Town | Hollywood Casino at Charles Town Races | | x | x | | |
| Chester | Mountaineer Casino, Racetrack & Resort | | x | x | x | |
| Wheeling | Wheeling Island Hotel, Casino & Racetrack | | x | x | | 1 |

West Virginia has four racinos, pari-mutuel facilities with slots and gaming tables. Two are at dog tracks and two at horse tracks. Listed below are the three racinos that permit RV parking.

## Charles Town

### Hollywood Casino at Charles Town Races
*750 Hollywood Dr*
*Charles Town, WV 25414*

www.hollywoodcasinocharlestown.com
304-725-7001

**DESCRIPTION:** Racing combined with 24/7 casino gaming. **GAMING:** slots, pit/gaming tables, poker room, sports book. Live racing all year Tue-Sat. Daily simulcasting, horse & dog racing. **FOOD & ENTERTAINMENT:** restaurant overlooking track, steakhouse, buffet, Asian, food court. Live music at lounge. Ticketed touring shows in event center. **LODGING:** The Inn. **CAMPING:** RV parking is across from the west garage structure. Overnight parking permitted for limited stays. **DIRECTIONS:** From I-81 exit 5, follow Rt-51 east for 12 miles.

## Chester

### Mountaineer Casino, Racetrack & Resort
*1420 Mountaineer Cir*
*New Cumberland, WV 26047*

www.moreatmountaineer.com
304-387-2236

**DESCRIPTION:** Casino resort nestled in scenic hills of northern WV. **GAMING:** slots, video poker, pit/gaming tables, poker room. Live Thoroughbred racing Apr-Nov. Simulcast parlor open daily. Casino shuttle during racing hours. **FOOD & ENTERTAINMENT:** steakhouse, trackside dining, buffet, cafe, quick food, sports bar. Live entertainment weekends in the lounge & cafe. Ticketed touring events monthly. **LODGING:** Luxury hotel, golf course, outdoor pool, gift shop. **CAMPING:** Free RV dry camping in south lot near the track. Call security for shuttle. **DIRECTIONS:** From Weirton, West Virginia, follow WV-2 north for 15 miles to Mountaineer.

## Wheeling

### Wheeling Island Hotel, Casino & Racetrack
*1 S Stone St*
*Wheeling, WV 26003*

www.wheelingisland.com
304-232-5050

**DESCRIPTION:** Greyhound racing & casino gaming at Wheeling Island. **GAMING:** slots, live pit/table games, race book, daily simulcasting, dog & horse racing. **FOOD & ENTERTAINMENT:** steakhouse, buffet, trackside dining, concessions, coffee shop, bars. Live entertainment in casino, ticketed events monthly in showroom. **LODGING:** Deluxe hotel. **CAMPING:** Parking for RVs is in Lot H; overnight is permitted. **DIRECTIONS:** From I-70 east, exit 225. Left at the end of the ramp, then right at first light. At the next light continue straight & cross the bridge onto Wheeling Island. At second light after the bridge turn right onto South York St. & follow to Wheeling Island. From I-70 west, after passing through Wheeling tunnel, in the left lane, use exit 0 (Wheeling Island). At the first light turn left onto South York St. & follow to Wheeling Island.

# Wisconsin

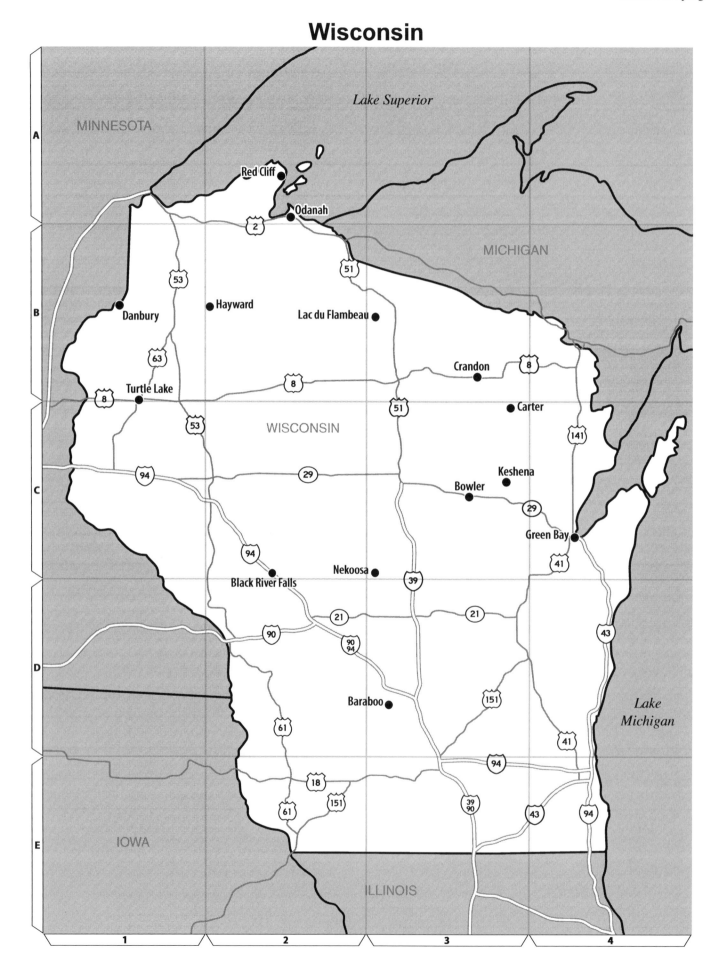

# Wisconsin

| City | Casino | 🚐 | 🅿 | 🛏 | 🏌 | 🛡 |
|------|--------|------|------|------|------|------|
| Baraboo | Ho-Chunk Gaming - Wisconsin Dells | p49 | x | x | | 3 |
| Black River Falls | Ho-Chunk Gaming | s4 | x | x | | 3 |
| Bowler | North Star Mohican Casino Resort | p57 | | x | | |
| Carter | Potawatomi Carter Casino Hotel | s10 | x | x | | |
| Crandon | Mole Lake Casino & Lodge | s3 | x | x | | |
| Danbury | St. Croix Casino | p35 | | x | | |
| Green Bay | Oneida Casino | s11 | | x | | 8 |
| Hayward | Sevenwinds Casino Lodge | p8 | | x | | |
| Keshena | Menominee Casino Resort | s42 | | x | | |
| Lac du Flambeau | Lake of the Torches Resort Casino | p72 | x | x | | |
| Nekoosa | Ho-Chunk Gaming | s8 | x | | | |
| Odanah | Bad River Lodge & Casino | s20 | | x | | |
| Red Cliff | Legendary Waters Resort & Casino | p18 | | x | | |
| Turtle Lake | St. Croix Casino | p18 | | x | | |

Wisconsin's Native-American communities have been offering traditional casino gaming in many locations throughout the state since 1987. Most casinos in the state welcome RV travelers.

## Baraboo

### Ho-Chunk Gaming - Wisconsin Dells
*S3214 County Rd BD*
*Baraboo, WI 53913*

www.hochunkgaming.com/wisconsindells
608-356-6210 • RV Park: 800-446-5550

**DESCRIPTION:** Casino resort in The Dells, popular vacation area. **GAMING:** slots, pit/gaming tables, poker room, off-track betting, bingo, non-smoking area. **FOOD & ENTERTAINMENT:** steakhouse, buffet, cafe, grill, sports bar. Live entertainment **LODGING:** Hotel, day spa, pool, meeting space. **CAMPING:** RV Park with full hookup sites, open May-Oct. Free RV parking available on the perimeter of the casino lot (where trucks park). **DIRECTIONS:** From I-90/94 exit 92, follow US-12 south to North Reedsburg Rd exit.

## Black River Falls

### Ho-Chunk Gaming
*W9010 Hwy 54E*
*Black River Falls, WI 54615*

www.hochunkgaming.com/blackriverfalls
715-284-9098

**DESCRIPTION:** Casino resort in the Jackson County Forest of northwest WI. **GAMING:** Open 8am-2am/ 24hrs (Fri-Sat), slots, live gaming tables, bingo. **FOOD & ENTERTAINMENT:** bistro, buffet, quick food. Live entertainment & ticketed touring shows. **LODGING:** Hotel, Wi-Fi, indoor pool, whirlpool, sauna. **CAMPING:** RV dry camping permitted in east parking lot. There are a few spaces with free electric hookups, first come-first-serve, at the northeast end; overnight OK. **DIRECTIONS:** From I-94 exit 116, take WI-54E (south) for 2.6 miles.

## Bowler

### North Star Mohican Casino Resort
*W12180 County Rd A*

*Bowler, WI 54416*

www.northstarcasinoresort.com

715-787-3110

**DESCRIPTION:** Friendly casino resort hosted by the Stockbridge-Musee Band of Mohican Indians. **GAMING:** Open 24 hours, slots, pit/gaming tables, poker room, bingo. **FOOD & ENTERTAINMENT:** restaurant, cafe, deli. Live local entertainment in the lounge. **LODGING:** Contemporary hotel, golf course. **CAMPING:** RV Park, 57 full hookup wooded sites (water turned off in winter), convenience store. Walking distance to casino, register at hotel front desk. NO dry camping in the lot. If staying overnight, please check in at the RV Park. **DIRECTIONS:** 50 miles northwest of Green Bay. From US-41 exit 169 take WI-29 west for 41.6 miles to mile post 217, then north on CR-U for 2 miles, continue on CR-A for 1.9 miles and continue to follow CR-A northwest for 7.5 miles.

## Carter

### Potawatomi Carter Casino Hotel
*618 State Hwy 32*
*Wabeno, WI 54566*

www.cartercasino.com

715-473-2021 • 800-487-9522

**DESCRIPTION:** Casino hotel in Nicolet National Forest near historic logging community. **GAMING:** slots, pit/gaming tables, bingo. **FOOD & ENTERTAINMENT:** restaurant, sports bar & grill. Live entertainment in casino. **LODGING:** Lodge, 24-hour gas station on property. **CAMPING:** Ten RV spaces with free electric hookup available. Must register at guest services in the casino. Maximum stay is 3 days. Dump station available. **DIRECTIONS:** 85 miles north of Green Bay. Take US-141 north for 23.7 miles, then WI-64 west for 20.1 miles and WI-32 north for 23.4 miles.

## Crandon

### Mole Lake Casino & Lodge
*3084 Hwy 55*
*Crandon, WI 54520*

www.molelakecasino.com

715-478-5290 • 800-236-9466

**DESCRIPTION:** Charming resort surrounded by beautiful scenery of northeast WI. **GAMING:** Open daily 7am-2am/3am (Fri-Sat), slots, blackjack tables, bingo. **FOOD & ENTERTAINMENT:** Cafe, bistro, quick food, lounge. Live entertainment. **LODGING:** Lodge, fishing nearby. **CAMPING:** Free overnight parking is permitted for self-contained RVs. Free electric hookups behind the casino. Please notify security if you plan to stay overnight. **DIRECTIONS:** From US-51 follow US-8 east for 39.1 miles, then south on CR-S for 2 miles and continue south on WI-55 for 4.5 miles.

## Danbury

### St. Croix Casino
*30222 State Rd 35*
*Danbury, WI 54830*

www.danbury.stcroixcasino.com

800-238-8946 • Campground: 715-656-4402

**DESCRIPTION:** Western-themed destination resort, near the Minnesota border. **GAMING:** 24-hr casino, slots, video poker, pit/table games. **FOOD & ENTERTAINMENT:** restaurant, buffet, cafe, deli, lounge, free live shows. **LODGING:** Hotel, gift shop. **CAMPING:** Campground in wooded setting, 35 full hookup sites, 10 electric-only, central dump, Wi-Fi, volleyball, horseshoes, basketball. Shuttle to casino. Fuel, groceries, canoe rentals nearby. Please check into the campground if staying overnight, reasonable rates. NO dry camping in the casino lot. **DIRECTIONS:** From I-35 exit 183 in Minnesota, go east on SR-48 for 23.4 miles (crossing into Wisconsin); continue on WI-77 for 4 miles.

## Green Bay

### Oneida Casino
*2020 Airport Dr*
*Green Bay, WI 54313*

www.oneidabingoandcasino.net

920-494-4500

**DESCRIPTION:** Flagship casino hosted by Oneida Nation of Wisconsin. **GAMING:** Open 24 hours, slots, pit/gaming tables, high stakes gaming area, poker room, smoke-free off-track betting room, bingo. **Food & Entertainment:** sports bar & grill, express food, deli, noodle bar, live entertainment in the lounge. **Lodging:** smoke-free Radisson Hotel, restaurant, lounge. **Camping:** 11 RV parking spaces with electric hookups located along the road on the north side behind the casino, first come, first served; no water or dump station. Register and pay at the casino Players Club desk. **Directions:** From I-43 exit 180 take SR-172 west 8 miles to Airport Rd.

## Hayward

### Sevenwinds Casino Lodge
*13767 W County Rd B*
*Hayward, WI 54843*

www.sevenwindscasino.com
715-634-5643

**Description:** Casino resort in the heart of the Great Northwoods. **Gaming:** Open 8am-2am/24hrs (weekends), slots, many progressives, pit/gaming tables, poker room, bingo. **Food & Entertainment:** buffet, quick food, free shows in the lounge. **Lodging:** Lodge. **Camping:** Eight campsites, water & electric hookups, near the casino; dump station is available. Register & pay at the lodge front desk. **Directions:** From junction of US-53 & US-63 go east on US-63 to Hayward, then Hwy-27 south for .5 mile to CR-B, then east for 5 miles to the casino.

## Keshena

### Menominee Casino Resort
*N277 Hwy 47/55*
*Keshena, WI 54135*

www.menomineecasinoresort.com
715-799-3600

**Description:** Luxury resort on the Menominee Reservation near Green Bay. **Gaming:** 24-hour casino, slots, pit/gaming tables, poker, bingo. **Food & Entertainment:** restaurant, cafe. Live entertainment in the lounge, Ticketed events in the ballroom. **Lodging:** Hotel, free Wi-Fi, indoor pool & hot tub, steam room, fitness center. **Camping:** 42 RV spaces, electric hookups, no water or dump, Wi-Fi, 24-hour security. RV guests have access to hotel pool, fitness

rooms, register & pay at the hotel. **Directions:** From US-41 exit 169 go west on WI-29 for 32.2 miles, take exit 225 for WI-22 north for 2 miles then north on WI-47/55 for 7.8 miles.

## Lac du Flambeau

### Lake of the Torches Resort Casino
*510 Old Abe Rd*
*Lac du Flambeau, WI 54538*

www.lakeofthetorches.com
715-588-7070 • 800-25-TORCH

**Description:** Casino on the shores of Lake Pokegama in Wisconsin's Northwoods. **Gaming:** Unique casino-in-the-round, open 24/7, slots, pit/gaming tables, high-stakes bingo. **Food & Entertainment:** restaurant bar & grill, music in the lounge. Ticketed touring concerts at events center. **Lodging:** Hotel. **Camping:** Free overnight parking for RVs is on the level gravel lot across the street from the casino next to the gas station. Note: RVs are not permitted in the casino lot. **Directions:** From I-39 in Wausau, north on US-51 for 73 miles to the town of Woodruff. Go west on WI-47 for 12 miles to the casino.

## Nekoosa

### Ho-Chunk Gaming
*949 County Rd G*
*Nekoosa, WI 54457*

www.hochunkgaming.com
715-886-4560 • 800-782-4560

**Description:** Friendly hometown casino, where the locals play. **Gaming:** Open 24 hours, slots, gaming tables, non-smoking slots area & poker room. **Food & Entertainment:** grill, snack bar, lounge; live entertainment. **Lodging:** There is no hotel at this location. **Camping:** Eight RV spaces in parking lot, free electric, first-come, first-serve. Maximum 3 day stay limit. **Directions:** From I-39 exit 136, follow WI-73 west for 20.8 miles; continue on WI-173 for 2.2 miles, then west on County Rd G for 3.7 miles. The casino is about four miles south of Nekoosa.

## Odanah

### Bad River Lodge & Casino
*73370 US Hwy 2*
*Odanah, WI 54861*

www.badriver.com
715-682-7121

**DESCRIPTION:** Friendly casino hosted by the Lake Superior Tribe of Chippewa Indians. **GAMING:** slots, video poker, gaming tables. Casino hours 8am–2am daily. **FOOD & ENTERTAINMENT:** restaurant, snack bar, smoke shop, gift shop. **LODGING:** Lodge. **CAMPING:** 20 RV spaces, electric & water, dump station, register and pay at the smoke shop. Gas station, food market, post office and convenience store with mini-casino nearby. **DIRECTIONS:** Located near Lake Superior ten miles east of Ashland on US-2.

## Red Cliff

### Legendary Waters Resort and Casino
*37600 Onigaming Dr*
*Red Cliff, WI 54814*

www.legendarywaters.com
800-226-8478

**DESCRIPTION:** Resort at the waters edge, hosted by Red Cliff Band of Lake Superior Chippewa. **GAMING:** Open 24 hours, slots, live-action blackjack, poker tables, bingo, cribbage. **FOOD & ENTERTAINMENT:** restaurant, cafe, concerts, shows, in event center, summer patio entertainment. **LODGING:** Hotel. **CAMPING:** Two campgrounds (seasonal), 34 sites with electric & water hookup. If staying overnight, register at the RV park (no space available for dry camping). **DIRECTIONS:** From points south & east take I-39 north toward Wausau, then take US-51 north to US-2 west. A couple of miles past Ashland, take State Highway 13 north. Red Cliff is located 3 miles north of Bayfield.

## Turtle Lake

### St. Croix Casino
*777 US Hwy 8 W*
*Turtle Lake, WI 54889*

www.turtlelakestcroixcasino.com
715-986-4777

**DESCRIPTION:** West Wisconsin casino resort hosted by St. Croix Tribe. **GAMING:** 24 hours, slots, pit/gaming tables, poker room, non-smoking slots area, high stakes area. **FOOD & ENTERTAINMENT:** buffet, smoke-free fine dining restaurant, snack bar, lounge, free live entertainment. **LODGING:** Hotel. **CAMPING:** RV Park open May-Oct, 18 sites, water & electric, dump station, shuttle to casino. NO free RV dry camping; if staying overnight pull into the RV park. **DIRECTIONS:** From US-53 exit 135 go west on US-8 for 20 miles.

# Wyoming

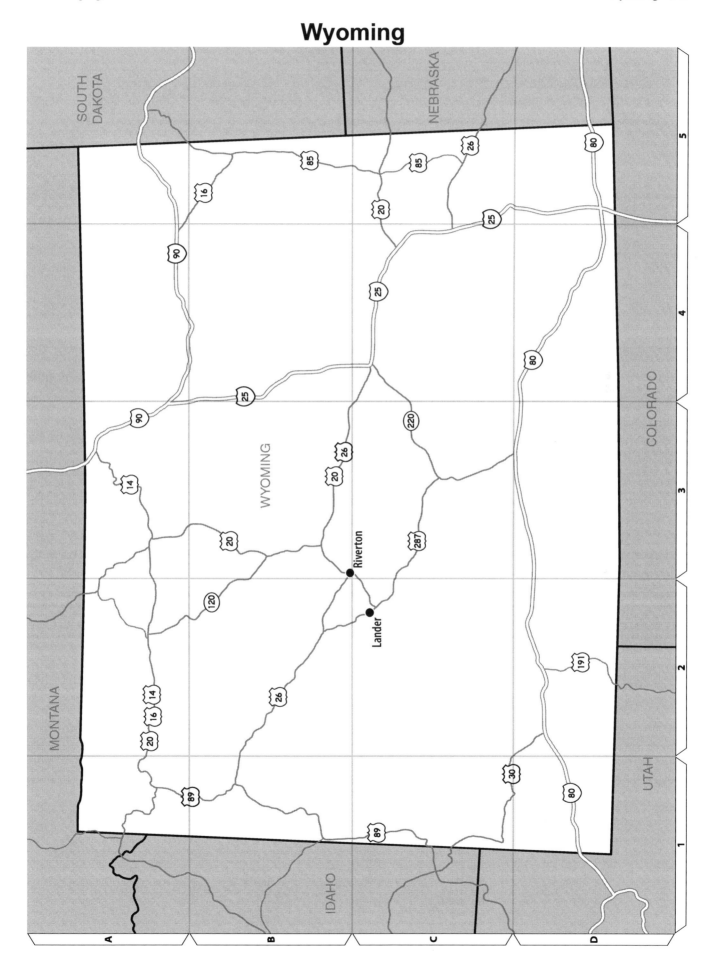

# Wyoming

| City | Casino | 🚐 | **P** | 🛏 | 🏌 | 🛡 |
|------|--------|------|------|------|------|------|
| Lander | Shoshone Rose Casino | | x | x | | |
| Riverton | Wind River Hotel & Casino | s20 | x | x | | |

Two Native American casino resorts in Wyoming listed below are RV-Friendly. Surrounded by the natural beauty of the West, they are near the Grand Tetons.

## Lander

### Shoshone Rose Casino
*5690 US Hwy 287*
*Lander, WY 82520*

www.shoshonerose.com
307-206-7000 • 307-335-7529

**DESCRIPTION:** Gaming in the heart of Wyoming, hosted by the Eastern Shosone Tribe. **GAMING:** Open 24 hours, slots, blackjack & poker tables, casino promotions. **FOOD & ENTERTAINMENT:** restaurant, quick food. **LODGING:** Modern hotel. **CAMPING:** Check in with Security for parking authorization. Free overnight parking permitted on the south side of the lot. **DIRECTIONS:** From I-80 exit 215, take US-287 north for 86 miles.

## Riverton

### Wind River Hotel & Casino
*10368 Hwy 789*
*Riverton, WY 82501*

www.windriverhotelcasino.com
307-855-2600

**DESCRIPTION:** Largest casino in Wyoming, hosted by The Northern Arapaho Tribe. **GAMING:** Open 24 hours, slots, live table games, video bingo. **FOOD & ENTERTAINMENT:** Restaurant, cafe, espresso bar. **LODGING:** Stylish hotel, gift shop has unique Native American items. **CAMPING:** 20 spaces with electric hookups, first come-first serve. Register at the hotel. **DIRECTIONS:** From I-25 exit 189, follow US-26 west for 108 miles.

# Appendix A

## How to be a Savvy Casino Discounter

Casinos are big on promotions. They are continuously offering discounts and other incentives designed to bring you into their facility and onto the gaming floor.

Senior citizen discounts are common. Most casinos cater to seniors by giving percent off food or 2-for-1 meals on Senior Days and some casinos even offer free breakfast or lunch. The definition of senior citizen also varies—some consider 65 and older to qualify for discounts while other casinos define senior as 60+ 55+ or 50+. People over 50 should always ask about senior discounts.

Veteran discounts are also common at restaurants and hotels. Carrying your veteran ID can mean benefits, but only when you inquire about them.

Casino hotels and RV Parks generally extend the AAA and AARP discounts. Many RV Parks also offer the Good Sam and other RV-related discounts. When you book your room or campsite, be sure to ask about discounts available.

Other frequent benefits are percent off at restaurants and gift shops for Players Club members or weekly specials at the restaurants. Many casinos give Fun Books containing valuable coupons.

When going into a casino for the first time, stop at the Players Club desk and apply for a card. When you do, ask if the casino offers any incentives for new club members. Often they'll give you a free gift just for joining – cash credit toward $10 of gaming is typical. And, don't think that because you are just passing through for a one or two-day visit, you won't be able to accumulate enough points for comps. Often, even minimal points can amount to a discount at the buffet. It doesn't cost anything to join a casino club. There are no dues but many benefits. Casinos send discount coupons by mail, usually on a monthly basis. But, if you didn't join the Players Club, they won't have your mailing address and you'll miss out on some valuable comps offers.

A few national chains of casinos, such as Caesar's Entertainment as well as some regional casino chains have networked their Players Clubs, so you can accumulate points earned at any of their casinos to your single account on their centralized database. Be aware that points being earned on a Players Club card may expire after one year.

When playing at the casino, make sure your card is inserted into the gaming machine before you begin. If the card reader is flashing, try re-inserting the card until the welcome message appears. Points won't accumulate unless the card is properly inserted. For table players, put your card on the table and be sure pit personnel get your information. If you didn't bring your card, or lost it while moving around the casino floor, take time to go to the Club desk and get a duplicate card.

Bottom line: Always ask about discounts available, join the Players Club, even if just passing through, and take advantage of all the discounts, comps and free stuff being offered by casinos.

# Appendix B

## Casinos are Hospitable to RVers

Question: What is blacktop boondocking?

Answer: Free overnight parking for self-contained RVs, typically on the paved parking area of a business establishment, with the property owner's permission.

The key phrase in this definition is "with the property owner's permission." Consequently whenever RVers want to stay overnight in a parking lot they must obtain permission from the property owner. RVers who often look for free overnight parking know that the places most hospitable to RVers—those who are inclined to permit "blacktop boondocking" in their parking lots—are casinos and truck stops.

The casinos listed in this book are "RV-Friendly," that is they either have an RV Park or they permit free parking for self-contained vehicles in one of their surface lots. Most allow RVs to dry camp overnight. If you wish to secure free overnight parking, it is important to obtain authorization from management or security personnel. Those that do not permit overnight parking often allow day-use only.

Blacktop boondocking at a casino is safe and secure. We cannot emphasize enough that security personnel must be notified if you plan to stay overnight. Some will ask to see your driver's license or will ask you to complete a form showing your name, vehicle plate and drivers license number along with the date of your visit to the casino.

Casinos welcome adult campers because they know their facility is getting additional business. And the RVer gets a quiet, safe spot to rest and relax without being hassled. Since most casinos are open 24/7, security personnel are on duty all night. However, RVers should always be aware of your surroundings and be responsible for your own security.

A parking lot is not a campground. When your RV is in for a free overnight stay, you are there because the property owners allow RV parking. Don't take advantage of their hospitality. Be considerate, park in the area designated for RVs. If there is no designated RV area, use the perimeter of the lot, don't take up spaces reserved for customers with cars. Restrict your activity to the inside of the RV.

It is always a good idea to return the casino's hospitality by doing business with them. Treat yourself to a meal in the restaurant, buy something at the gift shop and (the obvious) participate in the gaming if you are so inclined.

Even though casinos have 24-hour security, the type of security provided at a large open parking lot is not the same as at an RV park or campground. It is not wise to leave your RV unattended overnight or for any extended period. If you are going to be in the area for more than a day or two, check into an RV Park or campground!

RVers should never abuse the hospitality of private businesses that allow free overnight parking. The Escapees RV Club has established eight simple rules for proper "free overnight parking" etiquette. FMCA and other national organizations have adopted the code as a model for their members as well. Please observe these rules:

1. For dry camping, stay one night only.
2. Obtain permission from a qualified individual.
3. Obey posted regulations.
4. No awning, chairs or barbecue grills.
5. Do not use hydraulic jacks on soft surfaces (including asphalt).
6. Always leave an area cleaner than you found it.
7. Purchase gas, food or supplies as a form of thank-you when feasible.
8. Be safe. Always be aware of your surroundings, and leave if you feel unsafe.

Note: Many casinos have fee-pay RV parks or campgrounds. Some of these casinos will also allow free overnight parking in their parking lot. But others expect you to stay and pay at their RV Park and do not permit free overnight parking. If you want to dry camp in the parking lot of a casino that also has an RV Park, it's imperative to clear it with Security.

# Index

## Numbers & Symbols

### D

### E

### F

### G

## T

## U

## V

## W

## X Y Z

Made in the USA
Middletown, DE
29 June 2019